D0212472

Chronometric
Explorations of Mind

THE EXPERIMENTAL PSYCHOLOGY SERIES

Arthur W. Melton • *Consulting Editor*

Chronometric
Explorations of Mind

The Third Paul M. Fitts Lectures
Delivered at the University of Michigan
September 1976

MICHAEL I. POSNER
University of Oregon

 LAWRENCE ERLBAUM ASSOCIATES, PUBLISHERS
1978   Hillsdale, New Jersey

DISTRIBUTED BY THE HALSTED PRESS DIVISION OF

JOHN WILEY & SONS
New York   Toronto   London   Sydney

Lawrence Erlbaum Associates, Inc., Publishers
62 Maria Drive
Hillsdale, New Jersey 07642

Distributed solely by Halsted Press Division
John Wiley & Sons, Inc., New York

Library of Congress Catalog Card Number: 78-13120

Printed in the United States of America

Contents

4   PSYCHOLOGICAL PATHWAYS

5   ALERTNESS

6 CONSCIOUS ATTENTION

7 ORIENTING

8 IMPLICATIONS

BIBLIOGRAPHY

Preface

Graduate school is an exciting time of life. For most, it is the first time one feels a part of what is a vast effort devoted to collecting, understanding, and transforming knowledge. At the time of my graduate training, a group of psychologists at the University of Michigan under the leadership of Paul M. Fitts was trying to discover a unity underlying studies of the human mind.

Different schools with their own questions and methods were busily engaged in the study of psychology. Behaviorists explored the nature of reinforcement, usually following the work of Skinner, but sometimes of Guthrie, Hull, Tolman, or another of the behavior theorists of the time. Those influenced by the computer developed programs capable of solving complex problems such as those found in symbolic logic. There was a great interest in the nature of language and the underlying grammar from which it is derived. Sensory psychologists were influenced by the growth of knowledge about the physiology of sense organs, and classical psychophysics was being enlarged by the scaling ideas of Stevens and the detection ideas of Tanner and Swets. Mathematical formulations of learning and decision making were emerging from laboratories at Michigan. Physiological psychologists were pushing electrodes deep within the brains of rats and discovering sites that would lead rats to work for stimulation and other sites they would work to avoid. It was an exciting world. Only rarely did psychologists attempt to find unity in this diverse activity, but the efforts of Hebb (1949) and then of Broadbent (1958) to do so made a profound impression on our group. We did not have the techniques needed to explore Hebb's ideas, but Broadbent's were something else again.

Our group was somewhat embarrassed by this rich corpus of material. Fitts set as his goal the development of a performance theory that would unify this complex field, at least insofar as it applied to the performance of people in real-life tasks. We were not to deny any of these insights but rather to find a unity that would handle them all. On every side we found specialists making discoveries in isolation from one another, all determined to explore their own special fields. Perception, learning, memory, sensation, and skill were fields of study in which one majored and did one's work. Lesions, rote learning, straight alleys, tachistoscopes, and computers were the tools of the trade. They defined the problems that would be investigated and delineated the literature that would be appropriate.

Fitts' work was similarly shaped by a set of problems and a methodology. He took his problems from the things people did in working environments: driving automobiles, reading, listening to words in noise, etc. He used the methodology of careful, empirical measurements of time. His thinking was heavily influenced by the new metrics made available by information measurement, allowing us to combine such independent manipulations as number of events, their probabilities, sequential dependencies, and instructions given to people to stress speed or accuracy. He was struck with how well people could adapt to new situations and also with how rigidly they often carried forward inappropriate habits learned outside the laboratory.

As I began to develop a line of research work of my own, I became intrigued by the speeded methods I had learned to use from Fitts. Why did they work so well? Could it be that their ability to provide useful measures of performance revealed a fundamental fact about the nature of mind and its relation to brain? I came to believe that the answer was yes and that it might be possible to achieve a unification of different strands of the study of mind and brain by their systematic application. The type of unification sought was not to reduce one field of investigation to another, but to find methods that would allow their discoveries to converge on common models. In so doing, I departed considerably from Fitts' fascination with naturalistic tasks but retained his methods and his pursuit of knowledge via empirical generalization rather than simulation or speculative theory.

Some of the results of my 15 years of effort along these lines are contained in the following pages. They clearly do not qualify as a theory of mind. I have tried to avoid tempting extrapolations to problems that I have not specifically studied. Nor is this a textbook that reviews and critiques the results obtained in a given field. I have elsewhere attempted to integrate my results with others in the form of textbooks. But this is a personal statement of my own convictions and, more than that, of the evidence upon which they are based. I would not have had the nerve to impose it upon others without the explicit encouragement of the committee charged with these lectures—that in their view it could serve some useful purpose. The best that I hope is that these pages will provide a sufficiently encouraging picture of our ability to study the workings of mind to facilitate and not inhibit future efforts to realize the unified theory toward which Fitts labored.

In addition to Professor Arthur W. Melton and the committee sponsoring the Fitts lectures, I would like to express my appreciation to a number of other individuals and institutions who helped make it possible for me to carry forward this research. The majority of the studies reported here were supported by a series of National Science Foundation grants to the Universities of Wisconsin and Oregon. For more than 10 years, my colleagues at Oregon, and in particular Professors Steven Keele and Ray Hyman, have spent endless hours contributing to my education. Many students and colleagues were involved in aspects of the research reported here, and I have tried to acknowledge their individual contributions in the references cited. It remains to thank them collectively for their assistance in this work, which is so much a collective enterprise. A number of colleagues were kind enough to comment on an earlier version of the manuscript. In particular, I am grateful to W. R. Uttal for exceptionally detailed comments. The preparation of the manuscript for publication was aided by Marge Eldridge and Joyce Mills, as well as my wife, Sharon.

Eugene, Oregon   Michael I. Posner

Chronometric
Explorations of Mind

1 Mental Chronometry

LANGUAGES OF MIND

Psychology is a discipline that can be approached from many different starting points. In particular, the study of mind can be viewed from the position of self-awareness (introspection), neural activity, or behavior (performance). Each standpoint gives rise to a particular language and set of methods. Although each language has its own unique advantages and disadvantages, it is a theme of this book that a common set of methods can serve as a basis for observations that tend to unify these different languages. In this chapter I seek to inform the reader about these methods and to indicate how they relate to the languages in which mind is usually discussed.

Introspection

The systematic experimental study of mind is 100 years old. It began appropriately with the method of introspection. All people have a window on the operation of their own minds available to them alone.

Psychologists sought to train systematic verbal reports based upon such introspections.[1] They hoped that from such systematic observations would come a

---

[1] The term *introspection* as used here includes all efforts to use reports based upon the experience of the subject. Of course, different theorists had rules for what could be allowed as systematic introspection and what would be considered as naive. I do not wish to distinguish between introspections based upon systematic training in a theory and those of naive observers who might be induced to speak aloud as they solve problems or make judgments. They are both based upon the phenomenal experience of the judge. The term *phenomenal* will be used in the same way as *introspective*.

precise description of internal mental operations involved in our knowledge of the world. The method of introspection was used by "structuralists" not only because of its potential power as a tool to reveal mental processing, but because psychology was defined in terms of processes of which one could be aware. As a "science of conscious mental life," psychology was confined to processes that could be made available to introspection. Thus two of the early theorists in the field, Wilhelm Wündt and Franz Brentano, in arguing the fundamental nature of psychology dealt with what processes could be brought to consciousness. Wündt argued that mental structures could be made conscious but that mental acts could not; Brentano argued the reverse. For Brentano, structures were unconscious and therefore amenable only to physiology, whereas mental acts alone were available to introspection and thus were the true subject of psychology. Wündt and Brentano agreed that the definition of psychology was limited to the study of those things that were conscious.

The revolutions in thought introduced by Darwin and by Freud showed clearly that a science based only on conscious content would miss much of what is vital in human life. The evolutionary continuum between humans and other animals emphasizes the adaptive significance of a brain that has evolved not to underlie the introspective mental life of philosophers but to produce actions and thus survival in the environment (Jerison, 1973; Razran, 1971). Freud popularized the idea of the unconscious and forced acceptance of the view that unconscious motives were a significant factor in the explanation of human behavior.

Thus introspection had serious problems both as a technique for the investigation of mind and as a definition for the field of psychology. But the failure of phenomenology and introspection as complete techniques for the study of mind and as a definition of the field should not be interpreted as meaning that introspective reports are unimportant. Current objective psychology relies a great deal on introspective reports of the subject. For example, modern psychophysics requires observers to introspect about the nature of their sensory experiences. These introspections are standardized by requesting such operations as matching or assigning numbers to indicate perceived intensity. Nonetheless, psychophysics is based on the conscious introspections of normal human subjects and depends upon the commonalities present in such introspections. Its success surely gives the lie to claims that introspection cannot provide systematic, quantitative, and reliable data but gives no assurance that introspections will be sufficient by themselves.

Similarly, much recent work on problem solving relies heavily upon the use of introspection through the method of speaking aloud (Newell & Simon, 1972). Subjects speak aloud during the process of solving a problem, and the investigator seeks to develop a computer program that mimics the protocol provided by them. This technique bases theories of problem solving upon those processes that are easily available to the conscious introspections of the subject. Although the verbal reports may themselves distort problem solving, it is often not difficult to speak aloud while thinking. Thus, introspection serves to open for the study of problem solving a window through which a formidable body of studies have examined the workings of normal human minds. Once again, there is no need to assume that all of problem solving can be explained in terms of operations available to introspection, but surely some of it can.

Perhaps the largest use of introspection in current psychological investigation is in the study of memory. Recall and recognition both rely on subjects being able to introspect into their past experiences to decide whether a given event is or is not familiar. The study of ''memory judgments'' makes most explicit the importance of controlled introspection as a method (Underwood, 1969).

Not all memory studies rest on introspection. The recollection of a skill or relearning of old material may show evidence of memories of which we ourselves are not aware. Perhaps the most striking case is of the patient, H. M., who showed roughly normal improvement for the skill of learning to trace a star in a mirror without ever being able to remember from day to day that he had participated in previous sessions (Milner, 1967). The distinction between introspective and skill memories is not limited to motor activity. Warrington and Weiskrantz (1968) have shown that amnesics who do poorly on introspective tests of memory do almost as well as normals when the tests involve a perceptual skill such as learning to recognize a familiar word or picture from limited cues.

Much of psychology is based upon introspective evidence; yet since the development of behaviorism, most psychological theories have been reluctant to deal directly with the distinction between conscious and unconscious mental activity. It is one goal of these lectures to do so.

There are two important ways in which introspections figure prominently in this book. First, on rare occasions, introspective methods will be used as they are in studies of memory or psychophysics. Thus the introspective technique will be one way of attempting to understand mind. However, more important will be the effort to develop a better understanding of the systems involved in introspection itself. At points in the book, I will discuss the mechanisms that underlie introspections and the way in which these mechanisms are accessed by input information. Consciousness or awareness will not be used to explain behavior but rather the reverse; behavioral data will be applied to understand how conscious introspection may fit within a general theoretical analysis of mind (Shallice, 1972). The history of the mind–body controversy within philosophy and the methodological arguments of behaviorists have convinced many psychologists that a theory of mind should be erected without distinguishing between conscious and unconscious activity. Even if this is a reasonable final goal, at this stage it has generally had the effect of making psychological theories appear very incomplete. The extent to which our conscious intentions and strategies control our thought and behavior is a question that seems important to consider. Yet most theorists in psychology, by leaving aside the distinction between conscious and unconscious processes, are unable to deal with this question except by extreme emphasis on either conscious control or behavior. For example, many writers stress the active and constructive nature of all psychological operations (Kolers, 1972; Neisser, 1967), even those that may appear introspectively to be effortless and automatic; whereas others tell us that human memory is an associational machine that operates entirely without control by the subjects' strategies (Anderson & Bower, 1973). Only an explicit distinction between conscious and unconscious operations may allow us to study separately those events that are passive—in the sense that we can do little to prevent them—from those that are active—in the sense of resulting from a deliberate strategy that the subject could as freely reject as adopt. Nor is it necessary that the issue be left as a dichotomy. Later (in Chapter 7), methods of dealing with the degree of conscious control (set) will be developed.

It is of vital importance that psychology be able to understand the role that introspections play in the mental life of organisms. To do so, psychology must deal with both conscious and unconscious processes, rather than ignore the distinction between them. To ignore the distinction is to avoid an account of the subjective experiences that accompany only those processes we call conscious. Would a cognitive psychology that described in the utmost detail the kinds of activation patterns in memory—but that could not tell us which ones were conscious and which were not—be a satisfactory account of human behavior? I feel that it would not be, and thus it is an explicit goal of the work here to attempt to determine how it is that the subjective experience of awareness is related to information processing in general. As Powers (1973) has recently pointed out, the term *perception* is used in two senses. In one sense, it is the *process* of the accumulation of information in sensory-memory systems independent of what the subject might be able to report. In another sense, it is *awareness* itself that is of interest. A goal of this book is to examine both of these meanings and their interrelationships.

Brain Processes

A second language for psychological theory has grown up through direct study of the brain. Some investigators have supposed that it would be possible to reduce the study of mind to the study of brain, thus providing both a way of ensuring the unity between humans and other organisms and a sound basis for an entirely material analysis of mental phenomena. The study of brain process via electrical recording, lesions, and stimulation has provided a cumulative and growing objective base of data that represents an impressive achievement of scientific analysis. We know a great deal about individual elements (neurons) that compose the brain and of their method of communication with one another across those tiny gaps called synapses. We know something about the great influence of chemicals upon brain processes. We know the brain changes state between waking and sleeping and that its dominant electrical rhythms change and vary over the course of a day and with different tasks and goals.

Still there is a great chasm that yawns between the study of brain and the study of mind. No electrode yet has been sufficiently subtle to seek out the mechanisms by which subjects perceive and act. Even if one remains reductionist in principle, supposing that all of psychology could be reduced to physiology, there appears no more likelihood that the principle will be realized than there is that complex social phenomena will be predictable by individual personality. Fourteen billion nerve cells responding in complex ways with multitudinous connections to each other give little likelihood of providing a rational solution that would allow prediction of mental process.

Brain does constrain mind in important and complicated ways. The results of the split-brain work in particular (Gazzaniga, 1970) have had a substantial impact upon psychological analysis. Even though there was already considerable reason to suppose that language processing was a system separable from the physical characteristic of input and had a separate evolutionary history, the important results obtained by splitting the corpus callosum confirmed this view and pro- vided new methods for its study that would not be available in any other way.

Moreover, the study of disconnection syndromes in clinical neurology pro- vides some evidence that the principles of independent, specialized processing systems developed from the split-brain preparation extend to other neural sys- tems (Geschwind, 1968).

In the process of developing an experimental psychology of mind, it would be foolish to ignore the hints provided by modern neurophysiology. Moreover, there is current interest by neurophysiologists in studies that combine behavioral and physiological techniques. As Mountcastle (1976) puts it:

> ... It has been clear for a long time—at least since the time of Lashley—that the quantitative study of behavior, traditionally the domain of the Psychologist, and of neural events in the brain, called "Neurophysiology," are conceptually dif- ferent approaches to what are generically the same set of problems, an identity long emphasized by Jung (1972). What is new is that it is now possible to combine in one experiment the methods and concepts of each to yield a deeper insight into the brain mechanisms that govern behavior than is possible with either alone. In this "combined experiment," one controls and measures behavior and records simultaneously the signs of cerebral events thought relevant [p. 1].

In many cases, however, such as the study of color vision and central factors in perception of depth, psychological techniques and theories developed well in advance of neurophysiological methods for the study of the same systems. This is likely to be increasingly true as more central mental operations are explored.

Neisser (1967) suggested that psychology should not be viewed as just some- thing to do until electrophysiology comes around to solve the problems. In the pages to come, we shall see that even with the combination of all we know about physiology and all we can discern through performance tasks and introspection, the constraints upon our models are too slight; and the effort to wring from nature a more profound analysis depends upon obtaining constraints from different sources, not reducing the kind of information upon which models rest.

Information Processing

It might seem at first that the approaches of phenomenology and physiology to the problems that have been raised are simply too remote to be brought together in any fruitful way. The history of Western philosophy is replete with efforts to solve the mind–body problem. Although armchair analyses of this problem have not succeeded, one can perhaps hope to develop an experimental approach that has the long-range potential of forcing a language of sufficient breadth to relate theories that begin even from these basically different viewpoints. Efforts to do so through the study of conditioning were unsuccessful, because the view of mind adopted was too impoverished to be plausible; and efforts from the psychoanalytic and Gestalt viewpoints are too far removed from current physiology and from powerful, objective, psychological techniques to close the gap.

The language of human information processing provides a potential common vehicle for such analysis. On one hand, it can be related to phenomenology, since introspection often serves as a tool for the construction of models and can itself be viewed as the output of a specialized processing system that can have its own objective status within the theory. On the other hand, the language of information processing provides an analysis of psychology that is congenial to physiology by placing emphasis on different levels of processing and the time course of their activation. This book represents one effort to determine whether that potential can be realized.

The information-processing language has been influenced by computer models (H. A. Simon, 1969) and by the mathematics and insights of information and control theory (Shannon & Weaver, 1949). However, its experimental base rests in studies of human performance. Essentially, this work requires adapting the human to a particular task environment and then studying the detailed organization of mental processing that obtains in that task environment. The emphasis is not upon a direct comparison of these task environments but on the adaptive abilities themselves and on the common limits to processing that emerge in different task environments. This approach seeks to isolate elementary mental operations and to understand their relation both to subjective experience and to brain processes. This approach to understanding mind has some similarities to the study of lawful constraints and conservation principles in modern physics (Feynman, 1965) in that no prediction of what will happen is possible; instead, the theory tells us only what is forbidden or constrained from happening.

To realize this integrative goal, it is necessary to rely upon a methodology that can provide insight into questions that arise in each of the three languages constituting the background for this inquiry. A set of such methods is available in the use of mental chronometry as a basic tool by which psychology can seek to understand the nature of the mind.

MENTAL CHRONOMETRY

What most holds physiology and phenomenology together within the information-processing approach is the idea that mental processes are embedded in real time. This assumption is central to the book. It is quite natural to doubt the assumption, based either upon our lack of clear introspection about time or on evidence that our awareness of events is not necessarily identical to the times at which the internal processes corresponding to those events are taking place. For example, one might be aware of the meaning of the word *psychology* before realizing it is in italics and yet also suppose that the meaning depends upon abstraction of some aspects of the physical form of the word. Such examples tend to confound the cues upon which classification is made with our awareness of those cues. Chapters 2 and 4 are devoted to an effort to separate these aspects of internal mental activity.

William James (1890) stressed the temporal nature of our phenomenal experience. He viewed consciousness as being like the flow of a stream, narrow in some places and wide in others. Unfortunately for introspective methods, our ability to discriminate short intervals of time is quite limited; thus introspections about the details of internal processes distributed in time are weak. Generally we are aware only of the product of such processes. Experimental studies, as we shall see, suggest that bringing conscious attention to bear upon a stimulus is itself a time-dependent process.

Brain activity is clearly embedded in time. The neural code consists at least in part of spikes separated by blank intervals of time. In recent years, many physiologists have used poststimulus latency histograms as a means of studying the fine temporal structure of cellular activity.

Finally, the assumption that mental operations can be measured in terms of the time they require is fundamental to modern cognitive psychology. It has provided an objective tool for the systematic observation of mental events, whether or not they are conscious. As such, it provides a method that can transcend the limitations of introspection.

Mental chronometry can be defined as *the study of the time course of information processing in the human nervous system.* The stress on information processing and humans indicates that mental chronometry seeks systematic relationships between physiological indicants, changes in performance, and subjective experiences that relate to them. As such, mental chronometry serves as a means of relating the differing viewpoints of phenomenology, physiology, and performance at least in so far as the three languages can be applied to common topics close to the boundaries of their application. It seems clear that there are problems that can be approached by phenomenology that are too complex for systematic study by physiological or chronometric techniques. In the same way, mental chronometry will doubtless fail to illuminate many issues within the domain of neurophysiology. Some topics do fall at the boundary of these approaches, and it is those problems that I have tried to choose for discussion in these lectures.

Techniques

It is important to recognize that mental chronometry as defined above is not limited to any single method of time measurement. It is this methodological breadth that allows it to serve as a wide-ranging framework for the study of mental processes. Many current psychological studies employ chronometric techniques, as do many studies in physiology. The fields have a common theoretical strategy despite the diversity of their specific empirical techniques.

The most common method is simply to measure the time between two events. When the first event is a stimulus and the second the response to it, the measure is called *reaction time*. The use of reaction time as a dependent variable has a long history in psychology (see p. 13) and is enjoying great popularity just now. It is not a field of study, however, but simply one of many dependent variables that can be used to infer the time course of mental processing.[2] A very closely related technique is to provide an informative event (cue) and measure the length of time it takes before the reaction to a following imperative event has reached its minimum. This technique can be used to determine the time required to encode the cue event in an optimal way. Much of this book deals with what is encoded during the time to reach optimal performance. In this method, focus is not upon the latency by which a subject responds but rather upon the time required to reach this optimal latency. This method has the effect of freeing encoding from an immediate response requirement (see Chapter 6). The separation of encoding and reaction time is illustrated in Figure 1.1.

Some investigators prefer to control the time subjects have available to interact with the stimulus and observe the errors they make with a given exposure duration. One such technique (Kahneman, 1969)[3] is to follow a brief exposure of a target with a second masking event. The assumption is made that the mask serves to restrict the time that is available for dealing with the target. An alternative method to masking is to train subjects to respond at different rates of speed

---

[2]There is a story that psychology has only two areas of research: "reaction time and percent correct." The confusion between reaction time as a dependent variable and mental chronometry as a field of investigation is a natural one. However, many studies that record reaction time have no relevance to inducing an understanding of the time course of information processing, and many chronometric studies use percent correct as the dependent variable.

[3]References are frequently made to a recent review of the method and/or area rather than to the first study. In general, the review should provide references to earlier sources.

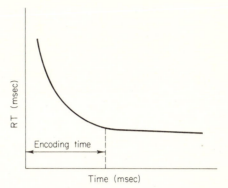

FIG. 1.1.   RT as a function of the time between cue and imperative stimulus. The interstimulus interval needed to reach the optimal RT (indicated by the arrow) is called the *encoding time*.

and then to observe the errors they make at each rate of processing (Pachella, 1974). This technique makes use of the fact that people can obtain greater accuracy by going more slowly.

Measurements of the accuracy of performance following different lengths of stimulus exposure are based on an implicit notion that quality of input builds up over time and that subjects can access this information at different places in its build-up. Faster access means lower information quality and thus greater errors until asymptote is reached. This idea is outlined in Figure 1.2. Although more precise theories can be stated as to the shape of the function shown in Figure 1.2 and thus the detailed nature of the speed–accuracy tradeoff, they have in common the monotonic assumption indicated in the figure.

All the methods discussed so far can be called *behavioral*, in that they require the subject to perform a task and thus provide an overt response. Another set of chronometric methods involves the use of electrical potentials that are time locked to events. In human subjects, time-locked-evoked potentials are usually

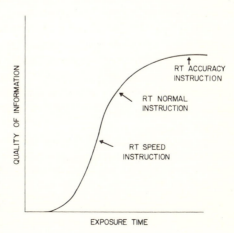

FIG. 1.2.   Quality of information builds up with exposure duration. Instructions, alertness, and other variable affect the time before the subject responds.

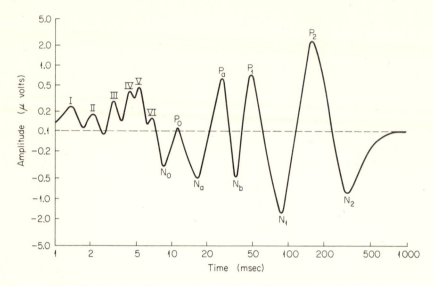

FIG. 1.3. Human auditory evoked potential to a 60-db click stimulus. The first six peaks represent subcortical contributions. (From Picton, Hillyard, Krausz, & Galambos, 1974. Copyright 1974 by the Elsevier/North-Holland Biomedical Press.)

taken from the scalp (Donchin & Lindsley, 1969; Regan, 1972). Thus, like reaction time and speed–accuracy curves, evoked potentials must be subject to a great deal of averaging in order to reduce the contribution of unwanted background artifacts.

Using auditory clicks as stimuli, it is possible to separate contributions from several subcortical relay stations as well as from different areas of the cortex, as illustrated in Figure 1.3. These contributions represent the activities of many cells distributed over a wide area, but when used as a part of systematic chronometric studies of behavior they can expand our understanding of information processing and serve to make the connection to brain activity apparent. The value of studies of evoked cortical potentials as aids to chronometric analysis is made clear when two curves collected in somewhat different conditions are superimposed, as in Figure 1.4. Here we are able to see when the two conditions first have a differential effect upon the evoked electrical activity.

It is sometimes possible to observe the activity of single cells or small groups of cells at one or another level of the nervous system. Although this method is usually confined to nonhuman organisms, the use of operant or classical conditioning methods sometimes makes it possible to develop tasks the nonhuman can do that resemble components of those frequently performed by human beings. Such single-cell studies can be linked to mental chronometry when the investigator plots a poststimulus latency histogram that indicates when in the sequence

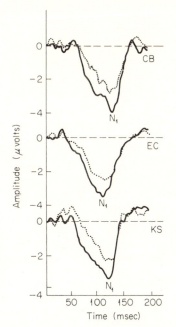

FIG. 1.4.   In this figure, evoked potentials to the same auditory stimulus
events for each of three subjects are
shown when the stimulus occurs on
an attended channel (solid line) and
on an unattended channel (dotted
line).   (From   Hillyard,   Hink,
Schwent, & Picton, 1973. Copyright
1973 by the American Association
for the Advancement of Science.)

of processing a particular cell is affected. The logic is similar to that shown in Figure 1.4 for evoked potentials. For example, in Figure 1.5 there is evidence that cells in the medial geniculate discriminate between previously conditioned positive and negative auditory events by 20 msec after input (Olds, Disterhoft, Segal, Kornblith, & Hirsh, 1972). We are still some way from being able to bring together the single-cell work with behavioral techniques, but the common language of mental chronometry does indicate the possibility.

Although the logic of the techniques using mental chronometry seem quite similar, there is a very rigid separation of this literature into different fields and journals. Partly for this reason, it is rare to find the various techniques brought together so as to reveal both relationships and problems. For example, serial models for processing of sensory information have arisen both in studies using single-cell recording from striate cortex in response to visual stimuli (Hubel & Wiesel, 1962) and from studies of reaction time to linguistic stimuli in humans (Sternberg, 1969). The use of different techniques, stimuli, and sensory systems has generally prevented the observations that confirm or deny these models from being discussed together.

Indeed, each literature has developed in isolation, and there is widespread feeling that the methods provide conflicting results and thus cannot be compared or used together. There are conflicts all through the psychological literature, both in studies using a single method and studies employing different methods. There

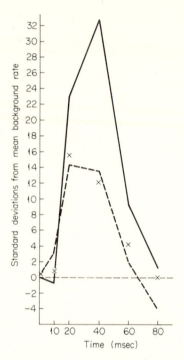

FIG. 1.5. Responses of electrodes in the medial geniculate to CS+ after conditioning (solid line), CS− before conditioning (dashed line), and CS− after conditioning (Xs). The conditioning affects the input signal by 20–30 msec after input. (From Olds, Disterhoft, Segal, Kornblith, & Hirsh, 1972. Copyright 1972 by the American Physiological Society.)

are few cases where such discrepancies have been definitely traced to the use of different techniques per se. In many situations, differences in the method are confounded with differences in the task configuration needed to employ a given method. An illustration of this is the finding that reaction time decreased and errors increased with warning interval in a task measuring reaction time to a signal that remained present until the response (Posner, Klein, Summers, & Buggie, 1973). This speed–accuracy tradeoff seemed to suggest a bias rather than a change in sensory processing, and it appeared to conflict with studies employing signal detection methods that showed improved d' as a warning interval increased from 0 to .5 sec (Klein & Kerr, 1974). Further analysis indicated that when brief signals were used, as is necessary in order to measure d' in this situation, both reaction time and errors decreased with foreperiod. Thus the apparent conflict was not due to different measurement techniques but to different physical situations being used in order to employ those techniques (Posner, 1975a). It would probably be foolish to suppose that there are no differences introduced by the method of measurement, but it seems likely that there is more to be gained than lost from systematic comparisons of results arising from differing techniques.

There are other problems in attempting to relate results using such widely different methods as those we have discussed. One of the most serious problems is the difference in the relatively long times required to get a human being to make an overt response to a stimulus (150–450 msec) as compared to the relatively short time it takes for stimulus information to travel from the peripheral nervous system to the brain (15–30 msec). Thus it is sometimes difficult to relate overt responses directly to the stages of processing found in the much faster single-cell results or the continuous evoked-potential techniques. This difficulty has become less severe as psychological techniques begin to break down the stages of information processing through the use of models that serve to analyze overt behavior.

A more severe impediment is the difference in questions that physiological and experimental psychologists ask about information flow. Physiological psychologists tend to be interested in the location of events so that they can work out the detailed neuroanatomical mechanisms that underlie the operations at a particular level of the nervous system. They have little concern with whether a given mechanism can be controlled by instruction or whether it influences the subjective state or activity of the organism. Experimental psychologists have less interest in the specific location of processes and more in how they relate to subjective experiences and overt behavior. For example, physiologists find the spatial averaging of the evoked potential recorded from the human scalp to be a blunt tool for research studies. This is certainly true if the problem is to understand the detailed operations of neural mechanisms. However, for psychological issues it may be a useful advantage to deal with activity that involves great masses of cells, such as the scalp-evoked potentials, because such activity may indicate processes with sufficient weight to control the subjective state or behavior of the organism in the face of competing events. The activity of single cells and of averaged massed responses both may aid in understanding the internal stages in the processing of information.

History

The basic idea of viewing information processing in terms of the reflex goes back at least to Galen, and—as illustrated in Figure 1.6—Descartes had a theory of the coordination of sensory and motor nerves in the processing of visual information.

However, the idea that mental processing is relatively slow did not arise until the middle of the 19th century. Until that time, it was thought that nervous processes were infinitely fast or at least immeasurably rapid. In fact, J. Müller felt that the time for nerve conduction could never be measured, since it was similar to the speed of light; and although we had the whole heavens within which to make our measurements of light, we only had the relatively confined size of the body in which to study nerve conduction. At first, it may appear puzzling that scientists prior to 1850 did not find obvious the delayed human response to stimuli that now seems so intuitive. In part, this must be due to the industrialization that has characterized the last 100 years. The late discovery of delayed processing reinforces the notion that there is poor awareness of rapid

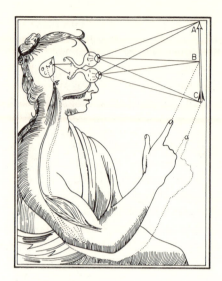

FIG. 1.6. A view of information
processing after Descartes.

processes. Even today, relatively sophisticated persons may find it surprising that
it takes about 20 msec longer to verify that 4 + 3 = 7 than to verify that 4 + 2 = 6
(Parkman & Groen, 1971). Perhaps more surprising is the longer time taken to
deny that 4 + 3 = 12 than to deny appropriate controls, due to the tendency
to respond "yes" because of the presence of a correct product (Winkelman &
Schmidt, 1974).

A short time after Müller's statement on its impossibility, his student, Helmholtz, measured the time for neural conduction in both frog and humans and
showed that far from being infinite, it was not even very rapid. His estimates of
neural conduction time were around 100 m per sec, thus requiring about 20 msec
for information to be conducted to the brain from remote parts of the periphery.

Within a few years after Helmholtz, F. C. Donders had begun to apply this
method to the study of human mental processes. He developed the subtractive
method, which assumed that reaction time could be divided into a series of
additive stages and that tasks could be invented that inserted or deleted these
stages, thus allowing us to measure by subtractraction the time required for each
stage.

For a period of time after Donders, there was considerable interest in exploring individual differences in response time and in studying the implications of
mental chronometry for the investigation of psychophysical questions. Wündt, in
particular, attempted to build upon the subtractive method by supposing that one
could directly measure the time for an event to enter the consciousness of the
subject. This was of particular theoretical interest, because the emphasis within
structuralist psychology on the study of conscious processes made it imperative
to know the relationship of processing time to the subject's awareness. Wündt's
effort to develop the so-called *d* reaction was unsuccessful. Subjects could not

reliably signal when an item entered consciousness, because this method depended entirely upon the criterion they adopted. Chapter 6 reviews recent attempts to analyze this same issue but this time through more objective techniques. Wündt's linking of the subtractive method to the study of consciousness in this way was a disaster for chronometric studies, because it eliminated the objective character of the methods developed by Donders. By the turn of the century, mental chronometry was only of secondary interest within academic psychology.

The subtractive method and mental chronometry continued to have practical applications, however. Frederick Taylor (1967), in his book on scientific management that became the basis of industrial engineering in the United States, referred to the experiments on mental chronometry as a reason for supposing that the measurement of time might give an objective basis for development of task analysis in industrial settings. The "Therblig" became a chronometrically defined unit for the analysis of complex motor behavior. Through time and motion study, mental chronometry had a practical impact on the technology of job design, but these results were not related to the development of psychological theory.

It was during World War II that experimental psychologists, coming into contact with the practical problem of equipment design, began to resurrect the use of reaction time, particularly in relationship to the new mathematical theory of information (Shannon & Weaver, 1949). The work of Hick (1952) and Hyman (1953) provided support for the idea that response time was linearly related to the amount of information transmission required by a task (see Figure 1.7). However, the hope that there would be some fixed human information-processing capacity that could be obtained from the reciprocal of these slopes was dashed by subsequent findings that showed that the slopes vary over a wide range and were even flat in some cases (see Figure 1.8).

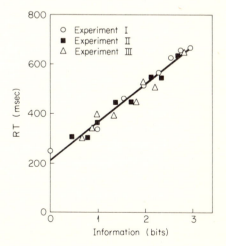

FIG. 1.7. The relations between information and RT for one subject. Experiment I manipulates number of alternatives, Experiment II probabilities, and Experiment III sequential dependencies. (From Hyman, 1953. Copyright 1953 by the American Psychological Association. Reprinted by permission.)

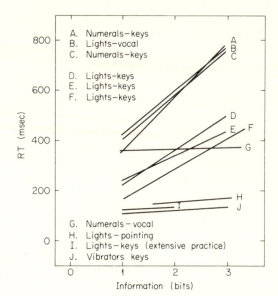

FIG. 1.8.   RT as a function of information for a number of experiments of varying compatibility. (Adapted from Fitts, 1964.)

These findings led most psychologists to abandon the information measure (Neisser, 1967). It was certainly correct that information measures could not provide a complete objective basis for the development of psychology, but it is probably a mistake not to continue efforts to teach it as an important, practical tool for psychology. Once again, as in the case of Donders' methods, theoretically oriented psychologists were quick to abandon techniques that could not provide a complete basis for psychological theory without much regard to the practical utility of the technique. Information measures have proven useful as a tool for the analysis of problems, as in the design of cockpits (Senders, 1964), and in the evaluation of complexity, as in aesthetics (Berlyne, 1974). The contribution of information theory to theoretical psychology was in emphasizing that humans are influenced not only by what occurs but also by what might have occurred. Our sensitivity to information so defined reflects the importance of expectancy as a controller of human behavior. Indeed, experiments with nonhuman organisms have also shown the importance of information in this sense in influencing behavior (Egger & Miller, 1962; Rescorla & Wagner, 1972). Moreover, information theory provides a way of combining a variety of different experimental manipulations such as number of events, probability of events, and errors into a single metric.

Information measures as used in experimental psychology were variants of stimulus–response theory, in that the main interest was in the correlation between some input variable (amount of information) and output (time). There was also interest in the internal processing stages that might mediate that relationship. For example, Hick (1952) proposed a serial dichotomization as the underlying basis for the logarithmic relationship between number of alternative events and reaction time. This proposal was consonant with the general emphasis in mental chronometry of a series of additive stages that eventuated in the overall response time. However, a dichotomization process did not seem too plausible, particularly for symbolic input codes. There was no introspective impression of performing such a dichotomization, and there was little reason to suppose that all internal search processes would best be viewed as a series of successive dichotomizations.

Efforts to extend information analysis beyond transmission tasks (Posner, 1964) to those in which people were required to condense or create information were not successful, because they too remained at the level of input–output relationships. This problem and the failure of information theory to provide a reliable value for the information-processing capacity of the human mind helped turn attention to the examination of internal processing stages that might mediate between the occurrence of stimulus and response.[4]

Serial Assumptions

A fundamental basis of mental chronometry since the time of Donders has been the assumption of a sequence of serial stages mediating between stimulus and response. This is essentially an elaboration of the reflex arc idea. When psychologists began to look inside the organism, it seemed useful to use the assumption of serial processes as a working hypothesis. Moreover, a variety of results from such disparate directions as artificial intelligence, physiology, and performance at first seemed to favor the assumption of serial processing.

Physiology. In the study of visual pattern recognition, serial processing ideas received support from findings in neurophysiology (Hubel & Wiesel, 1962) that indicated a serial progression of processes from simple to complex and hypercomplex cells—each type of cell responding to more general features of the input and each formed from a concatenation of cells at lower levels. Although these units dealt with only the earliest levels of visual processing, they were expanded by theories postulating gnostic units based on the same general principles that serve to recognize complex visual patterns (Konorski, 1967). The single-cell recording results and their theoretical elaboration had profound influence upon studies on information processing. The serial principle appeared to describe the early stages of visual processing in the striate cortex, and it seemed reasonable to

---

[4]I want to stress that unlike others, I do not see the use of information measures in psychology as a failure or of only historical interest. There are many practical reasons to desire a summary of input–output relations that do not deal with the specific, internal manipulations involved. Moreover, the basic conception arising from this approach—the importance of expectancy—has remained viable.

extend that basic idea through the rest of information processing. Moreover, the assumed correspondence between the Hubel and Wiesel results and the task hierarchy outlined by Donders 100 years before seemed to provide a unified basis for mental chronometry.

The use of evoked cortical potentials also provides a chronometric method for the study of electrical activity, at least for that which could be recorded from the scalps of human subjects. These potentials also appeared to support serial models in that early sensory-specific components of the evoked potential occurring within the first 50 to 100 msec were quickly replaced by sensory-nonspecific components (Donchin & Lindsley, 1969). These nonspecific components could be obtained from either vertex leads or those over the modality of stimulation. Such findings were compatible with the hierarchy emerging from the single-cell work in the sense that they showed that short-term, sensory-specific processes were replaced quickly by more nonsensory effects.

Artificial intelligence.   Work in artificial intelligence also seemed to favor a serial model. Part of this emphasis undoubtedly arose from the serial nature of digital computers of the time. In addition, however, Newell, Shaw, and Simon (1958) developed the General Problem Solver program, which stressed the point of serial organization of information processing. This program was not only mated to the capacity of the digital computers being used but also reflected the necessarily serial output in verbal protocols obtained from subjects. The power of the General Problem Solver and the theoretical ideas that stem from it also provided additional support for a serial organization of processing stages. If a serial model was capable of proving the theorems of *Principia Mathematica,* it seemed reasonable that it could handle the information processing that was required by most psychological tasks.

Computer models were not always strictly serial in their operation. The pandemonium model of Selfridge (1959) involved both serial and parallel processing. Demons at lower levels shouted in parallel, even though higher level mechanisms were contacted serially. Selfridge's idea is compatible with the hierarchical notions arising from the studies of Hubel and Wiesel; but neither is an entirely serial system, since within a stage many analyzers operate together. The stages themselves, however, operate in serial order.

Performance analysis.   The most persuasive evidence for a serial stage approach to the organization of internal processing emerged from the work of Sternberg (1966, 1969). He showed it was possible to maintain the idea of a series of additive stages composing the reaction time without having to adopt Donders' rather awkward method of creating tasks that inserted new stages without otherwise changing the ones already present. Sternberg studied tasks in which a number of items called a *positive set* were presented to the subject followed by a single probe item. The subject was to respond as quickly as possible, indicating whether or not the probe was a member of the positive set. A linear relation between the reaction time and positive-set size was found.

The task could be divided into four logical stages: encoding, serial scanning, binary choice, and response execution. Sternberg (1969) argued that any two variables that affect different stages would have additive effects on the overall reaction time and that those affecting the same stage would have interactive effects. This additive factors method has been used subsequently to explore the duration and coding of internal operations involved in successive stages. Given its assumptions, it has become a very powerful method. It assumes that the input is undergoing a continual abstraction process in which each successive stage replaces the last. Thus a single input code is compared against the stored positive set. It is only the output of this comparison process that feeds into the binary selection stage, and no earlier code is available for reevaluation. It should be no great surprise that these restrictions do not always apply (see below) and that the brain more often operates with multiple codes that are present in parallel and among which complex selection processes select. What is impressive is that despite its restrictive assumptions, the additive factors method has proven as useful as the work of the last several years has shown it to be. Although it cannot be readily accepted as a complete basis for the study of mental processing like information analysis, it is an extremely valuable tool. Its value will increase still further if we can discover more of a fundamental nature concerning the conditions under which it applies.

Parallel Processes

The findings of the last several years in each of the areas discussed above have not supported a strictly serial-stage view of the internal mental operations involved in the recognition of patterns. However, these studies have generally used some variant of mental chronometry and serve to strengthen the notion of mental chronometry as a general approach for the study of pattern recognition and mental processing in general.

Single-cell studies designed to explore the latency of input to simple, complex, and hypercomplex cells (Stone, 1972) have shown that complex cells receive faster input from geniculate levels than do simple and hypercomplex cells. This result suggests that the logical hierarchy discussed in Hubel and Wiesel is not necessarily a temporal hierarchy. Though this need not upset the logical hierarchy of feature abstraction so attractive in the earlier Hubel and Wiesel work, it is obviously inconsistent with the strictly serial view. On the other hand, one does not know what aspects of the physiological signal are being used at higher levels. As long as one supposed that the only input to complex cells was from simple cells, it did not matter which aspect of the signal was being used by higher levels. However, if complex cells have multiple inputs both from simple cells and directly from other levels, then it becomes crucial to know what aspect of the signal at a given level is being used by higher levels. This is just the question to which current physiology by itself cannot provide a satisfactory answer. '

Results obtained from depth electrode recordings of evoked potentials (Goff, Williamson, Van Gilder, Allison, & Fisher, Note 1) suggest that the idea that sensory-specific components of evoked potentials are rapidly replaced by nonspecific components is too simple. Sensory-specific components seem to persist at deep recording sites within the modality of stimulation, although they are swamped by nonspecific activity as the electrode placements are made toward the surface of the cortex. This suggests that sensory-specific activity is maintained in parallel with the elaboration of nonspecific components.

This result is very consonant with the efforts of behavioral psychologists to examine the persistence of memory at various levels of processing (Broadbent, 1958; Sperling, 1960). If sensory-specific memories persist and if the subject had access to these sensory-specific memories, then even though a hierarchical abstraction system may operate serially, the information at each level will be available to influence experience and behavior.

Studies of human performance also raise problems with a strictly serial analysis even when applied only to pattern recognition. Experiments have suggested that a full analysis of the input probes is carried out during the first stage of the Sternberg model (Atkinson & Juola, 1973; Meyer, Schvaneveldt, & Ruddy, 1975; Posner, 1972). For example, changes in the signal–to–noise ratio interact with prior activation of semantically related items, indicating that the two affect the same stage. Other studies show that information on the familiarity of the probe input (Atkinson & Juola, 1973), its name, and its semantic classification are often available before subjects begin to match the probe against items in the positive set. This is particularly true when the positive set is highly familiar and thus in long-term memory, as is obviously the case in pattern recognition. Thus the serial-stage assumptions of the additive factors method, though useful for the study of mental operations, are inadequate to deal with the process of recognition itself or with problems where memory codes persist following input.

As I hope to illustrate, the study of mental chronometry does not depend upon the truth of the serial assumptions. Where such assumptions hold, as they frequently appear to do, we have an especially powerful tool in additive factors analysis for the study of the internal stages of information processing. However, even where serial processing is seriously wrong, it is possible to examine the time course of information flow. As I hope to demonstrate, such studies can provide consistent data and can reveal a great deal about the structure of internal mental processing.

TOPICS OF THE LECTURES

Related Efforts

The purpose of these lectures is to bring together the languages of introspection and brain processes around a consistent information-processing framework. I recognize how distant the goal still is and how weak and primitive this effort to realize it. The goal is one that various physiologists, psychologists, and philosophers have attempted repeatedly for over 100 years. These efforts have been diverse, beginning from different metatheoretical assumptions and based upon different views about the nature of the brain. One such effort stems from the study of reflexes, another from observations of brain injury, another from the principles of evolutionary theory, and more recently, from the analogy between the brain and a computer. Each of these approaches has had a strong effect on the shaping of the current lectures, and it may be useful to examine these relationships briefly.

The earliest systematic effort to base the workings of the human mind on the known physiology of the reflex stems from Sechenov's 19th-century classic *Reflexes of the Brain* (1965). In this work, Sechenov sought to extend the experimental model of the reflex developed in German physiology to the workings of the normal human mind. Sechenov's main thesis was that perception and thought could be viewed as early stages of reflex activity, the latter stages of which were inhibited by central systems. The theoretical brilliance of this simple but powerful idea was unfortunately not complemented by comparable empirical analysis. However, subsequent work in experimental physiology summarized by Sherrington (1906) helped to flesh out with experimental detail and technique the Sechenov thesis.

The basic ideas remain with us in current works that stress the role of reflex systems in the understanding of mind. A recent treatment by Razran (1971) emphasizes the behavioral work in America and the Soviet Union in this field, and Konorski (1967) attempts to tie the operations of reflex activity more closely to known brain function. There can be little doubt that the reflex idea—perhaps elaborated with feedback and feed-forward concepts (Arbib, 1972; Powers, 1973)—has persisted, because it does capture much of the organization of mind in performing habitual tasks. Those who follow these lectures will note that the reflex concept, in much the way Sechenov proposed it, is used heavily in Chapter 4.

Two points must be made that serve as important qualifications of the reflex idea. First, most psychological attempts to explore reflex ideas in an empirical way have relied upon the conditioned-reflex methodology (Pavlov, 1960). Because these operations involve learning of new reflex connections, they combine voluntary and involuntary operations in very complex ways, making it hard to know how much of the conditioning procedure reveals fundamental processes that are imposed upon a human by the procedure and how much involve strategies adopted for experimental situations. The study of interoceptive reflexes (Razran, 1971), the use of biofeedback methods (Miller, 1969), and the effort to separate automatic from volitional responses by time course or topography (Grant, 1972) are all ways of avoiding this difficulty. In Chapter 4 I will argue that mental chronometry provides another and to some extent a more satisfactory way of exploring this difficult relation between the voluntary choice of the subjects and reflex-like actions imposed upon them. In any case, I believe that the conditioning literature, particularly with such concepts as expectancy, orienting, and blocking included, is not very remote from models appropriate to highly automatic tasks in human subjects that have been fruitfully explored by mental chronometry.

The second qualification represents one of the most important points of modern experimental psychobiology. Sechenov assumed that the central system activated by input was basically simple, like the mechanism involved in the spinal reflexes he had studied. The great complexity of central systems that underlie the internal state of the organism and that allow association of input with past experience have been discoveries of this century and have seriously undermined the reflex model. The discovery in biology of endogenous rhythms (Brunning, 1973), of motor programs operated from internally stored subroutines (Hoyle, 1975), and the complex dissociations that occur in brain injury (Gazzaniga, 1970; Geschwind, 1968) all testify that a model that treats the central mechanisms as passive switching systems or relays will be hopelessly primitive. Hebb (1949) was probably the first to dramatize the need to place increased emphasis on the central systems in the construction of brain models, and many others have followed. Though it appeared, following the work of Lashley, that it might not be possible to subdivide these central processes by experimental analysis, subsequent studies of disconnection syndromes and in particular of the split brain (Gazzaniga, 1970) have given support to the idea that these central systems have sufficient specificity and localization to be separated for experimental study.

Faced with the great complexity of central systems, psychologists interested in the human mind have adopted one of several metatheoretical positions. Some have continued to study the reflex or associational model in the hopes of finding some task, internal system, or organism in which the central systems would be of sufficiently small import that nonreflex concepts could be avoided. The boldest such proposal by Anderson and Bower (1973) is that the memory system operates in a strategy-free (i.e., reflex-like) way in organizing input information. This strategy-free assumption allows the preservation of a reflex-like model, although one that in this case is embellished with many complex parsing operations. This view assumes a minimum of cognitive control.

Other psychologists have held that the memory system involves the use of many optional strategies and cannot be seen in terms of an associational machine.

Neither side has attempted to adduce direct evidence on this issue but instead have tried to argue that evidence consistent with an overall model can be used to support their metatheoretical view. I believe that chronometric studies show it to be possible to observe strategy-free connections in habitual processing tasks, even those involving learned semantic content. Like Anderson and Bower, I believe that these are only part of the story; but unlike them, I believe that it will prove impossible to argue that memory storage as a whole is a process that operates without regard to the conscious strategies and intentions of the subject.

A second metatheoretical approach adopts principles of evolutionary theory (Garner, 1974; Gibson, 1966). This idea appears to me to be as follows. The human information-processing system is very complex, and it cannot be disentangled by empirical study, at least within psychology. Instead, let us assume that the system has adapted via evolution to perform in a way that is optimal for the environments that have exerted selective pressure. Given that assumption, it is really unnecessary to analyze the processing system directly; instead, we will seek understanding of the environments to which the human system has adapted. Jerison's (1973) important work on the evolution of brain size provides rationale for this argument. It has been adopted to a greater or lesser degree by Gibson (1966) in his study of perception and by Newell and Simon (1972) in their study of problem solving; more recently, Garner (1974) has applied the idea to information processing in general in the previous Fitts lectures. This approach has the attraction of viewing psychology in close relation to other fields of biology and bringing to bear the powerful concepts that have developed from evolutionary theory (Wilson, 1975). On occasion I have relied upon this method, particularly on the evidence provided by Jerison on the separate evolution of sensory systems. Basically I am unconvinced that the evolutionary argument can provide precise enough constraints to develop answers to many of the questions regarding human performance and information processing that one would like. However, it is important to bear in mind this approach, because it holds the promise of adding important new developmental dimensions to what are too often relatively static models of human performance.

A third metatheoretical viewpoint for the study of mind arises from the analogy between it and the computer. It proposes that analytic attempts to carve out small, experimental domains for the study of human performance have not been successful, because overall strategies, intentions, and active processes guide all of our behavior and cognition. Thus until we obtain an overall model of the process, we cannot begin to understand the subsystems that operate within it. In many ways the computer simulation effort has been based on the same view of mind that inspired Gestalt psychology 50 years ago. One of the contentions of this view is that all behavior, even the simplest, is subject to cognitive control from higher levels. Thus any reflex-like or associational efforts will be doomed to failure, because they are artificial abstractions. It seems to me that this view places too much reliance on cognitive control. Although central systems are both complex and important, they do not replace the simpler principles of association, even within the human mind. Any acceptance of an evolutionary model could hardly argue otherwise. Even if one uses the computer analog, it will still be necessary to come to understand the elementary mental operations that constitute the basis of the particular models that are used for simulation. If these are totally arbitrary, the models that adopt them must themselves be completely arbitrary. The experiments described in this book can be viewed as an effort to develop an account at both the information-processing and physiological levels of the elementary mental operations needed to construct such models.

It should be noted that I have not tried to dismiss any of the three views that I have discussed above. They are neither exhaustive nor mutually exclusive. They all carry important insights and represent valid approaches to the problems of the human mind. However, my emphasis in these lectures is on a fourth approach that is most similar to that adopted by D. E. Broadbent in the first Paul M. Fitts Lectures. Like his, it is basically an empirical approach in that it seeks direct evidence on such questions as whether reflex-like activity can be found within human mental processing and if so, for what kinds of tasks, under what circumstances, and at what levels. Second, like his view, it distinguishes between sensory systems that collect and organize evidence from the environment and central decision systems. At two points, there is a departure from his understanding of this issue. The information-collection systems are seen as involving both sensory and memory systems at many different levels. For this reason I cannot rely upon too close an identification of d' with the operations of the information-collection systems. A criterion (beta) at one level of such a system can affect the discriminability at the next level. I have also taken much more seriously than he the need to connect certain operations with our awareness of input. I have also tried to be as explicit as possible about the chronometric framework that provides unity to the methodologies employed in these investigations. Finally, I have approached rather different questions than occupied Broadbent. The rationale and organization of these choices are outlined below.

ORGANIZATION

One cannot cover all topics of experimental psychology in an attempt to develop a theoretical framework. I have chosen to limit the topics to those on which I have specifically worked in the last 10 years. Thus both the chronometric techniques employed and the specific topics discussed will be idiosyncratic and selected to illustrate rather than to exhaust the current state of the field.

The materials are organized to provide a coherent development of the overall framework and to demonstrate how processing studies can serve to illuminate aspects of introspection and of physiology.

In Chapter 2 I start by developing the notion of independent (isolable) processing systems for dealing with linguistic material. Since only some systems can be isolated by surgery, I use behavioral operations to define such systems.

The properties of these independent processing sytems are outlined in Chapter 3, and efforts are made to discuss some of the ways they are coordinated in behavior and in subjective experience.

Such independent systems may be viewed as pathways mediating information flow. I explore efforts to prime and inhibit these pathways by prior input. The experimental investigations reviewed in Chapter 4 illustrate the reality of such pathways, even though we do not understand their physical basis.

The human organism is both active and passive. No more fundamental result has emerged from the last 100 years of psychobiology. Chapters 2 and 4 largely concern the human as a passive system viewed in accordance with the reflex model stemming from Sechenov. But there is evidence that endogenous, cognitively controlled processes make as much difference for human information processing as do habitual pathways. For this reason, a reflex model is an inadequate way to view human information processing.

The activity of organisms wax and wane over time in accordance with endogenous rhythms and with rapid changes in internal state. In Chapter 5 the effects of such phasic and tonic changes in state upon human information processing are discussed. We are all familiar subjectively with the high energy of peak alertness and with the low points that sometimes follow a heavy meal or occur late in the evening. These changes that we experience subjectively also make differences in our information processing that can be used to tell us something of their nature.

Introspection itself rests upon a particular subsystem that underlies conscious experience. This system is isolable in the sense that various kinds of experimental operations can make it more or less available for the analysis of input. Moreover, the time course of such conscious processes can be observed and studied. Chapter 6 reviews attempts to do so.

Sets induced from central strategies are an important aspect of human information processing. Some have viewed this aspect as so important as to render useless any passive view of human mind. In my view, these active strategies are elaborated on top of automatic processing. Chapter 7 attempts to bring new experimental results to bear on the question of how central endogenous factors come to control the information-processing pathways developed in earlier chapters. In Chapter 7, simple experimental techniques are used to investigate sets created to orient the subject toward input pathways.

Finally, in Chapter 8 I try to apply the principles we have learned in earlier chapters to an understanding of complex psychological issues such as reading, intelligence, and personality. Unfortunately, the principles provide only minimal constraints and do not allow prediction of complex task performance. There are some lessons to be learned that provide a basis for application of performance principles in complex environments.

With this overview, you may decide to quit reading. If you wish to follow the book, you should read it pretty much in the order in which it is presented. Each chapter builds upon conclusions developed in the preceding chapter; each introduces methods understandable only after having reviewed earlier methods. The core of the material introduced in the succeeding chapters is from my own work and that of my associates and students. I have tried to reach out to deal with many of the studies that have relied upon similar methods and that have provided criticisms, warnings, and cautions about the success of our own empirical approach. I undoubtedly have not incorporated answers to all the questions raised by critics, nor have I been able to deal with all the important findings obtained by others using these methods. I have walked a narrow line in attempting to deal with only those questions for which an empirical analysis was available and not with all the questions about the human mind to which one would like an answer. I leave to others the decision about whether the framework developed is sufficient to handle the materials presented here and whether it can be extended to handle a broader range of results on the nature of mind.

2 Processing Systems

INTRODUCTION

As we have seen in Chapter 1, the pendulum in psychology swings between extremes of precise localization of function in brain centers and doctrines such as mass action and equipotentiality, which emphasize the operation of the brain as an undifferentiated whole. A localization viewpoint is helpful because it provides a method of dividing the problem of human information processing into more manageable units of analysis. For example, the ability to localize the primary projection areas of the great sensory pathways supports the division of sensory psychology into the study of different modalities.

On the other hand, introspection reveals a world that seems superficially at harmony with a mass-action viewpoint. Sights, sounds, and smells blend into a unified subjective experience of the world around us. Even if physiologists argue that this unity is assembled from the operation of quite distinct processing systems, it may seem unlikely that such systems remain in any sense independent for the purposes of psychological analysis.

Careful chronometric studies have indicated that even an experience that seems as unified as a single, visual letter gives rise to a set of quite different internal codes, which can be isolated by experimental analysis. By a *code* I mean the format by which information is represented. The visual code corresponding to a word consists of representations that are based upon the form of the letters and their interrelations but does not involve the phonetic character of the letter string. These codes can be made operational by behavioral techniques. However, they also correspond to the organization of the brain in terms of different sensory systems. Thus if there is a separate visual code for a word, it seems likely that it

27

is represented within the brain's visual system. The neural representation of internal codes, however, is a question that is separate from their psychological organization. This functional independence of internal codes arising from the same stimulus event provides experimental psychologists with their own operational means of exploring the separation of internal codes. It provides objective methods for realizing the old structuralist effort to obtain evidence of internal psychological structures whose independence from specific mental acts is sufficient to serve as underlying representations. If a single stimulus event provides the basis for independent activity within these separate structures, their independence should be even more clearly evident when separate events are presented, as they inevitably are in the real world. In this chapter I wish to dwell at some length on the consequence of the functional independence of internal codes.

LEVELS OF PROCESSING

Definition

The idea of processing levels arises naturally from the structure of sensory systems. Neurons synapse in structures between peripheral sense organs on their way to and from the primary projection areas of the cerebral cortex. Thus in vision it is natural to think of retinal, lateral geniculate, and cortical levels (see Figure 2.1). This idea was extended, for example, by Hubel and Wiesel (1962) to include simple, complex, and hypercomplex cells within the visual cortex. Theorists like Konorski (1967) extended it still further in an attempt to provide an

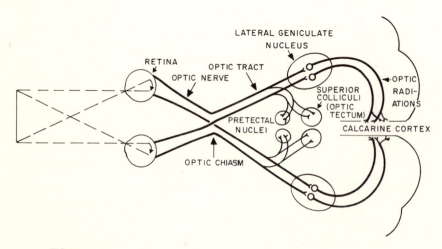

FIG. 2.1.   The visual system provides a natural basis for a processing-levels approach.

account of pattern recognition in which higher-level cells (gnostic units) serve to abstract information at levels beyond the hypercomplex cells. Other sensory systems such as audition (Webster & Aitkin, 1975) and pain (Melzack, 1973) can also be analyzed in terms of processing levels.

The concept of a processing level begins as a purely anatomical description of the location of successive synapses. Sometimes special functions can be identified with these levels. In vision, for example, a level (e.g., the lateral geniculate) has been closely related to a function (e.g., the processing of opponent color information). There is an experimental advantage to a levels approach for physiological research, because electrodes can be inserted at a given level, and the detailed mechanisms that lie at that level are then available for study. However, this sense of isolability of a level may not be as strong as it first appears. Since information can be fed back from higher levels, there is no guarantee that the information picked up by an electrode at a particular level is influenced by processing at that level alone. For the earliest stages of sensory input, where pathways can be traced precisely, it is easier to assure onself that the output of a given electrode is due to input information coming from lower centers; thus processing is at the level being examined and is not influenced by feedback from higher levels. However, for more central levels of processing, it becomes an impossible task to determine directly by pathway tracing the sources of information that might influence a given electrode. For these levels, careful chronometric analysis (Olds, Disterhoft, Segal, Kornblith, & Hirsh, 1972) of the latency at which a given cell is affected by some input may provide a potential means to insure that the processing being measured is taking place at or prior to a particular level. In any case, the isolability of levels requires a special argument from the logic of the data obtained.

Under the influence of the serial processing assumptions of mental chronometry discussed in Chapter 1, it was tempting to identify the levels of processing concept in physiology with a similar idea in psychology (Craik & Lockhart, 1972; Estes, 1975; Posner, 1969). However, there are some serious problems in too close an identification of psychological and physiological processing levels at the present time.

First, such a close identification leaves psychologists without any independent definitions to explore new levels or to determine the organization of levels. This is particularly critical at higher levels where physiologists have not obtained data and where pathway tracing is difficult or impossible. If psychologists had their own operational definitions of levels, these could be checked against the physiological analysis for lower levels; then the argument might be extended to levels where no physiological analysis is available. Psychological studies could then aid in understanding the type of mechanisms that might be required at a given level. This approach is of particular value if psychological findings are to be useful in guiding and directing neurophysiological research in such areas as language and attention.

Second, the levels approach has a strong bias toward serial processing and leaves only the most highly abstracted information available to control experience and behavior. Each successive level serves to produce a more and more abstract code. Yet it is clear that behavior is often influenced by the physical characteristics of a message as well as by its highly abstracted semantic content. The identity of a voice may be as important to behavior as the semantic interpretation of the words spoken. Activity at each level persists, providing a memory of the code at that level that is undoubtedly available to consciousness in parallel with the more highly abstracted information from higher levels (Posner & Warren, 1972). This simple fact is underemphasized in serial models of information processing. It is often the case that higher levels of processing (e.g., the phonetic or semantic codes of words) are more easily available to influence conscious awareness than lower levels (e.g., visual codes), which are activated earlier. Since different codes of the same stimulus event are active in parallel, there are options within the processing system.

TEMPORAL HIERARCHY

A number of years ago, I published a paper (Posner, 1969) attempting to carry over the levels of processing view to psychological analysis of visual letters. Prominent in that paper was a view (see Figure 2.2) that adapted the levels of processing approach to the analysis of letters and later of words. The visual system analyzed the physical stimulus. This analysis included contact with information stored from previous visual experiences. The outcome of this visual system process was linked at a higher level to a letter name.[1] The name could in turn be connected to a semantic category. When I wrote the paper I already knew that there were problems with this basically serial analysis. These problems related both to control from higher levels (which I called *generation*) and to the doubtful idea that all that was available for the subject's later analysis was the most abstract level. However, I left for further empirical work (Posner, 1969) to determine how realistic the level of processing view would be: "It must not be assumed that these levels are steps in a serial chain or that each successive code obliterates the last. Rather, the analysis of how subjects pass from one code to another and what remains of previous codes is the empirical question with which the chapter was concerned [pp. 44–45]."

The reason for developing the levels of processing approach in that paper was straightforward: It rested on the temporal hierarchy we found in matching exper-

---

[1]I have adopted the term *phonetic* to stand for the code that underlies the internal naming of visual and auditory stimuli. The existence of a common phonetic code is supported by the empirical studies developed in this chapter. The term *name* code is a theoretically neutral term for the instruction to equate the stimuli based on whether or not they have the same name.

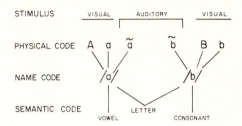

FIG. 2.2. A logical progression of codes from auditory and visual letters.

iments. Subjects were to respond "same" in some conditions if the letters were physically identical (physical instruction), in other conditions if the letters had the same name (name instruction), or if they were members of the same semantic category (rule instruction). It was found, as indicated by Figure 2.3, that using the instruction to base judgment on semantic category (e.g., both vowels or both consonants), the time for letter pairs that were physically identical (e.g., AA) was about 70–100 msec faster than the time for pairs that had only the letter name in common (e.g., Aa). It seemed reasonable to postulate that the retrieval of the phonetic information involved in the name was the source of this extra reaction time. Two aspects of the data argued for this theory. First, in separate experiments using physical and name instructions, one can examine the RT to respond "different" to single letter pairs like "AB," which requires the response "different" under all instructions. The reaction time for such pairs was about 80 msec faster with physical instructions than for name instructions, indicating that the advantage for physically identical letters could not have been due to the physical configuration of the input letters or to the redundancy between form and name, but rather to the kind of processing the subjects performed in making the match.

Second, when the instruction involved physical matching of letter pairs that had the same name but were not physically similar (e.g., Aa), RTs were no longer than for pairs with different names (e.g., Ac).[2] This result was striking, not only because of the long overlearned common naming response having no effect, but also because reaction times were delayed to pairs that had physical similarities (e.g., EF).

One important methodological advantage of research on physical and phonetic matching of visual letters that has emerged since my original studies is that different chronometric techniques have been used to explore the basic finding discussed above. For this reason, it serves as a model system for exploring convergence of chronometric methods.

---

[2]This important result has been disputed in some studies (e.g., Anderson, 1975), but it has been replicated both in this laboratory in unpublished studies and in published studies from other laboratories (Pachella & Miller, 1976; Well & Green, 1972). As we shall see, the model adopted in this chapter does allow for some violations of this finding when physical code matches are relatively long or phonetic access times particularly short.

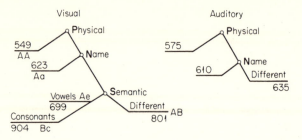

FIG. 2.3. A temporal hierarchy of RTs obtained from studies of auditory and visual letters (left panel after Posner, 1969; right panel after Cole, Coltheart, & Allard, 1974).

Taylor and Reilly (1970) used accuracy as a measure of performance. By following the stimulus with a masking field, they attempted to confine information sampling from the second of the two stimuli to a maximum of 9 msec. The results were clear: Under conditions of time-limited information access, individuals made fewer errors when making a physical match than when making a name match.

Blake, Fox, and Lappin (1970) attacked the relation between speed and accuracy in this task directly. They encouraged their subjects to tolerate different error rates. In some sessions they were to respond relatively quickly and accept a low accuracy level. In other sessions they were to take more time and increase their accuracy. When Blake et al. plotted discrimination accuracy against speed (see Figure 2.4), they found that at every speed compared, individuals were more accurate on the physical identity trials than on the name identity trials. Pachella (1974) has replicated this basic result using three levels of emphasis on speed.

Evoked-potential data also reveal the time course for matching letters at different levels. Figure 2.5 (Posner & Wilkinson, Note 2) shows the evoked potentials to the second of two letters that occur .5 sec apart. The dotted evoked

FIG. 2.4. Accuracy of performance (discriminability) as a function of response latency (RT) for letter-matching tasks. (From Blake, Fox, & Lappin, 1970. Copyright 1970 by the American Psychological Association. Reprinted by permission.)

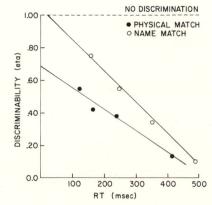

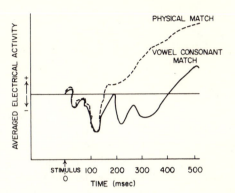

FIG. 2.5. Average visual evoked potentials to a second letter when subjects are required to do a physical match (dotted line) or vowel-consonant match (solid line). (From Posner & Wilkinson, Note 2.)

potential is for the instruction to match at a physical level, and the solid evoked potential is for the instruction to match based on whether both letters are vowels or consonants. The large positive upswing reflects the decision being made by the subject. In this particular experiment the first letter also serves as a warning signal and thus produces a large negative shift (contingent negative variation) that accompanies alerting (Walter, 1964). At the time the decision is made, this negative shift is released (Donchin, Kubovy, Kutas, Johnson, & Herning, 1973). This release occurs earlier for the physical match task than for the vowel–consonant task. The important point is that evoked-potential methodology provides another converging method that can be used to investigate the time course of mental processing. The advantage of this method is that it provides a continuous temporal record and that it may provide clues about the neural systems used in the task. A more extensive discussion of this method will be presented later (see Chapter 5).

The distinction between physical and phonetic codes has also been found in some studies of hemispheric function. It is widely accepted that among other things, the left hemisphere is more efficient for phonetic processing and the right for spatial processing (Levy, 1974). In agreement with this view, reaction times on name match trials are faster if visual letters are presented to the left hemisphere (right visual field) than if presented to the right. The reverse holds true for physical match trials (Cohen, 1972; Geffen, Bradshaw, & Nettleton, 1972).[3]

An important extension of the temporal hierarchy for linguistic information was its application to auditory phonemes. When subjects were asked to determine if two auditory letters were the same or not, they were faster when the two

---

[3]There has been considerable dispute about these hemispheric results. The use of single letter pairs—particularly when they are presented sequentially—leads to much of the dispute, since the time courses for physical and phonetic matches in this case are very close (Umilta, Frost, & Hyman, 1972). The problem will be clearer as I discuss the optional nature of the codes later in the chapter. The important point to stress is that the hemispheric results simply provide one source of support for the ability to develop functional separation between codes.

were physically identical than when they were uttered in different voices (Cole, Coltheart, & Allard, 1974) (see right panel, Figure 2.3). However, it is not clear with this design that the judgments made when two different voices are presented really use a nonphysical code. With visual materials, two letters having the same name (e.g., Aa) need be no more similar to each other visually than are two letters with different names (e.g., Ac). Thus it is reasonable to suppose that judgments of the former type require a phonetic code. Later in this chapter evidence is presented to show that a phonetic code is indeed used for these judgments (see p. 47). When visual letters in different cases are also visually similar (e.g., Cc), it is possible to match them based upon their similarity of shape (analogue match), rather than upon their names (see p. 59). In the case of auditory stimuli, the relationship between the physical and phonetic code is not arbitrary as it is with visual letters. Pairs of items having the same phonetic code must be aurally similar as well. Thus it is possible that judgments are made based upon an analogue code in this task.

Even with this difficulty, very important results have been obtained from chronometric studies of phoneme matching. Pisoni and Tash (1974) showed that reaction time for pairs of artificial stimuli varying only on the voice onset time dimension (*ba* to *pa*) were faster when pairs given the same phonetic label were also identical physically. This result showed that even for highly encoded stopped consonants (Liberman, Cooper, Shankweiler, & Studdert–Kennedy, 1967), physical information could be used in making speeded judgments. The doctrine of categorical perception (Liberman et al., 1967) had suggested a unique status for speech stimuli in that certain highly encoded physical dimensions required to classify the stimuli phonetically were thought to be unavailable for other judgments. Categorical perception represented an impressive case for a purely serial stage model, since information from an early acoustic stage would be unavailable for any psychological judgments. Pisoni and Tash's results show that physical information was not completely unavailable. Nonetheless, Pisoni and Tash still preferred a type of serial model for their phoneme-matching results. Subsequent results in our laboratory (Hanson, 1977) have shown that matching of auditory speech stimuli is best described by the same type of parallel system that will be developed for visual linguistic stimuli (see p. 42).

Processing speeds and accuracy are generally greater for auditory material if presented to the right ear (with predominant connection to left hemisphere) in a dichotic listening task, whereas efficiency is better on the left ear for stimuli requiring no phonetic analysis (Kimura, 1967). Using evoked-potential methods, Wood (1975) showed that there was a difference between left and right hemisphere sites when stimuli were classified along a linguistic dimension (place of articulation), but no such differences were found for these same stimuli when they were classified upon a nonlinguistic dimension (pitch). The hemispheric distinction in evoked potentials was found within 50 to 80 msec after input. However, in the Wood design subjects always knew in advance which dimension was to be processed, so these rapid times do not necessarily mean that the linguistic classification can be made by the brain within the 50 to 80 msec observed by Wood.

Though the distinction between physical and phonetic codes has not been explored with single-cell recording techniques, the evoked-potential and hemispheric data suggest that it would be possible to find systems of cells reacting to the phonetic codes of visual input sometime following those that respond to the physical input. Of course, one does not know whether such clusters would appear in only one place in the brain or whether they would have disparate physical locations.

The data I have so far presented surely indicate that the temporal hierarchy outlined in Figure 2.3 for visual letters holds over a wide range of chronometric techniques and experimental situations. What they do not tell us is the relationship between the physical and phonetic codes that the results support. If the temporal hierarchy resulted from a set of serial stages, each replacing the last, a levels of processing model would provide a complete and powerful description of our results. However, as we have seen in Chapter 1, the levels approach is simply too restrictive to use as a complete description of the processes involved.

ISOLABLE SYSTEMS

Models of Matching

The temporal hierarchy illustrated in Figure 2.3 does not imply that the processes involved at the different levels represent a strict series. One could imagine at least four ways such a temporal hierarchy might be obtained. These models are illustrated in Figure 2.6.

The first model is of a strictly serial process in which the nervous system first compares items on a physical level and moves to the next higher level only if no match is obtained. This view is consonant with a serial stage model of brain activity as viewed in Chapter 1. Second would be a system in which all matches are based on a single internal code, but the more bases on which two items are identical, the faster the match. This is called a *redundancy view*. A third view would be that the matches are always made at the highest level of the hierarchy but items reach that level faster the more similar they are. For example, one might assume that the time to extract the name of two identical letters is less than for two letters that have no physical similarity. This I call a *pathway activation view*. Fourth, there might be independent processing systems each capable of extracting a correct code and matching it. If the time courses of these systems differ, then according to the code involved, one could produce the temporal hierarchy of Figure 2.2.

These ideas are by no means mutually exclusive. Indeed I believe there is positive evidence supporting each of the last three in different situations. Many experimental papers have tested these notions in an effort to support one and

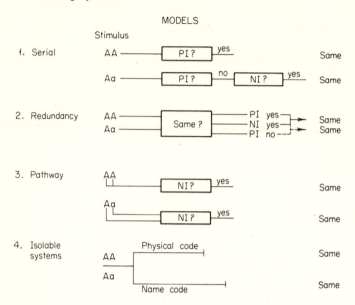

FIG. 2.6.   A number of logically possible models that would lead to the advantage of physical over name matches found in many matching experiments.

reject the remainder. I now feel that this method of inquiry is only likely to create confusion. Suppose the visual and phonetic codes of letters were processed in independent systems. Clearly they could not be as independent as though they were in two separate brains. There must be communication between such systems. If there is communication, it stands to reason that under some circumstances the information from the two systems would be combined (redundancy) or that output of one system would affect the activation of the other. Thus even if the systems underlying these matches were as independent as it is reasonable to expect, one would still find evidence for redundancy and pathway effects in different experimental paradigms (see Chapter 4). What appears to me to be a fundamental issue is whether experimental operations exist that can show the systems to operate independently in *any* reasonable sense. I adopted the term *isolable processing system* from George Miller (Note 3) for the sense of independence I feel is indicated by our data. Operationally, an isolable system refers to the existence of internal codes of a stimulus that are sufficiently separate so that an experimenter can independently manipulate their time courses. The idea of such independent processing systems receives some support from what we know of the organization and evolution of the human brain.

Separation

Though extreme views of localization of brain function have not found support, there is evidence favoring more general specialization of neural systems. Disconnection syndromes (Geschwind, 1968) argue that phonetic analysis may be disconnected from visual input by brain lesion while remaining available to audition. In at least one case, a reverse disconnection has been reported (Gazzaniga, Glass, Sarno, & Posner, 1973). Geschwind (1968) describes the theoretical implications of these disconnections quite clearly:

> For the past forty years there have been schools of thought which have stressed the importance of thinking of the patient as a whole, of seeing his responses as those of an integrated unitary structure, even in the face of damage. The ramifications of this thinking in neurology, psychiatry, psychology and other fields must be well known to most readers. It should be clear from much of our discussion that this principle, while it may be useful in some cases as a stimulus, may be actively misleading when it is regarded as a philosophical law. When Edith Kaplan and I were studying our patient, we constantly found that many confusions about the patient in our own minds as well as those of others resulted from failure to do the exact opposite of what the rule to look at the patient as a whole demanded, i.e., from our failure to regard the patient as made of connected parts rather than as an indissoluble whole. We were constantly dealing with questions such as "If he can speak normally and he knows what he's holding in his left hand, why can't he tell you?". We had to point out that we couldn't say that the patient could speak normally, since that part of the patient which could speak normally was not the same part of the patient which "knew" (nonverbally) what was in the left hand. This is at first blush an odd way to speak—it is hard not to say "the patient" and yet it is clear that this terminology is misleading [p. 637].

The extant data suggest that disconnection of the two cerebral hemispheres (Gazzaniga, 1970) divides a processing system that is heavily linguistic in orientation, although its evolutionary history may be based not so much on language as upon general temporal processing (Levy, 1974), from one that is spatial in orientation and that therefore can underlie the analysis of many kinds of analogue codes.

The analysis of the evolution of brain size (Jerison, 1973) also suggests the independent evolutionary history of brain systems for auditory–linguistic and visual–spatial processing. Jerison (1973) outlines this view as follows:

> Probably from the very beginning of this great Tertiary radiation of the mammals, the mammalian orders (especially Primates) responded to the selection pressure to use photic information and reevolved a visual distance sense. But their visual sense was not the same as the ancient reptilian vision. It was now represented by much more extensive neural networks in the brain itself. Just as hearing as a distance sense had been modeled after the natural reptilian sense of vision, so it may be assumed that the newly reevolved mammalian diurnal vision was modeled after the, by then, natural distance sense of mammals, the auditory sense, which had been evolving for more than 100 m.y. of the previous history of the mammals. The assumption that a new system is modeled after a preexisting system is one of my basic general assumptions [p. 21].

It is not clear how this separate evolution of visual and auditory modalities relates to disconnections between linguistic codes. Nor has any detailed model emerged that could predict the kinds of disconnections one obtains due to lesions from the evolutionary history of the brain. However, both lines of evidence suggest that the brain consists of specialized information-processing systems that can be forced into independent operation and have separate evolutionary histories.

This evidence makes psychological investigations of isolable systems more tenable by showing them to be generally consistent with a view of partial localization of function within the brain. The physiological data that argue for isolable systems are not crucial to the form of independence that might emerge at the psychological level. The physiology exists to support different psychological organizations.

It is critical that psychologists determine which of the physiologically possible organizations is consistent with the results of information-processing studies. Our work with linguistic material provides strong empirical evidence that supports a particular class of models concerning the operation of such systems. Because isolable systems must be coordinated in any actual performance, it is as necessary to consider evidence for coordination between codes as it is to establish their separation. The remainder of this chapter deals with the first problem, and Chapter 3 discusses the second.

PSYCHOLOGICAL INDEPENDENCE

One view of the kind of independence between processing codes that can be supported by psychological evidence is outlined in Figure 2.7. Suppose subjects are shown a single visual letter. Following a common pathway, two different

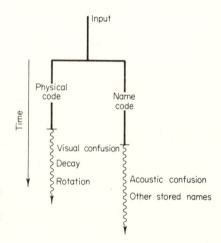

FIG. 2.7. A diagram of a horse race model of matching processes. (From Posner, 1975b. Copyright 1975 by John Wiley & Sons.)

internal codes are formed. One represents the visual code of the letter and the other its phonetic recoding. Neither code fully reproduces the raw physical input, but both exist as internal representations of the input. Though the two codes may communicate, it is possible to show with appropriate tasks that the experimenter can manipulate the time course for use of these two codes independently from one another.

The view outlined in Figure 2.7 leads naturally to a horse race model of the matching task. Simultaneously, the two codes are used to achieve matches based upon internal representations of the physical and of the phonetic codes respectively. Depending upon the parameters chosen by the experimenter, the physical match may be uniformly faster than the phonetic match, the two may overlap, or the phonetic code may be available earlier than the physical code. Evidence supporting this view is outlined below.

Simultaneous Matching Experiments

In a simultaneous matching study, subjects are provided with a pair of items on each trial and asked to indicate as quickly as possible whether or not they are the same with respect to some criterion (e.g., physical identity). This method has the great advantage that when a large number of stimuli can occur (such as all the letters), subjects develop little in the way of conscious expectancies about what specific item will occur on any trial. Of course they are sensitive to the probability of a match (i.e., "same" response) and to any nonrandomness in the sequence (sequential dependencies) introduced by the experimenter; but otherwise their attention is generally not directed to any specific feature, letter, or other characteristic of the stimuli.

Irrelevant features.   A number of studies have varied the similarity of irrelevant visual features of the two letters presented to the subject. These include color, contrast, size, and orientation. The results support the notion that such variations affect physical matches more than name matches.

Corcoran and Besner (1975) manipulated the size and contrast of simultaneous letter pairs. Thus the pair of items might differ physically either in size or contrast or both. They found that these two variables each increased times for physical matches while having no significant effect on matches based upon letter names (see Table 2.1).

A striking manipulation of the physical code can be obtained by rotation. Cooper and Shepard (1973) rotated a single letter and asked subjects to judge whether it was a correct (real letter) or mirror-image item. They found large and regular increases in RT as a function of the degree of rotation (see Figure 2.8). Though they did not specifically measure the effect of such rotations upon naming, it is clear from inspection that the effect of rotation on obtaining the

TABLE 2.1
RTs for Physical and Phonetic (Name) Matches as a Function
of Irrelevant Information[a]

Irrelevant Differences	Physical Match (BB)	Phonetic Match (Bb)
None	510	565
Size	534	575
Contrast	536	581
Size and contrast	560	578

[a]After Corcoran & Besner (1975).

name of the letter is slight. In the case of rotated letters, one often is aware of knowing the name of the letter before being able to complete the rotation in order to determine whether it was a correct or mirror image. This means that operations on the physical code can be extended in time so that they are actually longer than the processes involved in achieving the letter name. If this occurs, the horse race model suggests that phonetic processes will begin to have an effect upon physical matches. In agreement with the prediction, Buggie (1970) found that when one of the two simultaneous letters was rotated in a situation where subjects were required to respond ''same'' when two letters were physically identical, pairs that had the same name (e.g., Aa) took longer than pairs without the same name. When both letters were upright (Posner & Mitchell, 1967), phonetic identity had no effect on physical matches. By slowing down the physical match process, the

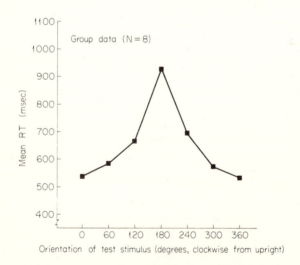

FIG. 2.8.   Time to determine whether a form if rotated to the upright is a letter or a mirror image of a letter as a function of degree of rotation. (From Cooper & Shepard, 1973. Copyright 1973 Academic Press.)

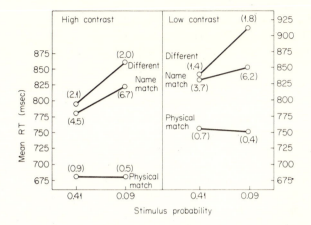

FIG. 2.9.   RTs as a function of contrast and probability for physical and phonetic (name) matches. Contrast affects both matches but physical matches more strongly, whereas probability affects only phonetic matches. (From Pachella & Miller, 1976. Copyright 1976 by the Psychonomic Society.)

phonetic code has a greater chance to accrue and thus produces interference with the physical match latencies.

Pachella and Miller (1976) manipulated both the relative frequency of particular letter pairs and the intensity of the pairs. Relative frequency might affect either physical or name codes. However, given results in short-term memory favoring storage of letter names (Conrad, 1965), one would probably expect frequency to affect phonetic level processes more than physical processing. The frequent letter name would presumably be more available in memory in somewhat the same way as any auditory item. The results are shown in Figure 2.9. The relative frequency variable had its effect only on phonetic matches. The intensity variable affects physical matches more than phonetic matches, though this interaction was not statistically significant. Intensity should have some effect on name matches if it improves the speed of processing a common input pathway.[4]

One of the simplest ways of varying physical codes while preserving a common phonetic code is to vary the modality of the input items. This method was in fact the earliest experiment that I performed with the simultaneous matching task. Simultaneous pairs of digits were presented either both aurally, both

_____

[4]The differences between the results of intensity manipulation by Pachella and Miller (1976) and by Corcoran and Besner (1975) are instructive in light of the model outlined in Figure 2.7. Corcoran and Besner varied the contrast within a pair of letters and found time differences were confined to physical match pairs. Pachella and Miller manipulated the intensity between letter pairs so that both members of any pair were of the same intensity. This manipulation might be expected to affect the encoding time common to all input, and indeed effects are found on both physical and name matches, though they are greater from the former.

visually, or one visual and one aural. Since the experiment was originally designed to study switching time between modalities, two instructional conditions were run. The first required subjects to respond "same" if the two stimuli were the same digit, and if not they were to respond "different." The second required the subject to respond "same" if both digits were odd or both even. The latter experiment showed no increase in RT if the stimuli were in different modalities, thus causing us to reject a switching interpretation. The first condition, however, showed that time for cross-modal matches was about 60 msec longer than for within-modality matches. The results support the idea that the extraction of a common phonetic code was necessary in order to match a simultaneous visual and auditory digit. The study suggests that obtaining the common phonetic code takes about the same time regardless of the modality from which it is extracted. It is particularly striking that varying input modality should require subjects to make the match based upon a phonetic code, since the learned correspondence of a visual digit and its auditory equivalent is so strong.

The data on cross-modal matching suggest that the phonetic code extracted from auditory phonemes involves the same representation as does the phonetic code extracted from visual letters. As pointed out earlier, there are problems in separating auditory input from phonetic recoding by use of a matching task, because of the intrinsic similarity between auditory and phonetic codes. Nonetheless, it should be possible to determine whether or not the same general model applies to auditory input as to visual input. To determine this, Hanson (1977) presented subjects with pairs of artificial phonemes varying in voice onset time. Subjects could be required to perform either physical matches or phonetic matches. Only a minority of subjects was able to perform the physical match task with better than chance performance. Those subjects who could make the physical distinctions were uniformly slower in doing so than they were in making matches under phonetic instructions. They also showed large influences of the phonetic boundary on their physical match performance and faster phonetic matches when stimuli were identical than when they were not identical but within the same phonetic category. These results all are consistent with the idea that physical and phonetic codes accrue in parallel, and that in making difficult judgments such as these, the time course is such that subjects can base their responses upon phonetic cues more quickly than upon physical cues. No subject in this task seems able to deal with the physical cues in complete isolation. Although the results are empirically different than for visual letter matching, the same underlying parallel model is appropriate for both.

Further evidence for similarity between visual and auditory processing of letters comes from studies of the categorical nature of the perceptual process. As I pointed out earlier, one of the most impressive facts of speech perception was the difficulty subjects have in retaining any information about the physical stimulus once it is recoded into phonetic form. Further support for this comes from the inability of most subjects to perform a physical match task with auditory phonemes as described above. This seemed quite different than what would be obtained with visual letters. However, recent studies of tachistoscopic presentation of visual words have shown that subjects, though recognizing words in a single case at somewhat lower durations than words when cases are randomly mixed (Coltheart & Freeman, 1974), are often completely unaware that unfamiliar case mixtures are being used. Thus, with low exposure durations, a kind of categorical perception is also found for visual linguistic material.

One area in which the effects of physical variation on matching has been disputed is in the study of changes in color. Well and Green (1972) found equal effects of variation in color on physical and phonetic codes in simultaneous matching. However, Kroll, Kellicutt, Berrian, and Kreisler (1974), using short delay interval between letters presented for matching, found effects only for physical matches unless the attention of subjects was deliberately called to the color dimension. When the subjects had to report color as part of the task, effects appeared on both physical and phonetic codes. The Well and Green study presented the letters in one color on 75% of the trials, only rarely changing the color of one of the two letters. This method may well have caused a generalized orienting to the color change that produced a result similar to deliberately advising subjects to attend to that code. Of course it is often possible to come up with some ad hoc explanation of a discrepant result. However, one general point should be made: The use of a small number of stimuli that become very predictable often leads subjects to develop active expectancies that influence the results.

Another result that appears at first to pose serious problems for independence between systems processing physical and phonetic information are studies that show that the physical similarity of two letters affects the time for rejection in a name match task (Coltheart, 1972). For example, letter pairs like "Ac" are classified as "different" faster than pairs like "AC," which look more alike (see Coltheart, 1972). Pairs like "EF" take longer to classify as "different" than pairs that have no form similarity (Cole, Note 4). If classifications in such a task are performed on the phonetic code, one may ask why relevant visual similarity of this sort should matter. Two answers present themselves. First, the physical match test may be performed before or simultaneously with the phonetic match, and the output of the physical test would bias subjects toward a "same" response when visual similarity is present. Second, the system corresponding to the phonetic code of one letter (e.g., F) may be partially activated by the similar form (e.g., E) and vice versa, giving a greater tendency for a "yes" response when the forms are visually similar. Both of these mechanisms probably operate; neither poses any special problems for the model outlined in Figure 2.7.

Summary.   Manipulations of such physical variables as intensity, size, color, contrast, and orientation have usually led to strong effects on physical matches with weaker or in some cases no effects on phonetic matches. Cross-modality matches appear to be based upon a phonetic code.

These results are confirmed by studies that have examined time delays between letter pairs. The time delay technique also allows further examination of the ability of subjects to select and control different codes developed from a single input stimulus. We next turn to this technique.

Successive Matching

According to the isolable systems view, a visually presented letter is stored both as a physical configuration within the visual system and as a relatively independent phonetic representation. If the letter is shown for a time sufficient to extract both codes, it should be possible to study their fate over time in store. This basic situation was investigated in the late 1960s (Posner, Boies, Eichelman, & Taylor, 1969; Posner & Keele, 1967) and has since been explored by many investigators (Kroll, 1975). The results indicate quite strongly that two codes are available, that they can be manipulated independently by the experimenter, and that aspects of the physical situation and the subjects' processing strategies affect their fate.

In the first studies of this situation, a single visual letter was presented for .5 sec and then removed to be replaced by a test letter after varying intervals. The results were very clear and straightforward. Name matches were unaffected by delays up to 1 sec, but physical matches, especially in mixed blocks, increased dramatically over the interval as indicated in Figure 2.10. Several studies using slightly different physical configurations provided nearly identical results. These are summarized in Figure 2.11, which shows the difference between physical and name matches obtained as a function of delay interval.

A number of investigators (Cohen, 1969; Dainoff & Haber, 1970; Thorson, Hockhaus, & Stanners, 1976) have sought to explore the hypothesis that the

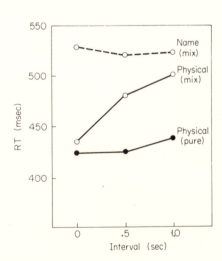

FIG. 2.10. RT for physical and phonetic (name) successive matches. (From Posner et al., 1969. Copyright 1969 by the American Psychological Association. Reprinted by permission.)

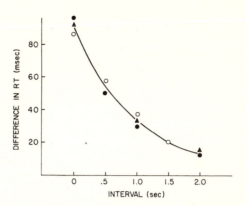

FIG. 2.11. Difference in RT between physical and phonetic matches as a function of time following a .5-sec exposure of the first letter. Closed circles, open circles, and triangles represent data from three separate experiments. (From Posner et al., 1969. Copyright 1969 by the American Psychological Association. Reprinted by permission.)

name match times are based upon phonetic codes and that the physical match times are based on visual codes by manipulating the confusability among letters. The results are reasonably comparable across different studies but have been obtained most clearly by Thorson et al. (1976). In their experiment, they compared a letter set that consisted of visually confusable items with one consisting of acoustically confusable items. A single upper-case letter was presented for .5 sec followed by a blank field that lasted during the interval. The matching letter was also upper-case, so in theory it would be possible for the subjects to make their matches based either on the physical or the phonetic code. The critical data were from the "different" responses that involved letter pairs that could be either visually or acoustically similar. They are shown in Figure 2.12. They indicate that acoustic confusability has no effect at very brief intervals, but starting at 1 sec it begins to have a very strong interfering effect. On the other hand, visual similarity has a great effect at short intervals, but by 2 sec these pairs are handled quite efficiently. These results, together with similar studies by Dainoff and Haber (1970) and by Cohen (1969), indicate quite clearly the presence of two different bases on which subjects make their match.

Using cross-case letters in these situations seems to insure primary reliance upon a phonetic code, but using letters with identical cases does not necessarily

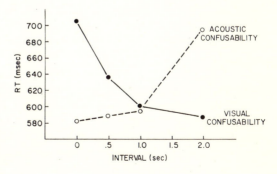

FIG. 2.12. RT for physical matches as a function of delay following the first letter for visually and acoustically confusing letter sets. (From Thorson, Hockhaus, & Stanners, 1976. Copyright 1976 by the Psychonomic Society.)

mean subjects will rely upon a physical code in making the match. Rather, the basis of their match seems to change over the course of an interval and with the type of material used, as would be predicted if they resulted from the horse-race process model outlined previously. A related result by Cohen showed that with a 5-sec interval between the original exposure and the test letter, it was necessary to have letters that were both visually and acoustically similar before an increase in RT due to confusability was presented. It was as though subjects could make the match on the physical basis of acoustic confusability was present alone or on an acoustic basis if visual confusability was present alone. Only when both were present was the system in some way disturbed by the presence of similarity. I suspect that the difference in detail between Cohen's study and Thorson's result that showed very specific effects of confusability has to do with the delay interval. The long delay in Cohen's study means that no code is very active at the time of the probe. Thus, as in simultaneous matching, one would expect temporal overlap in the times needed to complete matches based upon the two relevant codes. With shorter intervals, the active nature of the internal codes generally produces one code that dominates in speed, leading to a function of the type traced by Thorson et al. (1976) (see p. 45).

External Information

When subjects are presented with a visual letter and are required to retain it, there is strong evidence for rivalry among different codes. Conrad (1965) presented subjects with a number of visual letters that they were to recall later. He found strong evidence for the presence of acoustic or articulatory confusions in their recall. Under the influence of a single code theory, this finding was sometimes interpreted as meaning that visual information about letters could be stored only in a phonetic code. However, more recently it has become clear that the kind of code used is very heavily influenced by the degree of interference present from other codes. For example, Parks, Kroll, Salzberg, and Parkinson (1972) presented a single visual letter during the course of an auditory shadowing task. They found that instead of disappearing within 1 sec or 2 as shown in Figure 2.12, the advantage of physical matches over name matches was maintained for a full 8 sec. After 8 sec there was still a significant difference in favor of physical matches of about 30 msec. Thus in the presence of a considerable amount of acoustic confusability, there is a tendency for the relative advantage of the physical code of the first letter to remain.

A complementary finding was made by Boies (1971). In this study, subjects were engaged in a matching task with either a 0- or 2-sec interval between the letters. On half the occasions the letters matched physically, and on the other half they matched only in name. For half the trials an irrelevant set of auditory letters was presented to the subjects that they were to hold in store during the trial. Boies reasoned that the aural letters would interfere with the phonetic representation of the visually presented first letter but not with its physical representation. The results he obtained with a 2-sec interval between the first and second letter corresponded precisely to his intuitions (see Figure 2.13). For physical matches there was no influence of the irrelevant letter-set upon the matching process. For phonetic matches, however, there was substantial interference. The results of the Parks et al. and Boies studies confirm the idea that there are two relatively independent codes represented in the nervous system following the presentation of a visual letter. The relative advantage of the physical code over the phonetic code tends to decline over time. However, this cannot be interpreted as a complete loss or obliteration of the physical code, because its advantage can be shown when the proper kind of interference is imposed such as manipulation of phonetic confusability or presenting additional auditory letters. The results show that the physical situation has a great deal to do with the particular code that manifests itself in the subject's performance on any given trial. The Boies experiment illustrates another principle we have found before in simultaneous letter matching (see p. 38). The phonetic representation abstracted from a visual letter appears to occupy the same system as the code extracted from auditory letters. If this were not so, we would not expect the existence of the auditory memory load to interfere with the phonetic code more than it interferes with the physical code. Thus we have confirmation both of our ability to manipulate the codes of these letters independently and of the common code that seems to relate the visual and auditory linguistic processing systems.

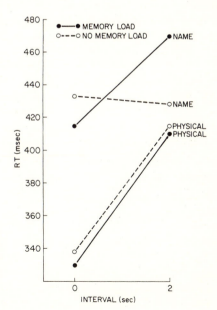

FIG. 2.13. RT for physical and phonetic matches as a function of interval between two letters for memory load and no memory load conditions. (From Posner, 1969. Copyright 1969 Academic Press.)

Exposure Duration

The use of confusability and of interfering items to manipulate the physical and phonetic representation of letters may suggest that these effects are mediated entirely by the physical situation and are not under the conscious control of the subjects. This issue is a complex one. In our original studies, we attempted to manipulate the effort that the subjects might give to the physical code of the first letter by making it a highly reliable cue for the subject's response (e.g., by making all matches physical matches) or by instruction. Neither of these manipulations was entirely effective in getting the subjects to rely on the physical code. They did, however, reduce the decay function we found for the physical code in the standard situation illustrated in Figure 2.11. Thus it appeared that the subjects had some control over the use of codes in this situation.

Additional evidence along these lines comes from studies that manipulate the exposure duration of the first letter. In our standard situation described above, the first letter remains present for .5 sec, is then removed and replaced after a varying interval by a second letter. Eggers (1975), in a series of experiments, varied the length of time that the first letter remained present in the visual field prior to its removal. She found results in accordance with those described above. When the first letter remained present for .5 sec, the physical matches increased in RT so that after 2 sec there was no significant advantage to physical over name matches. However, when the first letter was present for only 50 msec, the physical match remained superior to name match over a full 5-sec delay interval (see Figure 2.14). This result suggests that when subjects are exposed to very brief flashes of linguistic information, they tend to preserve the physical representation of that flash to a greater degree than when they are presented with a longer presentation. [Of course only post hoc explanations can be given for these

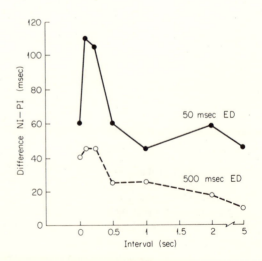

FIG. 2.14. Differences between physical and name matches as a function of exposure duration (ED) of letter 1 and interval between letters. (After Eggers, 1975.)

results. But as we shall see, they are in accord with some findings obtained from studies using brief exposure times for letters and words (see pp. 76–79)]. In none of these experiments that manipulate exposure duration or visual and auditory confusability has it been shown that the subjects can voluntarily determine the code used to make the match. All that has been shown is that the code that seems to be less susceptible to interference does turn out to be the one used. This might depend more upon the physical situation than upon the subject's intent.

More conclusive evidence favoring the ability of subjects to control the type of representation used in the letter match comes from experiments in which subjects' expectancies are led to a different stimulus code than is presented in the physical information given to them. These data on generation are presented in the next section.

GENERATION

Visual Generation

Several years ago I reported (Posner, 1969) that subjects could generate the visual representation of a letter after being presented with its acoustic equivalent. The evidence for this was quite objective. It involved our finding that the time for matching a visual stimulus following its aurally presented name declined over a .5- to 1-sec interval until it became as fast as for the same-case matching of visual letters and much faster than visual matches that involve switching cases. However, there was still a serious problem in this work. The time for physical matches always increased with delay, so that the generated match was never as fast as could be obtained when two physically identical letters were matched at short delays. Thus it was not clear whether the generated representation was sufficient to produce matching as efficient as physical matches at their best.

Boies (1969, 1971) performed a series of experiments that explored this problem and revealed important new points. At the time, we had thought that physical matches increased over a 1-sec interval because the code was reduced in availability or clarity. He eliminated any possibility of this occurring by leaving the first letter present in the visual field until the second letter appeared. In one study, the first letter could be either upper- or lower-case and was present for .5, 1, or 1.5 sec. The second letter could match physically, only in name, or be different. The results of this study showed that physical match RTs increased about 30 msec over a 1.5-sec interval. At 500 msec, physical and name matches differed significantly (83 msec); whereas after a 1500-msec delay, they did not differ significantly (15 msec). Although it appeared that generation had occurred, Boies had failed to prevent an increase in time for physical matches, even when the first letter remained present in the visual field.

There might have been several explanations for the upswing in physical match times, but Boies chose what seems at first an unlikely hypothesis. He felt that the time for physical matches increased because as the opposite case was placed in a visual code, subjects had a positive set of two through which to scan. This means, according to Sternberg's (1966) theory, that it should take them about 30 msec longer to make the match.

To explore this view, Boies set up three conditions. In one condition subjects had a first letter that was always upper-case (pure physical match). Boies reasoned that this situation involved a positive set of one, and there should be no tendency for physical matches to increase with exposure duration. The mixed condition was identical to the previous experiment. Finally, in a pure generation condition, the second letter was always opposite in case to the first. The predictions were that the pure physical match condition should be flat over all exposure durations; the pure generation condition should decline until it reached the same level. In both of these conditions subjects end with a positive set of one visual item, although in one case it was physically in the visual field, and in the other it was generated from the opposite case. The mixed condition should show an increase for physical matches and a decrease for name matches. With long intervals these two values should be equal and about 30 msec longer than the pure conditions. This, according to Boies, was because subjects had a positive set of two items. All these expectations were met as shown in Figure 2.15.

Boies also compared a condition where subjects were presented with upper and lower cases of the same letters to his generation condition. The data indicated that the dual case condition RTs initially lay between the physical and name match times for the single letter; and as exposure duration increased, all three conditions converged to a common value. Immediately after presentation, physical match times are identical, whether the subjects know that all matches are physical or whether they sometimes have opposite case matches. Thus having to deal with the two codes does not affect reaction time, according to Boies' data.

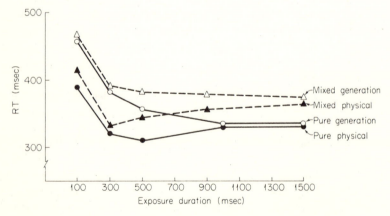

FIG. 2.15.   RTs for "same" responses as a function of condition and exposure duration of the first letter. (From Posner, 1972. Copyright 1972 Academic Press.)

It is only when subjects generate the opposite case and produce a positive set of two within the visual code that their times for physical matches increase to that of dual presentation. This same result has now been obtained by Elias and Kinsbourne (1972) using nonverbal stimuli in which matches could be made by physical identity or a learned classification. Similar results have also been obtained by Wood (1974). He presented stimuli either aurally or visually and inferred the basis of the match from confusability manipulations. He found that stimuli were matched on the basis of the modality of the second stimulus, regardless of the modality of the stimulus that had been presented first. His results suggest that the first stimulus was recoded to the modality of the second when the two are presented in different modalities, and that visual coding was as effective as auditory coding in performance of the task. Indeed the Wood result is like that obtained by a number of investigators who used multi-item input arrays (Cruse & Clifton, 1973; Swanson, Johnsen, & Briggs, 1972), in that matches are generally done in the modality of the second probe item rather than the modality of the array. It is powerful testimony to the general efficiency of recoding through generation that this should be the case.

The process of generation raises a number of important questions. One of these questions is related particularly to the condition when the generated item is a visual representation of a stimulus. There is considerable interest in the form of representation of such a visual code. Boies' study suggests quite strongly that whatever the representation, for the purpose of matches it behaves the same as a previously presented visual item. The representation of a visual code of this sort is discussed in more detail in the next chapter where I deal with the nature of analogue representation inside the visual system.

One of the strong objections to postulating a generated visual code was the idea that such representation is not scanned in a manner similar to actually presented items. Suppose one claims to have a subjective impression of a visual word such as *pumpkin*. When asked to spell *pumpkin* backwards, it is clear that it is not possible to scan this internal visual representation in the same way we scan an actually present word. Weber and Harish (1974) tested the notion that the reason the internal representation fails in the case of *pumpkin* is that the capacity to represent information in a visual code is limited. They found that for up to three items, a visually present item (percept) and the visual representation of a previously presented item (image) were scanned with equal efficiency. Only when the number of letters exceeded three did the advantage of the percept over the image arise. These data agree quite strongly with Boies' that the visual representation of a generated item is in pretty much the same system as would be used to hold or even to take in a visually presented letter.

Boies' results led us to another conclusion, however, that proved not to be correct. Recall that when a single letter is presented for 500 msec and removed, subjects do not tend to generate the opposite case. Rather the time for physical matches increases rapidly, whereas the time for name matches tends to remain constant. However, when the first letter is left present in the visual field, subjects do appear to generate the opposite case. These two findings led us to suppose that generation was both optional and difficult. Thus we thought of generation as a voluntary, attention-demanding translation, much like recoding binary to octal digits. This seemed to fit with the relatively long times required before generation was complete.

Attention Demands of Generation

The question of the difficulty of generation is important, because it bears upon the range of codes that might be automatically activated by input and among which the subjects can select. Our view in 1969 was that the presentation of a visual letter led automatically to activation of the letter name (abstraction), but that the reverse (generation) was an optional process that required attention and effort by the subject. This view has been challenged by the results of studies that involved matching of visual faces (see Figure 2.16) to their names.

Tversky (1969) found in her study of name–face matching that the match was in the code of the second stimulus even when that stimulus was unexpected. This indicates that subjects generate a face from the stored name. This result was surprising to us, because of the presumed attention demands of generation.

Tversky's data involved only a single interval between name and face and no direct comparison between face–face and name–face matching. Thus Rogers (1972) sought to replicate the Tversky result and see whether generation occurred as measured by the criterion of convergence of physical and name match RTs. Rogers used exposure durations of .4 and 2 sec and compared face–face and name–face trials. As shown in Figure 2.17, there was a clear convergence of same RTs. For the long delay, there were no significant differences between face–face and name–face trials. At the short delay, physical and name matches differed by about 70 msec. By this criterion, generation seemed to take between 400 and 2000 msec.

However, a finer analysis of the results indicated that at both intervals the match was based on a code of the face. This was shown both by the fact that faces

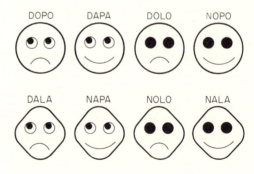

FIG. 2.16. Name and face stimuli used in experiments on generation. (After Rogers, 1972.)

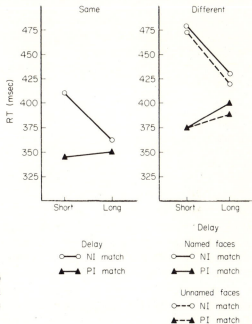

FIG. 2.17. RT for physical (PI) and name (NI) matches as a function of delay following exposure to the first face. (After Rogers, 1972.)

that had been given no names during learning were just as easy to match as those for which subjects had learned names and by a detailed comparison of individual feature confusions for the face–face and name–face trials. In the case of short delay, generation appeared to follow the second stimulus; in the long intervals, it was complete when the second stimulus was presented. These results agree with Tversky's finding that subjects prefer to transform the memorial stimulus rather than abstract the name of the second stimulus. This finding also agrees with much literature (see p. 51) suggesting that subjects make matches in the domain of the second stimulus rather than of the first.

Rogers (1974) followed this experiment with a second study. In the second study, she used eight faces (as shown in Figure 2.16) and their corresponding names. The faces and the names could be manipulated so that either one or two features differed between a pair. Some subjects were trained in abstracting the name of a face *and* in generating the face corresponding to a name; others were trained only in one of these two operations. Subjects indicated whether a name and face presented simultaneously or with an interstimulus interval of 2 sec were the same or different. Analyses of face and name confusability on "different" trials indicated both name and face information contributed to the decision on simultaneous trials. However, when the two stimuli were presented successively, the confusability was confined to the code of the second stimulus. These data are summarized in Figures 2.18 and 2.19.

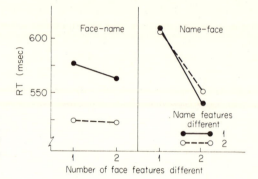

FIG. 2.18.   RT in successive matching tasks for face–name and name–
face different trials as a function of
face and name confusability. (After
Rogers, 1972.)

These results argue that on simultaneous trials in which name and face were presented, the abstraction of the name of the face and the generation of the face corresponding to the name go on in parallel. Otherwise it would be hard to see why both kinds of confusability affect the match. Of course, one could have a mixture of some trials in which it is based on generation, but the similarity of the results in this experiment to those obtained with simultaneous letter matching seems to argue for a race between the abstraction and generation process. If this were true, it seems unlikely that subjects could be devoting attention to generation.

However, something does happen when there is an interval between the two stimuli that is quite different than when they are presented simultaneously. Just as in the data for letter matching, when there is an interval between the stimuli, the subjects are able to confine their matching process to the code of the second

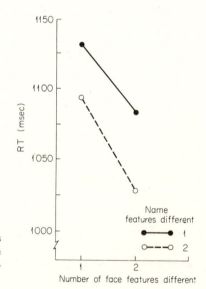

FIG. 2.19.   RTs in simultaneous
name–face trials as a function of face
and name confusability. (After Rogers, 1972.)

stimulus only. This corresponds to the subjective impressions of subjects that in the name-face trial they are developing an image that represents the face. Only under the conditions when there is a long interval does this subjective impression develop and is the response confined only to the code of the second stimulus.

These data are consistent with the idea that all available information will contribute to performance, provided that active attention is not allocated to any single code. Thus in the simultaneous task, the input information seems to automatically activate codes related to it from previous learning. The time course of those codes may overlap—as it seems to in the case of face-name matching—or may provide a clear advantage for one code over the other—as it usually does in the case of physical and name matching of letters. When subjects are given the opportunity to convert the first stimulus into the modality of the second, however, the decision is made on one code only. This result suggests the importance of a distinction between an image and a visual code. The visual code that partly indicates the decision on the simultaneous trials cannot be considered an image in the sense of being conscious. The subjects did not report being aware of this code. By comparison, on the delay trials, all subjects agreed that they constructed a pictorial representation of the face. The development of the pictorial image appears to take time. A visual code, however, can be accessed by a stimulus much more rapidly.

The potential importance of a conceptual distinction between a visual code and a visual image raised by the Rogers experiments cannot be stressed too strongly. We have defined a visual code in terms of evidence that the task uses visual characteristics of a letter that are separate from phonetic recoding. In simultaneous matching, the subjects have no clear awareness that they are using a visual rather than a phonetic code. The evidence shows that they are. With delayed matching, particularly when generation is involved, there are strong subjective reports of visual information. When such subjective reports are present, we should use the term *visual image*. There is strong evidence (Boies, 1971; Rogers, 1972) that it takes from .5 to 1.5 sec to generate a visual image of sufficient clarity to sustain a physical match that is as efficient as having the stimulus present and to give rise to strong subjective reports of imagery. Times for generation of such images are too slow for them to play a role in rapid tasks like reading or comprehension of spoken sentences. Visual codes, however, can be contacted very rapidly and do not necessarily give rise to the subjective reports found for visual images. The findings reported above suggest that the visual character of a stored representation is not something assigned when the item is sufficiently activated to be conscious but that it is a characteristic of the storage system itself.

Our conclusion is that the activation pattern of input is mainly influenced by the strength of past associations and that the direction of these associations (i.e., abstraction versus generation) matters less. When subjects are presented with a list of visual letters, the names are also activated, though they may not be conscious. Similarly, when subjects hear a list of concrete words, their visual code is increased in availability. Indeed, Boies' data on generation may be a rather special case where active attention is needed because they depend upon one case of a letter, "A," activating another case, "a." This association may be weaker than the link between either of these visual forms and the letter name. This view suggests that the input automatically activates a wide range of codes.

SUMMARY

This chapter began with an examination of data and theory related to a processing levels analysis of how information is processed. It was shown that data are consistent with a parallel version of the basically serial levels of processing viewpoint. According to this viewpoint there exist isolable codes derived from a single input. These codes are sufficiently separate so that their time courses can be manipulated by the experimenter. The existence of such isolable systems is established by data from matching experiments and is consistent with both physiological and neurological insights.

The matching experiments show that there are a number of principles related to the coordination of such isolable codes. For example, under some conditions, subjects translate one code into another. In successive matching experiments, this translation can be so complete that matching is based upon only one code. Under such conditions, subjects can report the code they use, and if it is visual, will talk in terms of an image. However, under simultaneous matching conditions, more than one code appears to be used, provided the time course of the codes overlap.

In general this chapter shows evidence that the nervous system consists of functionally independent systems that are brought into relation both through the associations developed from past experience and the use of active attentional mechanisms. The pathways that underlie the associations between such isolable systems will be dealt with in Chapter 4, and the question of the role of attention in their activation and maintenance will be dealt with in Chapter 6. We turn now to a more detailed analysis of some of these isolable systems and in particular to the representations that underlie visual codes and visual images.

3

Coordination of Codes

It is possible to develop theories at a level of representation common to all codes. For example, computer languages can be used to represent any code. However, there are reasons to believe that the efficiency of thought may depend critically upon the form of representation. In Chapter 2 it was shown (pp. 46–47), that although subjects tend to code items phonetically in visual memory-span tests, in the presence of competing auditory input a visual code is used. The ability to solve a problem represented spatially is reduced by a simultaneous spatial task, whereas verbal representation is affected more by a verbal task (Brooks, 1968). Subjects who report themselves as good in visual imagery have an advantage in solving problems that involve manipulating internal visual symbols (Snyder, 1972). Functional fixity that serves to block the ability of a subject to associate the visual form of an object with a particular use may leave intact the object name-to-use association and the reverse (Glucksberg & Danks, 1969; Glucksberg & Weisberg, 1966). These are examples of why it might prove useful for a theory of thought to preserve the distinction between internal codes.

Developmental psychologists (Bruner, Oliver, and Greenfield, 1966; Piaget & Inhelder, 1969) have emphasized the multiple bases upon which the same external situation may be represented. Bruner views the child as shifting from a primary reliance upon enactive (motor) codes first to iconic (visual) and finally to symbolic (e.g., language) representation.

Experimental psychologists working with adult subjects have also been studying different forms of representation of information in perceptual and learning tasks (Kosslyn & Pomerantz, 1977; Paivio, 1969). Despite these experimental results, there has been a strong desire to view complex tasks as involving only a single form of coding (Pylyshyn, 1973). The exact form has often been a matter of dispute. However, even if one accepts a multiple code view such as outlined in the previous chapter, it becomes important to understand how these codes operate together in actual performance.

My original intention in this chapter was to try to develop a general theoretical analysis of how visual and phonetic codes of letters and words were coordinated during the behavior of familiar tasks. As we have seen in the last chapter, these two codes appear to be complementary when activated by input but appear as rivals for the active attention of the subject. Unfortunately, I have not been able to develop a theory that does justice to the complexity of data already obtained concerning these codes.[1] Instead I have attempted to deal with several central topics concerning these that would have to be accommodated by a theory of code coordination.

The first topic involves an attempt to deal with operations that occur upon visual codes and images. The visual system is an extremely complex processing system that has been studied from many perspectives. The approach outlined in the last chapter seems to provide some new insights into analogue operations performed upon visual codes and images. In particular, chronometric analysis of matching tasks might tell us more than other methods have about the way information from the external world makes contact with memory systems in the process of pattern recognition. The term *analogue operations* refers to evidence that the visual codes produced by stimuli resemble the objects that they represent in the sense that operations such as rotation or expansion, which can be performed upon them during matching, produce similar latencies to those that would be expected if the actual object were to be physically transformed. Shepard (1975) called this characteristic of visual forms *second-order isomorphism*. It is second order, because the visual codes are not isomorphic with the input; rather the similarity relations among visual codes bear a resemblance to the similarity structure among the objects that produced them. The matching task is a natural one for the study of these similarity relations. It also provides some evidence on whether or not the operations performed during matching are similar to those that take place during the recognition of an individual item.

There is also interest in how past experience serves to structure internal representations. Printed words are familiar chunks consisting of letters. Does this familiarity operate within the visual code, or does it operate only upon a

---

[1]The major problem is that we are unable to specify the conditions under which attention will be dominated by a particular event or code. Codes that build up earlier and for which the subject is set by a previous instruction do seem to have an advantage. However, the predictions one would make from such principles are probably not adequate to account for the results obtained in different experiments. For that reason, it is difficult to predict whether or not attention will be committed to a single code or item and if so, which code or item will dominate.

phonetic recoding of the visual string? Of course, words are represented in more than one code, and this gives rise to questions of the coordination of visual, phonetic, and semantic representations. The middle part of this chapter is concerned with these questions. The study of visual and auditory word processing provides a vehicle to test the isolable code principles developed in Chapter 2.

A new direction in the study of code coordination is the hope that it may shed light upon differences among people in linguistic ability. A few experiments conducted on this question provide converging evidence on the general issues of code coordination and also indicate some new approaches to the study of individual behavior. The chapter ends with a consideration of these issues.

ANALOGUE REPRESENTATION

Form Matching

There are two basic questions concerning analogue processes with which we will be concerned. The first is representation in the absence of a current external stimulus (i.e., imagery). The term *imagery* is used because such studies often involve clear subjective reports on the nature of representation. The second is the question of normalization of input during the process of recognition. These studies almost never involve subjective reports of visual imagery but may involve visual codes. The studies reviewed below deal with both questions.

In our 1967 paper (Posner & Mitchell, 1967) on matching of simultaneous letter pairs, we found that the reaction time for cross-case matches that looked similar (e.g., Cc) was longer than their physical identity controls (e.g., CC, cc), but by much less than the 80 msec needed for cross-case matches that were not similar in form (e.g., Aa). This result proved to be somewhat of an embarrassment for those who wished to emphasize the discrete nature of the physical and phonetic codes. However, a glance at Figure 2.7 will suggest the meaning of this result. The existence of a size difference extends the time for the visual system to determine that the physical similarity of the two stimuli is sufficient for a "same" response. We assumed some size transformation was involved.

To study this "analogue" process more thoroughly, we set up an experiment using the four pairs of Gibson figures shown in Figure 3.1. Subjects learned to give each pair a common name (1, 2, 3, or 4). The pairs differed respectively in size, continuity, rotation, or were completely different forms. Having taught subjects the names for these visual forms, we gave subjects a simultaneous matching task with instructions to respond "same" if a pair had the same name. Figure 3.1 displays the difference in the mean reaction time for "same" responses to the physically identical pairs and those that were not identical but had the same name. In the case of size, rotation, and random pairings, these mean differences are statistically significant from zero. The size transformation had an

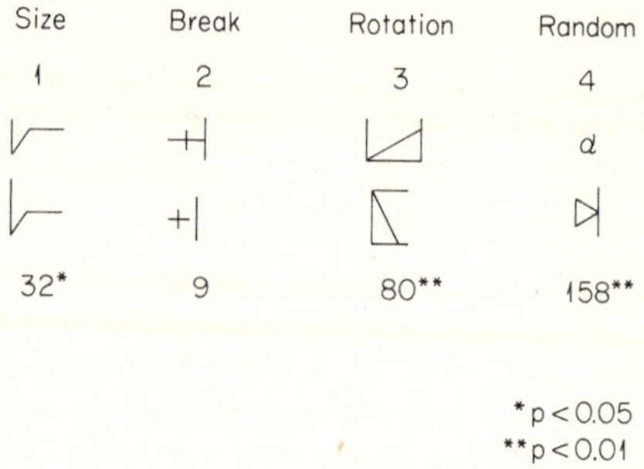

FIG. 3.1. Times for matching various pairs of forms to which subjects had learned a common response (1, 2, 3, or 4) as a function of the similarity among the forms. Times are differences in RT (msec) to the pair shown as compared to its physically identical controls. (From Posner & Mitchell, 1967. Copyright 1967 by the American Psychological Association. Reprinted by permission.)

Size	Break	Rotation	Random
1	2	3	4
32*	9	80**	158**

*p < 0.05
**p < 0.01

absolute difference of 32 msec, which is quite similar to the 19 msec by which the "Cc" exceeds the mean of "CC" and "cc." The continuity transformation did not show a significant increase over its physical identity control. We concluded that the method appeared to be a good one for determining the overall similarity of various types of perceptual transformations.

Our results did not show conclusively that an analogue process was involved, but they did provide evidence that small differences in physical form could be measured by chronometric techniques.

Orientation

I did not myself pursue the study of systematic transformations by means of mental chronometry. However, Shepard and his colleagues (1975) have made this one of the most active and instructive areas of mental chronometry. Shepard and Metzler (1971) explore systematically the times to determine whether two simultaneously presented forms could be made congruent by rotation. The results showed a beautiful linear increase in reaction time as a function of the degree of rotation (see Figure 3.2). Indeed, the results were so reproducible that Cooper

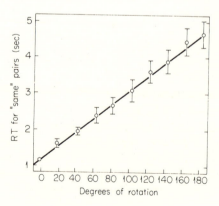

FIG. 3.2. RT to determine if two complex forms are identical as a function of angle of rotation between them. (From Shepard & Metzler, 1971. Copyright 1971 by the American Association for the Advancement of Science.)

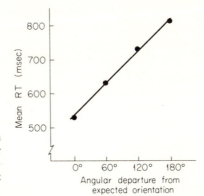

FIG. 3.3.   RT to respond to form probes as a function of the angular departure from an expected orientation. (From Cooper, 1976. Copyright 1976 by the Psychonomic Society.)

(1976) was able to calculate the rate of mental rotation for individual subjects. She presented a cue to instruct subjects to begin rotation of an upright form and presented a test pattern at varying distances from where her calculations said the subjects would be in their internal rotation. The results produced a linear relation between reaction time and the distance between calculated position of the subject's internal rotation and the actual orientation of the test pattern (see Figure 3.3). These results provide evidence of an internal analogue process underlying rotation of these forms. What is more, when subjects are provided with a single form and a cue about what orientation to produce, the rotation they perform on their internal image closely resembles the rotation rate for simultaneous pairs of forms. This impressive evidence favors the close similarity between visual operations upon images and upon percepts (see pp. 50–51).

Cooper and Shepard (1973) extended the rotation studies to letters. Using letters, it is possible to show that the mental rotation process goes on at the very same time that subjects derive phonetic descriptions of the letter names, as pointed out in Chapter 2 (see pp. 50–51). This evidence supports the isolable systems approach that has been taken in Chapter 2 rather than a single, underlying common code.

Size

Bundesen and Larsen (1975) have applied the simultaneous matching method to the study of differences in size. Once again they found close chronometric relations between the amount of transformation in size required to match the pair and reaction time. Corcoran and Besner (1975) had shown that size manipulations affect physical but not name matches of simultaneous letter pairs. It can thus be assumed that such manipulations are done on a visual code.

Because Bundesen and Larsen used complex polygons in one experiment, it is possible to compare the general level of their reaction times with those obtained by Cooper (1975) for rotation with the same type of figures. This is done in Figure 3.4. For the zero rotation and size ratio of one, the reaction times for "same" responses in the Cooper data are very similar to those obtained by Bundesen and Larsen. The relative similarity of the results gives us faith in a comparison of the two studies. Though it is not of much interest to compare effects of size and rotation quantitatively, it is important to note their linear effects upon matching RTs.

In another study, Bundesen and Larsen used as "different" stimuli pairs of items that were different figures. Cooper and Shepard (1973) always used reflections of the same figure as the "different" pairs. Thus in the orientation experiments the figures to be judged were always very similar. It is important that size differences increase reaction time even when the distractors are different figures. If subjects were able to respond to the identity of the stimuli irrespective of their size, one would not expect any increase in reaction time as a function of a change in size. Subjects should have been able to respond "different" to different forms irrespective of the size. The results obtained by Bundesen and Larsen, like those of Posner and Mitchell (1967), suggest, although they do not prove, that transformations in size and rotation may well be part of the normalization process by which single stimuli are classified.

Shepard did not distinguish between operations upon visual images and visual codes. His task of requiring subjects to determine whether a letter when rotated would be a correct form or a mirror image gives rise to clear subjective reports of imagery and is relatively slow. However, the methods used by Buggie (1970), Bundesen and Larsen (1975), and Cooper (1976) are simultaneous matching tasks. They give rise to little in the way of subjective reports of imagery and yet still appear to depend upon analogue processes, because they show systematic increases in RT with transformation size.

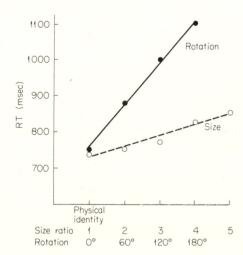

FIG. 3.4. RT as a function of degree of angular rotation (after Cooper, 1975) and of differences in size (after Bundesen & Larsen, 1975).

The results we have discussed for size and rotation conflict with widely held principles of shape and size constancy. We are often told by textbooks in perception that the human perceptual system is indifferent to changes in the size and orientation of objects, that it recognizes them irrespective of such distortion. Of course it is often said that such constancy breaks down in such cases as looking at a face upside down or viewing from an airplane. In fact from a chronometric view it appears likely that any distortion of the identity between two figures leads to an increase in reaction time to make the match.

Studies of size–distance constancy constructed within a chronometric framework (Broota & Epstein, 1973) show an increase in reaction time to determine if two stimuli are the same when they occur at different distances over when they are at the same distance. This increase occurs under conditions that produce near perfect constancy by judgmental criteria. Thus differences in physical size seem to have an effect on matching latency even when the two objects look identical in terms of perceived size judgments. A similar increase in latency was obtained when a single item was exposed for identification at a distance different than the one at which it was originally experienced. These data suggest that distance correction plays a role in identification of an object as though its stored representation has associated with it a particular physical size. Unfortunately, the results obtained so far have only explored distances greater than the one at which the object was originally exposed and thus cannot be considered definitive.

The data reviewed so far all come from simultaneous matching tasks. It is clear, however, that the same results are obtained when one deals with successive matching or with matching of an input item to an active visual image that the subject is asked to generate (Holyoak, 1977). In all these cases discrepancies in size or orientation between the internal representation held in memory by the subject and the presented item lead to systematic increases in reaction time in the same way as is found for simultaneous matching.

The next step is to ask whether the same analogue normalization process is also involved when subjects recognize an object presented to them. Shepard (1975) has rejected this view, because the times for mental rotation are simply too long to be involved when subjects are required to identify a letter. There is little evidence that rotation has much effect upon the time required to name a single letter (Buggie, 1970; Snyder, 1972). In addition, analogue distortions such as rotating letters often have larger effects upon "same" responses than upon "different" responses (Egeth & Blecker, 1971). This finding indicates that normalization is not a serial stage prior to making any response to a stimulus input. On the other hand, whether one views stored information as consisting of feature lists or templates based upon past experience with figures, it is hard to conceive of any way in which current input can be brought into contact with past visual experience that does not involve some form of matching process.

If the simultaneous matching method can give us an experimental model of the internal processes by which stimuli are normalized during recognition, it represents a potent experimental method for coming to understand a critical aspect of pattern recognition. Before pursuing this idea further, it is necessary to examine the stability of the results of matching tasks.

Diagnostics

One of the most impressive aspects of the comparison of the Cooper (1976) and Bundesen and Larsen (1975) results is that when a pair is physically identical, the reaction times are similar even though the overall tasks performed by the subjects are quite different (see Figure 3.4). This suggests that the process of matching two items maintains its integrity even when embedded in rather different task environments. It reinforces a notion that was strongly stated in our paper (Posner & Mitchell, 1967):

> If the perceptual comparison process remains relatively stable it may be possible to use it as a unit in the analysis of many cognitive skills in much the same way as the reflex serves as the unit of analysis within S–R theory. The present experiments seem to provide some hope that a stable empirical referent can be found for at least the comparison portion of the abstract TOTE process [p. 408].

Such stability is consistent with the idea that matching is an appropriate model for a part of the normal perceptual process.

One challenge to the view that matching serves as a unit for perceptual processes has been from proposals that subjects develop specific strategies or "diagnostics" for the analysis of input and that there is very little of a general nature that occurs when task formats are changed. Such a view has been held by Fox (1975). In his experiments, simultaneous letter pairs that differed in symmetry were presented. Thus a letter pair like "HH," which is symmetric around the vertical axis, could be responded to faster than "BB," which is not. Fox argued that vertical symmetry was a "diagnostic" for the letter-matching task. He argued that displays with vertical symmetry would give faster RTs than those without this diagnostic (see Figure 3.5). If this were true, it might be possible to account for differences between physical and phonetic matches as an artifact of the presence of vertical symmetry in some of the physically identical pairs, whereas vertical symmetry would never be present in the phonetic identity pairs. Obviously converging operations indicating the ability to manipulate physical and phonetic codes of simultaneous letter pairs argue that the Fox explanation could not itself be a complete one. However, it might still be that within the physical matching task, vertical symmetry serves as a diagnostic that subjects could adopt in the same way that they can decide to rotate or match stimuli of different sizes.

The similarity of data obtained by Bundesen and Larsen (1975) and Cooper (1976) in their very different tasks argues against the diagnostic view, as does

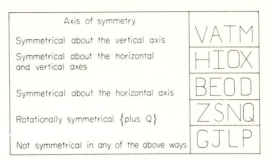

Axis of symmetry	
Symmetrical about the vertical axis	VATM
Symmetrical about the horizontal and vertical axes	HIOX
Symmetrical about the horizontal axis	BEOD
Rotationally symmetrical {plus Q}	ZSNQ
Not symmetrical in any of the above ways	GJLP

FIG. 3.5.   Axis of symmetry of letters. (From Fox, 1975. Copyright 1975 by the American Psychological Association. Reprinted by permission.)

much of the material that I reviewed in the last chapter. Fox did present evidence that vertical symmetry aided matching. This, however, turned out to be difficult to replicate in even slightly different situations (Egeth, Brownell, & Geoffrion, 1976). Moreover, even if it is the case that vertically symmetric letter pairs are responded to somewhat more rapidly than pairs that are not vertically symmetric (e.g., see Richards, 1978), it is not necessarily the case that subjects can control the use of vertical symmetry as a diagnostic. In fact, almost no subjects running in these experiments came to recognize vertical symmetry as a diagnostic; nor, despite the many hundreds of letter-matching experiments that I ran, did I ever become aware of the vertical symmetry diagnostic except through reading Fox. Finally, the effects of vertical symmetry in letter matching are small (Richards, 1978) when they are found at all.[2]

Thus the evidence of the stability of matching in a variety of task formats seems to argue both against the diagnostic approach and other active approaches by which subjects adopt particular hypotheses designed to solve the tasks given to them. This is not to deny that strategies and individual task adaptations are important in the study of human performance but to emphasize the relative stability of the match reaction times as would be expected if they were closely related to normalization required as a part of recognition.

Random Perturbations

I have considered two dimensions upon which pairs of simultaneous stimuli might be compared. Results for both size and rotation seem to favor systematic transformations of visual information during matching. More evidence on the question comes from experiments reported in Posner (1964). In that study, pairs

---

[2]Although Richards (1978) found advantages for vertically symmetric pairs, he argued that these obtained because they made matching processes easier. In particular, vertical symmetry appears to aid segmentation of the field in cases where there is uncertainty involved in separating the pair of forms.

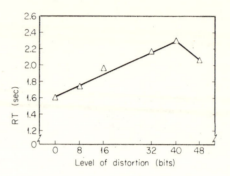

FIG. 3.6.   RT to equate two dot patterns as a function of degree of distortion (bits). (From Posner, 1964.
Copyright 1964 by the American
Psychological Association. Reprinted
by permission.)

of random dot patterns differing in similarity were equated by learning a common name for each pair. Later on, subjects were placed in a reaction time situation in which they were to report whether a given pair had the same name. The results in Figure 3.6 are plotted as a function of the degree of distortion between the two members of the pair. It is clear that the reaction time for "same" is a linear function of the degree of distortion between the two patterns.

This result can be explained in at least two ways. For example, it could be that the degree of learning differed systematically as a function of the difference between the paired patterns. Or the process by which the dot patterns underwent distortion may have left relatively more features in common among similar pairs than among nonsimilar pairs. Thus one could talk about the subject by equating particular features rather than by making a more direct, holistic comparison between the patterns.

In 1964 (Posner, 1964) I attempted no decision between these hypotheses. In retrospect, given the results obtained from both size and rotational transforma-tions that do not seem reasonably accounted for either on the basis of prior learning or on the basis of equating individual features, I now feel that the dot pattern studies represent a general point—namely, that a common way to match patterns of different distortions is through an analogue comparison process.

Templates

Our discussion so far has concerned itself mainly with the time course of compar-ing two input forms in order to determine if they are members of the same class. The hope is that the operations performed on visual codes in this task may tell us something about the internal comparisons made when people compare an input item against memory during recognition. One factor that is undoubtedly impor-tant in evaluating that position is some notion of how information is represented in memory. Often the problem of storage of past information and the problem of recognizing current input are dealt with separately: the former in the field of memory and the latter in the study of perception. The two problems are obviously closely related. The random dot patterns discussed in the last section have been used for both purposes. If an input item is recognized by comparing it as a whole against an internal representation of a previous stimulus, then the act of recognition could also serve as a means of modifying the stored code. In this way the summary of past experience with items in the class would drift slowly toward reflection of the most recent instances encountered. When we recognize an old friend who has grown a beard while away on vacation the stimulus is usually not sufficient to prevent recognition, but the change does give rise to surprise. After a time, shaving the beard produces the same surprise that growing it did previously.

The relation between storage and recognition can be described both as *accommodation* of the stored representation to the new input and *assimilation* of the input by the stored structure. The new pattern is rapidly assimilated so that even shortly after its removal, reports of it will be contaminated by the knowledge that it is of a particular class. But the nature of the structure is itself altered by the new instance.

These simple ideas have been incorporated into experiments designed to increase understanding of the nature of stored representations of categories. Several years ago, Keele and I (Posner & Keele, 1968) presented subjects with a variety of distorted dot patterns. We found that subjects stored a representation that can roughly be categorized as the central tendency of the set of patterns with which they were presented (Posner, 1969).

At the time we felt that our findings were support for the so-called composite photograph view that had been presented at the turn of the century by Galton (1907). This idea was that the visual system could be seen as behaving much like a composite photograph in that it organized related visual experiences by taking an average. Of course we knew that the category was represented not by the central tendency alone but also by information concerning the range of boundaries and—provided the learning was extensive—by specific information concerning the exemplars that had actually been presented during learning.

More recently, a number of results have supported this view of categories and have enlarged it beyond the operations of the visual system.

Bransford and Franks (1971) found that one could characterize the memory for previous verbal propositions by a kind of overall synthesis of prior statements. The analogy between our own results and those of Bransford and Franks seemed to bring new stimulation to efforts to describe the kinds of mental structures that might underlie semantics.

Also related were results of Rosch (1973), Rips, Shoben, and Smith (1973), and Tversky and Kahneman (1974), which argue that the human mind often operates from a representative case. Rosch (1973) first showed that subjects represent color categories in terms of central instances. These typical instances were easily learned. Less typical instances near the boundaries were more difficult to learn. Rosch, Mervis, Grey, Johnson, and Boyes–Braem (1976) generalized the argument to deal with the storage system underlying natural visual objects. Rosch and then Rips, Shoben, and Smith (1973) applied this view to complex semantic categories viewed as consisting of typical instances, arrayed within a multidimensional space. Finally, Tversky and Kahneman (1974) argued that subjects reason from typical instances in probabilistic thinking.

An important general point that emerges from these studies is that one can predict the time to classify an input item as a member of a category from knowledge of its distance from the central exemplars of that category. In each of these areas prior distance measures have been used to predict classification times. The details of such classification times have sometimes been used to support spatial and sometimes network models, but clearly the simplest way to deal with the results is to suppose that an input item is compared in some way with an internal description of the category in whatever form it may be represented. Distances from the category center are related to the operations and thus to the time required to activate the stored system representing the category. This process involves the matching of input against stored categorical information in much the same way as is found in simultaneous and successive matching tasks. The results of classification experiments support the view that analogue operations are integral at least to those aspects of normal recognition that involve activating information about the classification of the input.

The first five sections of this chapter have reflected on two major questions concerning analogue representation. First, it appears that representation of visual information in its absence (imagery) involves an analogue system that has much in common with visual perception itself. A generated code is equivalent to one that has been presented visually both in the efficiency of matching and in the performance of mental operations such as rotation. It is less clear whether or not the analogue operations upon visual codes that are revealed in studies of matching are similar to those that occur when a single visual item is normalized in the process of matching it against information in long-term memory (pattern recognition). In favor of the similarity is the stability of matching results across experimental tasks and evidence that the memory system for past information involves abstraction of a central tendency from input. Less favorable to the analogy between matching and pattern recognition are findings that show little or no effect of size or rotation on the naming of letters and forms whereas they have a large effect upon matching.

Visual Dimensions

Our effort to deal with analogue representation within the visual system has relied upon different dimensions of form such as size and orientation. The time to match pairs of simultaneous forms for identity in shape is affected by the color of the forms used (see p. 40). It may be particularly useful to examine how color and form are combined in making such judgments. Color and form can be said to represent distinct dimensions of visual objects in the sense that there are different physiological systems that mediate their processing. Thus they may turn out to be good model systems for studying how the visual system combines dimensions signaled by separate mechanisms.

Schroeder (1976) in our laboratory has been working on color and form following a lead proposed by Garner (1974). Garner suggested that color might interfere with form more than the reverse, because a form cannot exist without a color, but the reverse is not true. One of Schroeder's experiments on color and form used the Garner technique. Colors or forms were presented either with only one of the two dimensions varying (simple), or with the two redundant or varied in orthogonal blocks. Another experiment used a simultaneous visual match requiring subjects either to match on form alone, color alone, or both color and form together. The literature on multidimensional matching tasks indicates that color and form are handled in parallel (Hawkins, 1969). The results were clear. In both the Garner technique and in the matching technique, color when made irrelevant interfered with the ability of subjects to make form judgments, but not the reverse (see Figure 3.7). Moreover, this occurred even when the reaction times for color and form taken alone did not differ significantly.

I do not know if it is best to view Schroeder's results as Garner does in terms of the properties of natural objects or whether the results suggest general characteristics of processing when separate physiological mechanisms are involved.

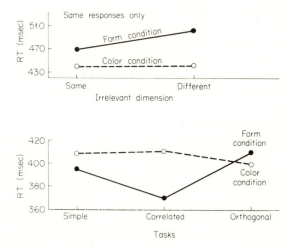

FIG. 3.7.   RT to stimuli varying in form and color. Upper panel uses a simultaneous matching task (same responses only are shown), and lower panel uses techniques developed by Garner (1974). Both panels show interference of irrelevant colors on form matching but not the reverse. (After Schroeder, 1976.)

The convergence of results from the matching task and the Garner task gives some hope that chronometric methods may eventually help us understand how information from separate mechanisms within the visual processing system is combined.

FROM LETTERS TO LETTER STRINGS

One of the most exciting areas of mental chronometry has been the investigation of the perception of words (Smith & Spoehr, 1974). This has been particularly true in the area of reading (Gibson & Levin, 1975), but there is interest as well in the relationship between individual, auditory phonemes and the phonetic code that combines them in words (Rozin & Gleitman, 1977). A number of techniques and concepts developed in Chapter 2 are applicable to the processes by which the visual system chunks individual letters into words. It is fruitful to compare the performance of people when receiving unrelated letters with their performance with words. It might seem at first that the advantage of words over random letter strings rests entirely in our ability to translate the word into a single phonetic unit. It is now known that this seductive theory is unlikely and instead that the visual code itself represents familiar letter strings in a way that differs from unfamiliar ones. In order to examine the evidence for this assertion, one has to find ways of breaking apart the rapid and complex process of recoding a visual string into its phonetic equivalent. Mental chronometry has succeeded in so doing.

Unrelated Letter Strings

For single letters, the nervous system simultaneously represents a visual and a phonetic code (Chapter 2). One would of course expect similar results to be obtained when a number of letters are shown simultaneously. Indeed there is evidence (Coltheart, 1972) that this does occur. A model developed by Coltheart is shown in Figure 3.8. It suggests that a virtually unlimited capacity iconic memory is rapidly replaced by a low-capacity, flexibly decaying, nonmaskable visual code and by a moderate-capacity, negligibly decaying, nonmaskable phonetic code. The usual tachistoscopic experiment draws upon a combination of iconic representation and the visual and phonetic codes.

The most direct evidence favoring the view that Coltheart outlines is that it is easy to mask items in the middle of a letter display but difficult to mask the ends of the display. Coltheart argues that the ends of a display are rapidly placed in a visual code that is not maskable. At the same time, a left-to-right translation process develops phonetic codes of the remaining material. Although one may well dispute the details of the model that Coltheart presents, it seems to be at least plausible—based on a large amount of tachistoscopic experiments—to propose

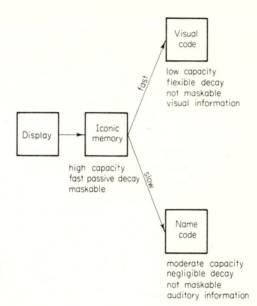

FIG. 3.8. A view of memory processes following a letter array. (From Coltheart, 1972, p. 75. Reprinted by permission of Penguin Books Ltd.)

that both visual and phonetic codes are represented from the multiple letters. It is unlikely, however, that the visual code developed from multiple strings is able to deal with very many items, at least not at a high level of availability (see p. 51). For that reason, if displays become larger than a few letters or if lag times become longer than .5 sec or so, the role of visual codes may become relatively minor with respect to the phonetic recoding. Thus to study chunking of words within the visual system, it is preferable to use tasks that involve either simultaneous presentation or very short time delays. In the next two sections I examine chronometric studies involving either simultaneous presentation of letter strings for matching or very minimal delays between the letter string and the test.

The use of simultaneous matching tasks flows quite naturally from the material presented previously. As a working hypothesis I view the simultaneous matching tasks as an experimental model of the internal matching process involved in comparing an input string against stored visual information in the process of recognizing a word. Evidence on this assumption was discussed above (p. 68) and will not be reexamined at this point, but the assumption is critical in interpreting some of the results outlined below.

Matching of Letter Strings

Beller (1970) required subjects to indicate whether pairs of letter strings presented one above the other were the same or different. The letter strings consisted of one, two, or four adjacent items. Three categories of "same" pairs were used. All pairs could be physically identical; there could be one pair in the string that was identical only in name, with the remainder being physically identical; or they could all be identical only in name. Subjects were requested to respond "same" if the pairs were identical in name. The data are shown in Figure 3.9. The results show a linear slope of about 60 msec per pair for the time to respond to physically identical strings. If one name match was present within the string, the slope remained about 60 msec a pair, but the intercept was raised by 80 msec, as would be predicted from single letter data. Finally, if all the letter pairs were identical only in name, the slope was 140 msec per pair, again as would be predicted by the difference between physical and name matches for single letter pairs. The results could hardly be stronger confirmation that the processes involved in comparison of random letter strings are very similar to those involved in the processing of single letters.

Eichelman (1970a) used the same method to explore the times for unrelated letter strings as compared to strings that formed words. Eichelman's results in comparing physical matches for letter strings and for strings forming words are shown in Figure 3.10. Comparing the Eichelman and the Beller results for unrelated letter strings, one finds virtually identical slopes. This gives some support to the idea that the processes Eichelman was studying are very similar to those that Beller investigated and thus also similar to the single letter data.

Eichelman's results for words showed a slope of about 20 msec per item. Clearly something was happening with the word stimuli that allowed a physical matching process to proceed more efficiently than was the case with the random letter strings. One possible explanation that occurs immediately is that information about the phonetic interpretation of the string—that is, the word name—was used in making the supposedly physical match. To test this, Eichelman ran the

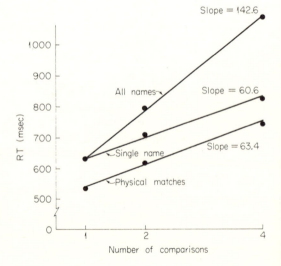

FIG. 3.9. RT for matching letter strings when all pairs are physically identical, one name match is included, and all pairs are identical in name. (From Beller, 1970. Copyright 1970 by the American Psychological Association. Reprinted by permission.)

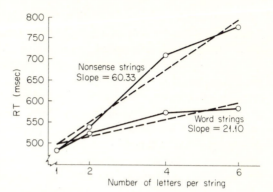

FIG. 3.10. A comparison of RTs for letter and word strings of varying length. (From Eichelman, 1970a. Copyright 1970 by the American Psychological Association. Reprinted by permission.)

same experiment using four-letter strings that were either physically identical or in opposite cases and were either random strings or words. Eichelman found (see Figure 3.11) that the cross-case random letter strings required about 250 msec longer or about 60 msec per pair longer than for the same-case pairs. Although this is not quite as much an increase as in the Beller study (80 msec per pair), it does seem to indicate that the random letter strings involved a process much like name matching. A likely reason for the relatively faster times per name match in the Eichelman study is that many of the vowel pairs (e.g., Oo, Uu) involve analogue matches that were excluded from Beller's study.

Name match pairs that were words required about 100–150 msec longer than physically identical word pairs. This increase is roughly the same per word as that obtained by Beller and Schaeffer (Note 5) in an experiment in which the subjects were required to determine whether two strings of two words were animal names or not. Thus there is independent confirmation that the time required to obtain a phonetic representation of two words appears to be about the value that Eichelman found in his study. These data argue quite strongly that only in the mixed-case condition is a phonetic analysis occurring and thus, by deduction, that in the pure-case condition physical matching was involved. Thus the advantage of words over random strings in the pure-case condition seems clearly to argue that something in the visual system is influenced by the use of highly familiar letter strings.

	Pure physical	Mixed physical	Mixed name	Name–physical
Strings	678	670	922	61 msec/letter
Words	643	602	754	28 msec/letter

FIG. 3.11. A comparison of physical and phonetic match RTs for four-letter word and nonword strings. (After Eichelman, 1970a.)

However, on the basis of these data alone, the capability of the visual system to be influenced by orthographic regularity of this sort may still be doubted. Proof that it is was developed in a later study of Pollatsek, Well, and Schindler (1975). In this experiment, pairs of letter strings were presented simultaneously for a physical match. In all cases the pairs were identical letters, but one or more of the letter cases could be changed, so that in half the cases the strings were not physically identical. Thus in this case, either words or random strings are presented for physical matching in which the phonetic representation is exactly identical for both strings within a pair. Despite this control, Pollatsek et al. found a familiarity effect with words being about 75 msec faster than nonwords. These results could not be in any way due to phonetic recoding either of the individual letter pairs or of the word as a whole. Moreover, there were some checks within the experiment as to whether phonetic differences between letter pairs facilitated the "different" response. A comparison was made between pairs that did or did not differ in the letters used. The size of the familiarity effect was quite similar. Moreover, there was no greater familiarity effect for homophones than for nonhomophones. Thus none of these tests suggests a role for phonetic comparison within the visual matching task; it seems determined by the visual code.

Familiarity of Units

One feature of the Eichelman data that has led to much controversy is the fact that reaction times for random letters and for words converge as the number of items in the string is reduced, so that with a single pair letters and words appear to be identical. The reason that it is interesting to determine whether a single pair shows the familiarity effect is that this would indicate that the effect does not result from the process of chunking together or putting together individual units, but extends to the presence of a single unit in the memory system. Unfortunately, it is always more difficult to determine the effect in a limiting case when one knows that it increases in magnitude as the number of items gets larger. Of course there are very few one-letter words, so the Eichelman finding may not be too general. Posner and Mitchell (1967) found that the reaction times for single letter pairs and for single pairs of Gibson figures (presumably less familiar to the subjects) were identical. On the other hand, Egeth and Blecker (1971) found that it is somewhat faster to respond to right-side-up letters than to respond to upside-down letters when they are mixed in a single block. Later, Ambler and Proctor (1976) showed that the advantage of right-side-up letters only occurred in mixed blocks and not when the two were embedded in pure blocks. Both the Posner and Mitchell and the Egeth and Blecker techniques can be faulted, because they employ different materials for the familiar and unfamiliar pairs.

A more thorough investigation by Ambler and Proctor (1976) appeared to show that it was possible to obtain differences in favor of familiar over unfamiliar items even when the same materials were used in both. Ambler and Proctor compared Japanese and American subjects exposed to Japanese and English letters. American subjects were faster to match English letters and Japanese subjects faster to match Japanese letters. This effect was obtained even when stimulus presentation was organized by letter type; and subjects knew what letter types to expect, so it was not limited by expectancy. The most important result of the Ambler and Proctor experiments, however, was from use of a memory search task in which a number of items were presented followed by a single probe item. They found that for American subjects the slopes of these functions were increased for Japanese letters over English letters, though the intercepts did not differ. This evidence, together with the fact that familiarity effects are greatly influenced by strategies [for example, differences between mixed and pure lists and whether or not the subject expects words to be present (Aderman & Smith, 1971; Schindler, Well, & Pollatsek, 1976)] and with the relative difficulty of obtaining familiarity effects with single item pairs, all suggest that the familiarity effect is limited to the comparison process itself and not to the processes that take place prior to comparison. This inference has been accepted by a number of readers of this literature (e.g., Krueger, 1970). They have suggested that the limitation of familiarity to the comparison process means that the effects of familiarity are relatively uninteresting. This judgment depends upon whether one believes that the comparison of external stimuli is in any sense a model situation for what goes on when the comparison of an input item is made against some canonical form represented in memory. Since I have taken the view that such an assumption is warranted as a working hypothesis, I believe that the limitation of these familiarity effects to the comparison process does not mean they are trivial but shows only what is logically necessary: That all processes prior to the comparison *must* be free of memory effects. In so far as the comparison of matching mimics pattern recognition, it must be the first place to show the effects of memory. Obviously, there can be no memory effect until the input makes contact with the internal memory code. In so far as the matching process mimics that internal comparison, then it must be the first place where one would find familiarity effects.

This point is a difficult one to grasp, because many investigators divide input processing into an encoding and comparison phase. Encoding is thought to involve all the processes prior to a match against some explicit positive set of items that the experimenter provides to the subject. Encoding in this sense involves several implicit comparisons (e.g., with internally stored visual codes) prior to the explicit comparison involved in matching against a positive set. It is these implicit comparisons that are used in pattern recognition.

I find it comforting that no processes prior to comparison seem to be influenced by familiarity and take this to be consistent with the idea that the simultaneous comparison task is a helpful model of what is occurring during recognition. Obviously, this hypothesis will always be subject to revision with additional evidence.

DUAL CODES IN READING

In recent years there has been a great deal of interest in the process by which one reads words. Obviously, the material we have outlined above on matching of letters and letter strings has implications for word reading. Many of the experiments on reading have been influenced primarily by linguistic rather than psychological considerations. Thus there has been much effort to search for *the* unit at either the visual or phonetic level around which word processing is organized. This corresponds to efforts by linguists and phonologists to isolate phonemes, morphemes, vocalic center groups, and other fundamental units around which to build their science. As psychologists, it should not surprise us that subjects can use many different units depending upon how they have learned language. Thus many of the questions to which the reading process has been subjected, though useful in the development of programs for teaching reading or for the human engineering of the reading process, do not provide very much that is fundamental about the analysis of mind.

To apply the matching techniques to the reading of words, it is important to understand what happens to the representation of a word string when a delay is interpolated between the array string and its matching stimulus.

For unrelated letter strings, Posner and Taylor (1969) found that same-case matches were faster than cross-case matches for only one or two letters. With letter strings that comprise a word, there is evidence for an advantage of physical over phonetic matches that lasts for a considerable period of time when subjects are instructed to remember the words and classify each of them as to whether they appeared before in the list (Hintzman & Summers, 1973; Kirsner, 1972). When the task does not involve any memory instruction, the same-case matches appear to show little advantage in reaction time (Scarborough, Cortese, & Scarborough, 1977).

For individual visual letters we had found that after presentation the stimulus is represented by two codes, one visual and one phonetic. The same seems to apply to simultaneous letter strings. However, logically speaking, one might expect differences between the internal representation of a word and a letter. There are abstract rules that specify the permissible orthographic character of a word. These rules are indifferent to differences between case; but they may still operate upon visual rather than phonetic codes, although they clearly lead to a phonetic representation. Thus it seems perfectly possible for a word to be represented visually but in a form that is abstract enough to be indifferent to changes of case. For letters, we found that cross-case and cross-modality reaction times provided about the same advantage of physical over phonetic matches. Moreover, converging operations such as use of a phonetic memory load and varying acoustic confusions argue that cross-case matches occur at the phonetic level. Unfortunately, little of this work has been done with words, so that the issue is less clear. There is an obvious advantage to defining the phonetic level in terms of cross-modality matches—that is, as a processing system that equates linguistic input from visual and auditory stimulation. It then becomes an empirical matter to determine for any kind of material whether a cross-case match is performed at a phonetic level so defined.

Posner and Hanson (Note 6) compared pure physical matching with both cross-case, cross-voice, and cross-modality matching of words. Subjects were asked to respond "same" when successive words were either both animals or both nonanimals. Physical matching was uniformly faster than phonetic matching. Rather surprisingly, in this study, cross-case, cross-voice, and cross-modality matches appeared to give comparable reaction times as though they were based on a common phonetic code. This result suggested that words were represented in terms of a visual code somewhat isomorphic to the physical properties of the stimulus and by a generalized phonetic code that was indifferent to the modality of input, just as is the case for individual letters. Unfortunately, in a subsequent study this simple result did not obtain; rather, cross-modal matches were considerably longer than cross-case and cross-voice matches. This lengthened reaction was not specific to the phonetic level matches but was found also for semantic matches and mismatches. Therefore, it might have been due to general factors of switching modalities rather than to a specific difference between the level at which the same word is matched when repeated in a cross voice, cross-case, and cross-modality form. Thus the results of Posner and Hanson need to be expanded by the types of converging operations that have been applied to single letters. For example, if cross-modal, cross-case, and cross-voice matches of the same word depend upon a common code, they should all be affected similarly by such operations as filling short-term memory with phonetic items.

Studies reviewed so far appear to show that there are separable codes available following the presentation of a visual word. These include the physical and phonetic codes found for individual letters. Since we know that familiarity with an item affects the time for visual matches, it is clear that some sort of visual code is influenced by information abstracted from past experience. Thus a word is treated as a chunk within the visual system in some sense. Whether the chunk is case specific or whether it is sufficiently abstract to be indifferent to case is not certain. In any event, such chunks must also include familiar stimuli that are not orthographically regular (e.g., FBI), since these have been shown to produce match RTs similar to words (Egeth & Blecker, 1971; Henderson, 1974). The idea that a word is represented as a visual chunk independent of its assigned phonetic code has a number of implications for reading tasks, some of which are examined below.

A problem in examining studies of reading is the expectation arising from serial models that the order in which codes are evolved predicts the ease with which that code can be accessed by awareness or can lead to overt responses (Ball, Wood, & Smith, 1975). The isolable systems notion developed in Chapter 2 suggests that codes exist in parallel, and the ease with which they can be accessed is a separate question from the order in which they are developed. Recently, Rozin and Gleitman (1977) have argued that semantic codes are more easily available to awareness than phonetic or physical codes. They point out the difficulty people have in becoming aware that a meaningful auditory unit (e.g., a word) consists of phonemes that can be arbitrarily assigned to visual symbols (letters). Although their point is well illustrated by this example, there are also many examples where the perceptual salience of the input stream masks the underlying semantics. For this reason, I feel it important to keep separate the question of the development of input codes from the issue of how they are accessed and used in various tasks. This point will become more important as we turn to results obtained in attempts to analyze reading.

If reading words conforms to the analysis already presented, studies should indicate evidence for separate visual, phonetic, and semantic codes and an ability to select among these codes depending upon whether the task of the subject is to comprehend, proofread, read aloud, or perform some other task related to word processing. To a large extent, results in word perception can be seen to fit in this way.

One of the most popular methods currently being used to study reading of single words (Reicher, 1969) is closely related to the matching task. In this chronometric paradigm, subjects are presented with either a letter, a letter string, or a word very briefly followed by a masking stimulus. Shortly thereafter, a pair of probe letters is presented. Since both probe letters make a meaningful word, the subject cannot guess the correct letter. This technique provides a powerful control over guessing strategies that have so badly flawed much older work comparing words with random strings.

The result that is most striking is that every letter of a visual word is better recognized than is a single letter presented in isolation. This is a most impressive result, because within the visual code one would expect that the preservation of a single letter would be equal to the individual letters of a word even if, as has been suggested above, the visual code of a word is a chunk. If only a phonetic code were present, one might expect a word to be better than a single letter. A word's relation to its phonetic representation must be closer than a letter's relation to its phonetic representation because of the strong tendency to read words.

Is it possible to explore how the word superiority effect arises? There appears to be some evidence that information about a word in this situation tends to be primarily represented in a phonetic code. Evidence favoring this view comes from a study by Polf (1976), illustrated in Figure 3.12. This study examines accuracy as a function of the time following the probe letters that the subject was given to respond prior to a forced deadline. Although information begins to accrue more quickly for an isolated letter display, word displays were more accurate given long accrual times. One explanation of this result is that it takes subjects some time to unpack the unified phonetic chunk representing the word in

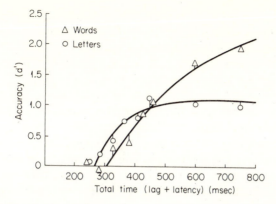

FIG. 3.12.   Accuracy of response (d') as a function of processing time for letter and word stimuli in an experiment requiring forced-choice identification of single letters. (From Polf, 1976.)

order to determine which letters are present. A unified visual chunk might also explain this result. However, Mezrich (1973) showed that forcing subjects to name the array prior to responding to the probe had no effect on word arrays but improved performance for individual letters so that they become better than words. McClelland (1976) showed that the advantage of words over isolated letters appeared to depend upon presenting a mask following the array. Finally, Hawkins, Reicher, Rogers, and Peterson (1976) showed that placing a small number of homophones (e.g., cent and sent) among the probes greatly reduced performance for the word arrays. All of these results are consistent with the idea that the word is held in a unified phonetic chunk while the isolated letters are present in a visual code that is affected by the subsequent masking stimulus (see Smith, Haviland, Reder, Brownell, & Adams, 1976, for a similar view).

Other results obtained by Hawkins et al. suggest that there is some option to the coding of words. They found that when a large number of homophones were inserted into the list, the subjects appeared to adopt a nonphonetic code for the word since homophones were no longer worse than control pairs. The code used in this case appears to be visual, since judgments are affected by visual similarity among the probes (Davidson, 1977). Under all these conditions words were still superior to isolated letters. This may mean both that there are optional coding strategies available to the subjects and that the word advantage arises within both visual and phonetic chunks.

There is still no full resolution to the question of the locus of the word superiority effect advantage, but the principles developed in its analysis are familiar ones from the letter- and word-matching experiments: First is the presence of physical and phonetic codes; and second is the evidence for a selection among these codes that is heavily influenced by aspects of the physical situation such as whether a mask is used and whether external interference such as homophones are present in the list. There have also been reports that individual differences among subjects in preference for coding is also important in the selection of codes for reading (Baron & Strawson, 1976).

Semantics

One of the most interesting questions involved in the reading of words is whether the visual code can make contact with the semantic representation without requiring a phonetic interpretation. A number of years ago I attempted (Posner, 1970) to study this question with a letter-matching technique. I compared the ability of subjects to make matches based on the classification, letter–digit, with their ability to do so based on the classification, vowel–consonant. I used letters that are difficult to match when subjects are given instructions to match on the letter name (such as b, d, p, q, g) together with easy-to-name controls. The experimental letters showed increased reaction times when the subjects were required to make a vowel–consonant distinction but not for a letter–digit distinction. Subjects were not required to go through the name in either condition, since all the experimental letters were both letters and consonants. It appeared that the subjects did use the phonetic code to make the vowel-consonant distinction but not the letter–digit distinction.

Baron (1973) performed what seems to be a crucial experiment in this field. He presented subjects with strings of words like "tie the not" or "walk the haul." Subjects were required to judge whether the string was meaningful or not. A string of words that was phonetically meaningful but visually meaningless (e.g., walk the haul) was classified as meaningless just as rapidly as a string of words that was both visually and phonetically meaningless. Thus the meaningful phonetics did not interfere with the ability of the subject to classify the string as nonmeaningful.

Once again this finding illustrated that the visual code seems to be a sufficient basis for reaching semantic levels of processing, at least under some circumstances. It is also true that semantic access can be by way of a phonetic code. Given what is already known about the ability of subjects to select between visual and phonetic representations for single words and letters, it appears that there ought to be a great deal of influence from strategies in this task as well. Thus one would expect that under some circumstances, people might understand phrases visually and revert to phonetic coding when reading is difficult, for example, in a very noisy environment. Nonetheless, it appears that the visual code is sufficiently complex to handle activation of higher-level semantic analysis just as is the phonetic representation. Obviously, the English language, with its heavily phonetic basis, gives additional incentive for subjects to use phonetic analysis.

The significance of these results on reading words for applications to the reading task will be discussed in Chapter 8. The main importance of the results for the book is to support the principles that have emerged from experiments using matching of single letters and letter strings.

INDIVIDUAL DIFFERENCES

The last section reviewed the idea of optional choices among different codes of the same event during reading. One would expect individuals to differ both in their ability to isolate codes and in their choice of codes. It is no trick to find vast individual differences in all of the experimental paradigms that have been reviewed so far. Indeed, one estimate (Hunt, Lunneborg, & Lewis, 1975) is that 85% of the variance in the letter-matching task is carried by differences among people rather than among conditions. This figure does not make it inappropriate to focus on the commonalities among individuals as I have so far done. For example, although people differ greatly, each of the several hundred subjects whom I have run has shown longer phonetic than physical match RTs in the simultaneous letter task. However, these differences indicate that there is much room for the study of indivdiual characteristics in these tasks.

Studies of individual differences have two goals. First, they may be designed to test theoretical notions through examining correlations between performance in different tasks (Underwood, 1975). Second, although a far more difficult goal, they may be designed to develop an analysis of the fundamental cognitive traits that differ among people (Hunt, Frost, & Lunneborg, 1973; Day, Note 7). A theoretical analysis of individual differences might then be used, for example, to redesign tests of intelligence from a theoretically derived perspective. The first goal is less difficult and is the one I focus on in this chapter. Some more general issues concerning the second goal will be addressed in Chapter 8.

Seeing and Imaging

One of the most important theoretical ideas outlined in this chapter is the notion that visual input uses much the same code as do generated visual representations. The evidence comes both from studies of letter matching (see p. 50) and mental rotation (see p. 61). This view suggests a relation between the speed of seeing visual input, as for example in duration thresholds, and the speed of operating upon mental images. These theoretical links have been supported to some degree. Snyder (1972) used three classes of activity related to imagery ability: self-report imagery scales, the ability of subjects to solve problems based upon manipulating blocks, and the speed with which subjects were able to match two complex patterns differing in orientation. He found small but significant correlations among these three tasks. Subjects who report themselves as being good in manipulating their images also solved the block problems more quickly and

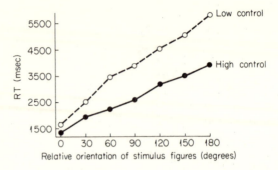

FIG. 3.13.   Time for mental rotation of subjects who report themselves as good
and bad in control of their imagery. (From Snyder, 1972.)

showed lower slopes relating reaction time to degree of rotation (Shepard &
Metzler, 1971). This last result is illustrated in Figure 3.13.

These findings were pleasing, because the block task involves a problem-
solving situation whereas the Shepard and Metzler task is much closer to perception. I have argued that matching two visual items that differ in size or rotation
taps a component skill involved in pattern recognition. It then follows that a
positive correlation between mental rotation speed and self-report imagery
implies that the ability to image is closely related to one component of pattern
recognition. The common component would be the speed at which one can
compare input with memory.

The implication that poor imagery means poor perception in this chronometric sense of speed of pattern recognition is thus important theoretically. Support
for this idea comes from a paper (Paivio & Ernest, 1971) showing that poor
imagers have higher duration thresholds for reporting the identity of pictures and
forms but not letters. Snyder (1972) confirmed this effect for some aspects of
letter identification. He found that subjects good in imagery control were faster
and more accurate in naming letters than those low in imagery control when the
letters appeared at unfamiliar orientations. Together, these results do provide a
link between imagery skill and speed of recognition for visually presented material. Surprisingly, since the Paivio and Ernest study, there has been no systematic
follow-up on this important result to the best of my knowledge.

Verbal Skills

A second confirmation of a theoretical notion based upon a comparison of different populations of individuals has been reported by Hunt, Lunneborg, and
Lewis (1975) in studies of verbal intelligence. They found that subjects high in
verbal intelligence showed reaction time differences between physical identity
and name identity trials of about 63 msec, and that those with low verbal skills

showed differences of about 90 msec. A similar result has been reported by Boies (1971), who compared subjects with chronic aphasia and normal subjects in simultaneous word-matching tasks. Some of the chronic aphasia groups showed no increased RT for physical matches in comparison with normal controls. However, they did show a large increase in phonetic match RT, thus producing a larger difference between name and physical RTs than normals. These results show that subjects with low verbal ability take somewhat longer to retrieve phonetic codes than those of high verbal ability even when the two are equated for physical match RTs.[3]

Language Bound and Language Optional

A related approach to individual differences has arisen from studies using speech stimuli. Day (Note 7) reported that subjects she termed "language bound" tend to fuse nonsense speech stimuli (e.g., banket and lanket) presented dichotically so as to hear a single word (e.g., blanket). They also make many errors judging which of two stimuli occur first when the actual order contradicts the normal order of English. Other subjects, termed "language optional," do not suffer as greatly from the tendency to organize ambiguous input by the structures of language.

In support of this idea, Poltrock (cited in Hunt, Lunneborg, & Lewis, 1975) reported that students low in verbal ability have difficulty in recognizing artificial speech stimuli but not other auditory input. A related result that provides support for this theory was reported by Hanson (1977). She investigated the voice onset time continuum using artificial speech and required subjects to make either physical or phonetic matches. She found that only those subjects who were capable of distinguishing different instances within a phonetic category in the physical match task showed the advantage in RT of physical over phonetic matches first obtained by Pisoni and Tash (1974) for the phonetic task. This evidence indicates that whatever mechanisms produce the advantage of physical identity in RT tasks are related to the ability of subjects to use these physical differences deliberately as the basis of judgments.

Clearly, Day's idea that subjects differ in the degree to which they rely upon phonetic codes would be quite consonant with the organization of the nervous system into isolable physical and phonetic codes and the evidence of code selec-

---

[3]In many ways the Hunt et al. (1975) result is weakened by a common problem in these studies. Low verbals are worse in both physical and phonetic matches, but the difference is greater at the phonetic level. The interaction might be due to the relatively longer times at the phonetic level. Boies' data are stronger in that some aphasic groups were equivalent to controls at the physical level but worse at the phonetic level. This finding is still subject to the objection that relative difficulty rather than code differences produce the interaction. It would be better to show that the effects were not due to difficulty alone, perhaps by showing that variations in spatial difficulty have no differential effects among the groups.

tivity that has been presented in this chapter. Moreover, Poltrock's evidence fits with the idea that low verbal intelligence is related to one's facility with phonetic interpretation. However, Day's ideas also suppose that there are cognitive traits that produce strong trans-situational correlations among individuals. This idea has been disputed in other domains (Mischel, 1973). If Day is right, the evidence of individual differences, which has so far been used mainly to provide converging support for some theoretical notions, might begin to form the basis of a more detailed theory of how people differ. Because few data on this question are so far available in the literature, it is premature to attempt to make a detailed analysis of whether such an enterprise will prove fruitful. Instead, I have left to Chapter 8 some speculations on the implications of findings within cognitive psychology for the study of the development of intelligence and personality.

SUMMARY

This chapter has examined some topics related to the coordination of codes processed within isolable systems. The second section dealt with analogue representation within the visual system as revealed by studies of matching patterns differing in size and orientation. The relation of these studies to the normalization process in pattern recognition was examined through studies of learning and matching random patterns. Some effort was made to deal with combining output of separate visual system mechanisms in studies of color and form processing.

In such natural tasks as reading of words, selection among coding systems was illustrated. Depending upon exposure duration, external interference, task demands, and individual differences, subjects are able to select different codes of the same stimulus event. This fact has produced many effects that are inexplicable from a single-code viewpoint.

Differences between individuals in the access to visual and phonetic codes have been shown in various paradigms and laboratories. Of particular importance is the possibility that individuals differ in their flexibility to select among and employ different codes.

4

Psychological Pathways

The delivery of a stimulus sets off a remarkably complex chain of events. Some of these events appear to be an inevitable consequence of the stimulus, whereas others depend heavily on the intentions of the subject. The very same action (e.g., moving the eyes 20 degrees to the left) may be automatic in that it is forced on us by the occurrence of a stimulus; or it may occur as the result of a decision to sample information from that portion of the environment in the absence of any external stimulus being presented. Normally, respiration goes on automatically without any feeling of control on our part, but it may also be controlled consciously by us. In this chapter it is my plan to try to separate automatic activities that take place without any conscious control from those processes that occur as the result of a conscious decision. Put another way, I wish to try to develop the role of reflex activity within human information processing. Despite the fact that much of psychology is built upon the concept of a reflex (for example, so-called stimulus–response theory), there is no generally agreed-upon definition of what characterizes a reflex. One can point to the innate, monosynaptic spinal reflexes as particularly good exemplars of an automatic system worthy of the name *reflex*, but it is by no means clear what critical features are necessary before an action should be called *reflexive*. In some sense, this is a semantic issue. I could simply use another term such as *automatic* and provide operational definitions for it. But I think some historical information will make it clear how closely related the concepts of automatic processing are to both traditional and current concepts of the reflex.

History

Though the idea of reflex connection goes back at least as far as Galen, the first extensive scientific effort to develop an entirely reflexive model of human performance and ideation stems from Sechenov, who proposed it in 1863. Sechenov believed that the motor activity involved in a reflex was not critical to its definition and that reflexes often terminated at their central phase—in what we call *thought*. Sechenov proposed that human thought should be viewed as the first two-thirds of a reflex arc. He said:

> Now the reader being aware of the properties of thought will understand how man learns to separate thoughts from the external acts which follow them. Indeed, in any man affected by sensory stimulation thought is sometimes directly followed by action; at other times movement is inhibited and the act seems to end with the thought; at still other times thought again leads to action, but the latter is different from that in the first case. It is clear that thought, as something concrete, must separate from action which also appears in a concrete form. Since the succession of two acts is usually regarded as an indication of their causal relationship (*post hoc ergo propter hoc*) *thought is generally accepted as the cause of action.* When the external influence, i.e., the sensory stimulus, remains unnoticed—which occurs very often—*thought is even accepted as the initial cause of action.* Add to this the strongly pronounced subjective nature of thought, and you will realise how firmly man must believe in the voice of self-consciousness when it tells him such things. But actually this is the greatest of falsehoods: *the initial cause of any action always lies in external sensory stimulation,* because without this thought is inconceivable [pp. 88–89].

Sechenov's proposal, then, is for an invariant relationship not between an external stimulus and a response but between an external stimulus and an internal state that does not necessarily find realization in behavior.

Forty years later, Sherrington (1906) proposed a rather different definition of a reflex. He viewed it as a form of nervous system coordination that "makes an effector organ responsive to excitement of a receptor, all other parts of the organism being supposed indifferent to and indifferent for that reaction [p. 7]." Sherrington recognized that this independence of a reflex is an abstraction perhaps never fully realized in any nervous system. He said:

> A simple reflex is probably a purely abstract conception, because all parts of the nervous system are connected together and no part of it is probably ever capable of reaction without affecting and being affected by various other parts, and it is a system certainly never absolutely at rest. But the simple reflex is a convenient, if not a probable, fiction. Reflexes are of various degrees of complexity, and it is helpful in analysing complex reflexes to separate from them reflex components which we may consider apart and therefore treat as though they were simple reflexes [p. 7].

Sherrington raised both the idea that the reflex can serve as a tool or unit of behavior and a conception of reflex whose pathway is separable from other reflexes.

Pavlov's (1960) experimental work on the reflex examined glandular activity in order to study conditioning to new stimulation. Pavlov's conditioned reflex model was an exciting account of a basic associational process. However, as soon as one attempts to extend Pavlovian technique to humans, there arises the problem with which we began this chapter—namely, that one does not know on a given trial whether the activity has been forced by the stimulus or whether it has been initiated via a control mechanism in which an external stimulus event plays only a small role. Thus one does not know whether the behavior is reflexive or voluntarily emitted by the subject. Defining a reflex as Skinner (1938) does in *Behavior of Organisms* in terms of an invariant relationship between a stimulus and response and then classifying reflexes into those resulting from a stimulus (respondent) and those that are emitted (operant) does not relieve the problem of determining the control mechanisms for the two types of behavior.

Studies of human eyelid conditioning, in particular, have attempted to develop operational distinctions between two forms of response. A true conditioned response (C response) with long latency can be separated from a voluntary response (V response) with low latency and a sharp onset (Grant, 1972). Unfortunately, these criteria have been disputed (Gormezano, 1968). The use of masking tasks to take the subject's conscious attention away from the conditioning process appears to have the effect of suppressing voluntary responding (Ross & Ross, 1976), as might be expected. Moreover, recent emphases in the animal conditioning literature have taken increasing cognizance of effects of context and predictability upon the probability that a stimulus will gain control over a response (Egger & Miller, 1962; Rescorla & Wagner, 1972).

In human behavior, effects of context and set can be extraordinarily subtle. It is somewhat doubtful that behavioral studies of conditioning that measure only changes in performance over successive trials can provide any detailed account of the level at which set or context effects influence the course of information processing. When the conditioning procedure is coupled with chronometric methods through recording of central nervous system activity (Olds et al., 1972; Thompson, 1967), such details could become available. Newer methods developing within the area of animal conditioning are more similar to the ideas developed in this chapter and should eventually provide means of studying the evolution of internal control mechanisms (Pfautz & Wagner, 1976). However, despite the venerable tradition of the conditioning methodology, chronometric studies outlined in this chapter seem at present to be further advanced in their ability to deal with internal pathways than are the conditioning procedures.

As the neurophysiology of behavior is pursued through the use of microelectrode recording in free-ranging animals, new information is becoming available

concerning reflex activity. Evarts (1973) attempted to examine the rapid responses of a monkey to the perturbation of a lever that he holds in his paw. Evarts
also seeks to define a reflex as follows:

> How should one classify short latency muscle responses which are under voli-
> tional control? A response occurring in man within less than 100 msec of a
> stimulus is commonly called "reflex," but perhaps this minimum time should be
> shortened for the special case in which the input has a strong and direct pathway
> to the areas of the cerebral cortex that control the output. Phillips has proposed
> that the PTN's [pyramidal tract neurons] of primate motor cortex may function in
> a transcortical servo-loop. The observations reported here are consistent with
> Phillips' ideas, and point to the need for further examination of cortical "re-
> flexes" and their possible role in motor plasticity [p. 503].

Evarts proposed that speed be taken as a basic criterion for reflex action.

This historical account has examined some views about the nature of reflex.
Note that none of these investigators requires that the reflex be innate, that its
pathway be entirely known, or that it be monosynaptic or spinal. Rather they
propose invariance, separability, and speed as criteria for defining reflex activity.

Chronometric studies have attempted to examine these same criteria in
human performance. Consider Figure 4.1, taken from the work of LaBerge and
Samuels (1974). The basic invariance idea of Sechenov is used in the notion that
a word produces representations in varying codes that are reflexively or automatically related to the occurrence of that word. These automatic pathways are
reflexive in the invariance sense of Sechenov. That such invariance exists at

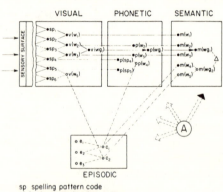

FIG. 4.1.   A modern version of the pathways activated by a visual input such as a word. The solid lines indi-cate automatic activation due to prior learning. The dotted lines indicate ac-tivation mediated by attention. (From LaBerge & Samuels, 1974. Copy-right 1974 Academic Press.)

sp spelling pattern code
v(w) visual word code
v(wg) visual word group code
p(sp) phonological spelling pattern code
p(w) phonological word code
p(wg) phonological word group code
m(w) word meaning code
m(wg) word group meaning code
e temporal spatial event code
c episodic code

some level in the nervous system would not be surprising. What is impressive is evidence that these invariant relationships occur at the level of learned semantic interpretation. This evidence will be reviewed in the next section.

The idea of separability that Sherrington proposed has also been examined within the framework of mental chronometry. Figure 1.7 shows that the time between stimulus input and response is often a function of not only those events that do occur on a particular trial but of those that might occur. This is the well-known relationship between reaction time and information. It implies that internal pathways interact at some stage in the process of determining which response is required. However, it is possible by manipulation of the input and output codes to develop flat functions between information and reaction time (see Figure 1.8). What are the reasons for these flat functions? The term usually used to signify the relationship between an input–output code that produces such a flat function is *compatible* (Fitts & Seeger, 1953). Compatible S–R relations give evidence of functional independence of each pathway and thus of separability.

There is also evidence that the activation of a given S–R system would shorten the time required for it to be reactivated when repeated. The repetition effect in reaction time was first reported by Hyman (1953). He found that a given stimulus–response combination would provide a faster response when it was activated in less than eight trials of a previous activation. Bertelson (1967) found that this effect occurs with a zero interval following a prior response and provided some evidence that it decayed with a delay of about 1 sec. Unfortunately it was not possible to say how these effects occurred. For example, if subjects expected a repetition for some reason, they might choose to bias their memory search process toward a repeated item. Indeed, Keele (1973) showed that under some circumstances there was no decline in repetition effects over time and that repetitions behaved very similarly to other sequential effects, suggesting that they resulted from a kind of expectancy by the subject.

There are hints, however, that suggest that the repetition effect includes an involuntary or automatic component. Hinrich and Craft (1971) had subjects predict which of two events they expected to occur on a given trial. They showed that more frequent events were processed more rapidly even when they were not expected on a given trial. Since the frequent event is also one that is more often repeated, this effect suggests that the repetition effect is somewhat independent of expectancy. Eichelman (1970b) found that when subjects were required to name letters, repeating the same letter twice in a row reduced reaction time. This effect was greater when the second item resembled the first physically than when it matched only in name, and both effects were reduced over a .75-sec interval. Kirsner (1972) found that having subjects study a list of letters with an instruction to remember the letters improved reaction time to naming a letter if it had been in the previous list. Marcel and Forrin (1974) found that when subjects were naming random digits, a repeated digit was faster than any other digit.

They also found a generalization gradient with a digit one number before or one after the previous digit being faster than a digit removed by two, etc. This occurred with an interval between a response and the next event close to zero.

If a subject is shown a letter and is required to determine if a second letter is the same or different, the advantage of "same" responses over "different" responses grows over stimulus onset asynchronies in the range from 0 to 500 msec (Posner & Boies, 1971). Thus as information about the first letter accrues, a strong bias toward matching letters develops. This kind of repetition effect is particularly persuasive, because one might think at first that any process that improved the decision to matches would enhance processing mismatches by the same amount. The relatively greater benefit for identical stimuli argues for an automatic enhancement of processing the same stimulus when it is presented again.

These findings all suggest an automatic increase in the ability to reactivate an associative connection following activation. They also indicate that new input need not be identical in physical form with the items just presented but also shows improvement if it shares the same phonetic or semantic codes.

Definition

I have attempted to carry forward some of the historical ideas about reflex in developing the idea of automatic connections between an input item and various isolable codes that are activated by that item. A psychological pathway is defined as the set of internal codes and their connections that are activated automatically by the presentation of a stimulus. The idea of a pathway builds upon the analysis of isolable processing systems activated by letters and words that was developed in Chapters 2 and 3 but switches the emphasis to the real-time activation of such codes. The use of the term *pathway* surely implies some sort of invariance between input and isolable systems representing its internal representation. I believe that the evidence for invariance in activation pattern, despite manipulations of such things as the linguistic context and intentions of the subject, is sufficiently impressive to be worth stressing against the usual view that such activation is determined by attentional strategies. However, such stress can be too strong, and it is not my intention to argue that no aspect of the activation pattern can be varied by context or intentions. Rather the idea is that automatic activation of complex codes may go on without the subject's intention or even despite intentions that it not take place. The pathway concept is also related to the idea of independence between pathways of different items (à la Sherrington). This view is stressed in showing that the activation of a given pathway has consequences only for items that rely upon that pathway and not for other items.

The problem of invariance of activation is a very complex one. The kind of example that impresses me with its importance is the inability of subjects to avoid influence from the color name in the Stroop test. In the next section I review some efforts to understand this effect and explore its significance.

AUTOMATIC ACTIVATION

We all are familiar introspectively with thoughts, ideas, or feelings that seem to intrude upon us rather than occur as a result of our intentions to produce them. I propose three operational indicants of whether a process is *automatic* as the term will be used here (see also, Posner & Snyder, 1975a). These are that the process may occur without intention, without giving rise to conscious awareness, and without producing interference with other ongoing mental activity. Even with these stringent requirements, it is possible to show that many complex but habitual mental processes can operate automatically and thus in principle be strategy independent.

To say that memory processes such as finding the meaning of a word may go on automatically is not identical to saying that they cannot be affected by conscious strategies. To use my previous example, respiration may occur either with or without attentional control. Many theorists have proposed a fixed processing stage at which limited capacity attentional effects are to be found. Sometimes the stage is early in processing and sometimes late, but the idea is that some types of operations are not capacity limited but others are. The view taken here is different: Attention is viewed as the result of a specific mechanism of limited capacity (see Chapter 6). This mechanism can be committed flexibly to different codes, depending upon many factors. Thus it is necessary to develop operational methods for distinguishing whether a given process is being performed in an "automatic" or "conscious" mode.

Intention

There is excellent evidence that subjects cannot always choose to avoid processing aspects of an input item that they desire to ignore. The Stroop effect is based upon this difficulty (Dyer, 1973). In Figure 4.2 the word *blue* is presented. Suppose the ink used was red. When given the task of naming aloud the ink color (e.g., red), one intends to avoid reading the color name (*blue*), but it is not possible to do so completely.

There is now a great deal of evidence that supports the kind of explanation for this effect, which is outlined in Figure 4.2 (Dyer, 1973; Hintzman, Carre, Eskridge, Owens, Shaff, & Sparks, 1972; Keele, 1973; Morton & Chambers, 1973; Murray, Mastronadi, & Duncan, 1972). First, the usual Stroop effect arises because of response competition between vocal responses to the printed word and the ink color. Keele (1973) demonstrated the importance of output interference by showing that noncolor words, which produce a small interference over non-

FIG. 4.2.   A schematic explanation
of the Stroop effect. Two internal
look-up processes produce representations of the ink color (dashed
line) and the word name (solid line).
If the task is one of physical matching, ink colors arrive at output first
and interfere with word matching. If
the task is one of naming, words arrive at output first and interfere with
ink colors. These interference effects
result from the time course of the
look-up process. (From Posner &
Snyder, 1975a. Copyright 1975
Lawrence Erlbaum Associates.)

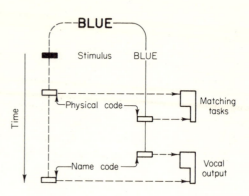

word controls with a vocal output, produce no such interference when a key press output is used. Second, the direction of interference depends upon the time relations involved. Words are read faster than colors can be named; thus a color-naming response receives stronger interference from the word than the reverse. Colors can be matched physically faster than words can, so that a matching response results in greater interference from colors on words than the reverse (Murray et al., 1972). Third, words often facilitate the vocal output to colors with which they share a common name (Hintzman, Block, & Inskeep, 1972).

These three results suggest that color naming and reading go on in parallel and without interference until close to the output. If they result in look-up of the same name, the overall reaction time is speeded; if they produce different names and a vocal output is required, however, the word tends to compete with the color name and reaction time is increased. One puzzle that remains is why a vocal response to color names interferes so much more than words that are not color names. After all, both have well-learned names stored in the memory system. The answer lies in the close semantic associations that exist between color names and in the fact that prior activation of an item affects the time for look-up of its name, a phenomenon to which we now turn.

One can use the Stroop effect to investigate the automatic activation pattern of a word in the memory system (Warren, 1972, 1974). Warren presented an auditory item or items followed after a brief interval by a single visual word printed in colored ink. The only task set for the subject was to name the color of ink as quickly as possible (see Figure 4.3). Warren's results showed clearly that the time for naming the ink color increased with the associative strength between the auditory word and the visual word. As shown in the lower panel of Figure 4.3, only associative strength in the forward direction is important; there is no effect of backward associative strength from the visual word to the prior auditory word.

The Warren effect can be explained by a logic quite similar to the one shown in Figure 4.2. An auditory word activates a pathway in the nervous system that consists of its auditory representation, its name, and a motor program for its production. When the visual word shares some of the same pathway (e.g., name and motor program), its processing rate is increased. Thus the word name is delivered more quickly and/or more strongly to the output mechanisms and thus produces more interference with saying the ink color name. There is no incentive in the task for the subjects to activate items related to the auditory word. They are not asked to form associations, nor need they be required to recall the auditory items to show the effect. Even when, as sometimes happens, subjects become aware that they are having difficulty in processing related items, they do not seem to be able to shut off the activation process.

The Warren results show why it is that interference in the Stroop effect is greatest for color names, intermediate for associated words, and least for unrelated words. This is due to a general tendency of a word to activate related items. This effect occurs without any apparent intention by the subject. The effect of automatic activation on reaction time drops sharply with delay (Warren, 1972), but the well-known tendency for related words to be reported as "old" on

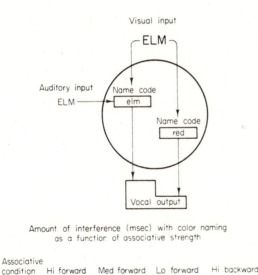

Amount of interference (msec) with color naming
as a function of associative strength

Associative condition	Hi forward	Med forward	Lo forward	Hi backward
	95	50	20	0

FIG. 4.3. An auditory word activates its name code. When the following visual word shares the same pathway, it will arrive at output first and produce greater interference with color naming. The lower panel shows supportive data for this theory from Warren (1974). (From Posner & Snyder, 1975a. Copyright 1975 Lawrence Erlbaum Associates.)

recognition memory tests (Underwood, 1965) suggests that at least on some occasions the effects remain present for a considerable time.

Awareness

Conrad (1974) has shown that the subject may be quite unaware of the activation pattern created by input words. She presented sentences to her subjects orally that ended with an ambiguous word (e.g., pot). The word was either disambiguated by context or not. Following the oral presentation of the sentence, she showed her subjects a single visual word in colored ink. The subject's task was to name the color of the ink. In agreement with the Warren effect, she showed that the time to name the color of ink was longer when the word was related to the sentence. This was true both for the ambiguous word itself and for words related to either one of the word's meanings. The size of the interference effect was approximately equal whether the sentence had been disambiguated by context or not. These results are illustrated in Figure 4.4. Since the sentences that were disambiguated by context are consciously perceived in only one way, the finding

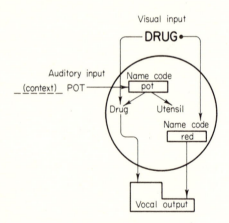

Amount of interference (msec) with color naming
as a function of context

Context	Word itself	Appropriate category	Inappropriate category
Ambiguous	73	----77----	
Unambiguous	58	61	50

FIG. 4.4.   The ambiguous word *pot* activates its lexical pathway irrespective of its linguistic context. A following visual word related to either pathway produced greater interference with color naming than a neutral word. Lower panel shows supportive data from Conrad (1974). (From Posner & Snyder, 1975a. Copyright 1975 Lawrence Erlbaum Associates.)

that both meanings of the ambiguous word are activated is evidence that the activation pattern is not dependent on the subject's conscious percept.

The results of the Conrad experiment seem to me to be striking support for the kind of automatic activation of lexical memory proposed by Anderson and Bower (1973). They postulate that individual items of a proposition look up related facts in parallel. Context has its effect as the activation patterns of the different lexical items are combined. The importance of context and the fact that we are rarely aware of ambiguity suggest that the equality of activation found by Conrad will change rapidly as one meaning or another comes to dominate. Her findings show that it is possible to develop psychological experiments that reveal memory processes relatively free of context and strategy effects.

There has been much dispute about whether ambiguous words look up their meanings, especially when they are in a context that disambiguates them. Using a lexical decision task, Schvaneveldt, Meyer, and Becker (1976) found no evidence of both meanings being present in the times to respond to a subsequent word. On the other hand, Warren and Warren (1976) found intrusions from the wrong meaning of a disambiguated word triad on the next trial of a short-term memory experiment. This is one area of research where conflict is to be expected and perhaps exploited. Clearly, if both meanings were activated to the same degree, we would be more frequently conscious of them than we are. That fact alone suggests that the activation patterns of the wrong meaning of a disambiguated item will be difficult to observe. Moreover, it is necessary for linguistic context to be able to allow one meaning to win out over another. Conflict is to be expected as different paradigms seek evidence for this fleeting multiple-activation pattern. What is most crucial is the development of a paradigm that will allow exploration of how linguistic context and set affect what activation patterns are present so that only a subset becomes conscious. In the meantime, the results so far obtained by Conrad (1974) give support to the idea that there is a degree of invariance to the semantic pathway activated by a word that can be tapped by psychological means.

The Stroop demonstrations all involve the automatic activation of a word meaning when subjects are attending to the channel on which it arrives. One might well argue that form and color are integral dimensions (Garner & Felfoldy, 1970), and thus the inability of the subject to ignore the word while attending to color is a very special phenomenon. Suppose instead that the subject attends to another set of items entirely. Will automatic activation still occur?

Much evidence on this comes from studies of dichotic listening. For example, Lewis (1970) has shown that when subjects are shadowing items to one ear, an item occurring on the unattended channel that has the same semantic meaning as an attended item will slow their rates of shadowing. MacKay (1973) and Lackner and Garrett (1973) have shown that an unattended lexical item may serve to disambiguate the meaning of an attended sentence. In these experiments, there is a semantic relationship between the attended and unattended items; thus the effect could depend upon having an already activated locus in memory related to the unattended item.

There is also conflicting evidence from dichotic listening studies that suggests that under many circumstances no such semantic activation occurs at the unattended ear (Treisman, Squire, & Green, 1974). Those inclined to favor the idea of automatic semantic look-up usually stress the difficulty of measuring the interference produced from semantic look-up on the unattended ear by most psychological tests; those inclined against semantic look-up stress the possibility of attentional shifts. For this reason, the dichotic listening experiments have not been as conclusive as they might. Perhaps even more interesting than the evidence for some degree of semantic look-up is its remarkable limitation discovered by Treisman and Geffen (1967). They found that when shadowing, subjects almost always tapped a key as instructed when the word *tap* occurred on the attended ear and almost never when it was on the unattended ear. Even if one believes in semantic look-up, it is impressive that so simple a voluntary output appears to demand more than automatic look-up.

Another approach to automatic look-up processes (Corteen & Wood, 1972; Von Wright, Anderson, & Stenman, 1975) is based upon the ability to obtain autonomic indicants of unattended items. In these studies subjects were first conditioned to produce a galvanic skin response (GSR) to particular words. They then show that the GSR occurs when these words are presented on an unattended channel during dichotic listening. In the Von Wright et al. data, the size of the GSR to semantic associates of the conditioned stimulus was as large when they occurred on the unattended channel as on the attended channel. These results could only occur if semantic classification of the unattended word had taken place. Thus the dichotic listening studies suggest that very complicated processing, including even stereotyped responses such as the GSR, occur when the subject's attention is focused elsewhere. Efforts to replicate these effects, however, have not always been very successful (Wardlaw & Kroll, 1975) for reasons that are not yet clear.[1]

In these studies the subjects have relatively little incentive to shift attention to the nonshadowed ear. Attempts to test awareness of unattended information have involved assessing breakdowns in shadowing, obtaining reports of unusual or obscene items, and measuring recognition memory for unattended items. Overall, it seems fair to conclude that some automatic processing occurs when the subject's attention is focused on different items.

---

[1]In nearly all of the paradigms studied, there have been some discrepant findings in which no evidence of a semantic effect of unattended information has been found. The more the indicant of activation relies upon an overt response occurring to the unattended item, the more difficult it has been to obtain consistent results. When processing of unattended information is indexed by interference with attended items, the sensitivity of the response to interference may be reduced with many variables such as amount of practice.

Parallel Processing

The Stroop method of studying automatic activation required subjects to attend to a particular position in space, although not to the particular dimension being studied. The dichotic method had subjects attending to a particular modality, though not the channel within that modality to which the unattended item is presented. Is there evidence that unattended items activate semantically related information even when they occur to an unattended modality? The results of several experiments (Greenwald, 1970; Lewis, 1970) indicate that subjects are not successful in filtering out information occurring on a modality that they are instructed to ignore when it has a close semantic relationship to the attended information. Thus it appears that the intention to ignore a modality will not prevent it from affecting attended processing.[2]

A chronometric technique for examining the build-up of information on an unattended modality is based on the finding that subjects are slow to respond to information that occurs on a channel that is not the expected one. This might suggest that pathway activation is being delayed because the subject is actively attending elsewhere. A more careful analysis raises doubts with this view, however. Consider the results of the following experiment (Posner & Summers, Note 8). In this experiment, subjects are required to classify a single item as to whether or not it is an animal name. On half the trials, the stimulus is an animal name; on the other half, it is not. On pure blocks the stimulus is always auditory or always visual, whereas on mixed blocks it may be either. In addition, sometimes the subjects have a warning signal in advance of the stimulus, and at other times they have no warning signal.

When the word is visually presented to the subjects, their reaction times are generally fast, provided that they either: (1) have a warning signal, or (2) know the channel of entry. But if neither of these obtains, their reaction times are quite long (see Figure 4.5). One might imagine that the subjects have their eyes closed or defocused. However, one feature of the data argues against this interpretation. Although the reaction times under these low attention conditions are long, the accuracy is high. It is as though the build-up of information goes on regardless of whether the subjects are attending or not. If they are not attending, the response time is slow; but since it occurs under a background of high information quality, it is accurate.

Suppose instead of merely making the subjects uncertain about the modality on which the information will arrive, their attention is carefully directed to the wrong modality. LaBerge (1973) reported such a study. The task involved a classification response on the auditory modality (1,000 versus 990 Hz tone) or on

---

[2]There is, of course, evidence that one can attend to information from one modality (see Chapter 7 for a review), but that does not mean that unattended information is blocked from access to semantic codes that are habitual to it.

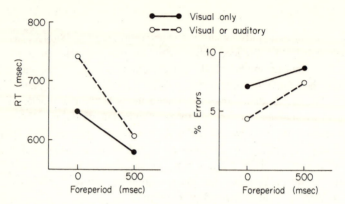

FIG. 4.5.   RT (left panel) and errors (right panel) in classifying a visual word as an animal name as a function of amount of warning (foreperiod) and whether or not the words are all visual or mixed visual and auditory. (From Posner & Snyder, 1975a. Copyright 1975 Lawrence Erlbaum Associates.)

the visual modality (yellow versus orange light). In pure blocks the subjects knew the modality that would be used. In mixed blocks they received the expected modality on .85 of the trials and the signal on the unexpected modality on .15 of the trials. A 1,000 Hz tone or an orange light was used as a cue stimulus to rivet the subject's attention on the expected modality prior to the signal stimulus. The results for reaction time show that the method was extremely successful (see Figure 4.6). On the pure blocks and when the expected modality was presented on the mixed blocks, the subjects were fast and reaction times were nearly equal. This suggests that subjects were attending to the expected modality. When a stimulus on the unexpected modality occurred, subjects were very slow but the most accurate. In this experiment, which requires high levels of

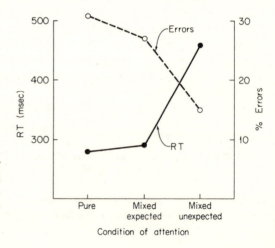

FIG. 4.6.   RT (left ordinate) and errors (right ordinate) as a function of whether signals are all in one modality (pure) or whether they are mixed and subjects are induced to focus on one modality (expected). (After LaBerge, 1973.)

discrimination, error rates are always high; but they are lowest in just those conditions when the subject's attention is directed to the wrong channel of entry. One explanation of these cross-modality results is that information from the unattended channel is building up in the normal way even though the subjects are not attending to it. When they switch attention, they are able to execute a response that is more accurate because the information quality is higher. Other interpretations are possible. Since the input remains present until the subjects respond, they may take longer samples once they have shifted attention. There are studies in the literature where errors occur more frequently to unexpected items than to expected ones. Indeed, the increase in accuracy so prominent in Figure 4.6 is not found in another condition of the same study in which subjects are involved in a detection rather than a discrimination task. In studies where errors increase when an unexpected event occurs, there are usually many rapid false responses that are made as though in anticipation of the expected event.

There is, then, a fair amount of evidence that purely passive activation of internal pathways does occur and that it has a measure of invariance in that it happens in much the same way whether or not subjects desire it. It is in this sense that the studies cited support the notion of reflex activation.

Clearly, the cross-modality data by themselves are not totally convincing. However, coupled with the results of the Stroop and dichotic listening studies, the data support a view of stimulus information automatically activating those internal representations that have been habitually associated with it.[3] Note that this view, which is similar to the one presented by LaBerge and Samuels (1974) and by Keele (1973), has the nice feature of making the automaticity of a perceptual pathway closely related to the degree of learning or experience that the subject has had to particular associations.

FACILITATION OF PATHWAYS

I want to try to distinguish between automatic effects of the activation of psychological pathways and effects that occur when subjects actively attend to a particular pathway in an effortful or conscious sense. Put simply, the idea is that automatic activation facilitates the passage of messages that share the same pathway; but since pathways can be active in parallel, such activation has no inhibitory consequences. This one-sided bias is quite different from the effects that occur after subjects begin to attend to the input pathway. Since attentional mechanisms are of limited capacity, facilitation of the attended pathway is accompanied by a widespread inhibition in the ability of information from any

---

[3]The concept of habitual association as a means of automating access to a semantic code is similar to the idea of automation of motor skill with practice.

other activated pathway to reach the mechanisms that subserve attention. The difference in the two forms of activation allows the psychologist to examine the automatic activation processes of an input item separately from these processes involved in conscious attention.

This separation requires a special nomenclature. In our lay language, the term *recognition* is given to both the activation of stored information about an item and our awareness of that activation. It is necessary for us to distinguish between these two processes in accordance with the operational distinctions outlined above. Thus in this chapter on psychological pathways, I deal with the activation of isolable subsystems that could include the physical, phonetic, and semantic code of the items presented. However, I will not deal with the operation of mechanisms subserving active or conscious attention, which will be left for Chapter 6.

In order to establish the reality of psychological pathways connecting isolable subsystems, it would seem useful to show that pathways exhibit properties such as facilitation, decay, and inhibition. One way that has been used to study the facilitation of pathways is priming of them by prior input.

Priming

Reaction time. Posner and Snyder (1975a, 1975b) attempted to establish the existence of automatic activation processes through a priming experiment. The basic design was to present a single priming item, which is either a signal of the same type to which a subject will have to respond, or a neutral warning signal. By manipulating the probabilities that the prime will be a valid cue to the stimulus array, it was hoped that subjects would vary the degree of active attention they committed to the prime. According to the theoretical view that was outlined above, when subjects commit little processing capacity to the prime, they will benefit from automatic pathway activation but would have no cost or inhibition. When they selectively attend to the prime, they should show benefits from both automatic activation and conscious attention and these should be accompanied by costs on those trials when the prime is not a valid cue to the target.

To calculate benefit (facilitation), the reaction time when the prime matched the array was subtracted from the reaction time obtained from the neutral warning signal. To calculate cost (inhibition), the reaction time obtained following the neutral warning signal was subtracted from that obtained when the prime mismatched the array. The error data were generally closely correlated with the reaction times.

The most favorable results were those obtained from "yes" reaction times when the arrays consisted of pairs of letters that must be matched for physical identity (e.g., AA) and the prime was either of high validity (prime matches both the array letters on .8 of the "yes" trials) or of low validity (prime matches both array letters on .2 of the "yes" trials). Figure 4.7 provides a cost–benefit analysis obtained from these studies as a function of the time by which the prime led the array.

Two features of these data are of interest. When the prime is of low validity (upper panel of Figure 4.7), there is benefit but not cost. When the prime is of high validity, the benefits begin to accrue more rapidly than does the cost. Benefits should begin to accrue rapidly after the presentation of the prime as the input pathways are activated. They should be closely time locked to the presentation of the prime. If cost is associated with the commitment of a central processor to the prime, it should be less tightly time locked to the input because of the subject's internal control of this system (see also Chapter 6, p. 153). The lower panel of Figure 4.7 confirms the striking asymmetry of cost and benefit in the condition where the prime is a valid cue.

The asymmetry between cost and benefit must be qualified by the distinction between two forms of cost or inhibition. Cost or inhibition may arise from the operation of the central processing mechanism, or it may arise from more local inhibitory effects due to interaction between stimuli. For example, if a visual mask is used following a visual target, a local inhibition due to masking between target and mask occurs that would depend upon their relative intensity and spatial position. Such inhibitory processes are not related to the operation of the central

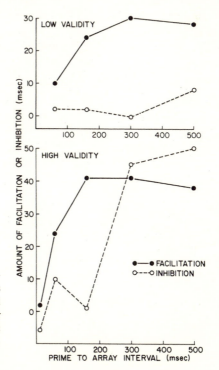

FIG. 4.7.   Time course of facilitation (benefit) and inhibition (cost) as a function of prime to array interval for low (upper panel) and high (lower panel) valid primes. (From Posner & Snyder, 1975b. Copyright 1975 Academic Press.)

mechanism. I use the expression *widespread inhibitory processes* to distinguish inhibition caused by masking, etc., from inhibition that results from the operation of the central processing mechanism. In the case of inhibitory effects produced by the commitment of the central processor, automatic activation of habitual pathways by the unattended stimulus would continue to take place.

Signal detection.   The priming of pathways can be studied by signal detection methods as well as through the use of standard reaction time methods. One study has applied the equivalent of the cost–benefit analysis using the signal detection method (Peterson & Graham, 1974). The results generally confirm the cost–benefit analysis that we have been developing.

Peterson and Graham used two conditions: Subjects were either provided with a descriptive sentence or were given no sentence prime. Subjects who received the sentence were asked either to construct a visual image corresponding to the sentence or simply to listen and understand it. The former condition serves as a high attention condition, the latter a low attention condition. Subjects were then shown a very dim picture that was either compatible or incompatible with the image. The results of the study were in terms of changes in d' from the neutral condition (no sentence) to the compatible or incompatible situations under both attention conditions. The results for the high-attention condition were substantial benefits in d' when the picture was compatible and costs in d' when the picture was incompatible. The low-attention condition showed benefits for the compatible picture, but no costs with an incompatible picture. In agreement with the cost–benefit analysis, when attention is directed to an interpretation of the sentence by the imagery instructions, both cost and benefits are found; and when attention is left undirected but a prime is provided, benefits still occur with a compatible picture.

Decay

If information presented to the organism serves to facilitate an input pathway, increasing the time between the presentation of the item and its being presented again should yield a reduction of facilitation. This result would be consonant with the idea of decay of activation that would appear to be a necessary property of the pathways. Unfortunately, most studies have not separated the loss of information in automatic pathways from the more conscious effort to preserve information in memory via rehearsal. One paradigm in which such a separation is possible involves repeating a stimulus twice in a reaction-time experiment. Such repetitions usually facilitate reaction time on the second occasion. However, there are both automatic and conscious expectancy effects involved in such facilitation (Hinrich & Craft, 1971). No single study has been entirely successful in separating them and in measuring decay at the same time.

Perhaps the most impressive single experiment along these lines is the work of Kirsner and Smith (1974). In that experiment, subjects were presented either with an aural or visual word or with a pronounceable nonword made by reversing the syllables of the words used. The subject's task was to classify each item as to whether it was a real word or a nonword. Items were presented every 4 sec. Use of this lexical decision task with distractors that are also pronounceable items (James, 1975) tends to insure that the subject's active attention operates at the phonetic and/or semantic level. There is no reason for the subject to attend or rehearse modality-specific information. However, items that come from the same modality would have more overlap in pathways prior to the phonetic level than those that come from different modalities. Kirsner and Smith (1974) showed that the response to the second of two items in the same modality was systematically faster than the response to the second item when it has the same phonetic realization but is presented to a different modality. By subtracting reaction time in the same modality from that in a different modality, the effects of phonetic and semantic levels are eliminated, and only the modality-specific component is left.

In Figure 4.8 the results of these subtractions are plotted against the time between the initial presentation of a stimulus and its being presented a second time. The delay time is filled with other items that occur every 4 sec. Thus we do not have pure decay, but an interval that is influenced by highly similar intervening items. In any case, it is clear that there is a rapid loss in the efficiency of having the same modality repeated. However, even after 1 minute, there is evidence that both visual and aural modality-specific information is present. The

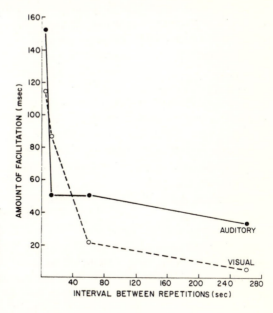

FIG. 4.8. Decay of facilitation of modality-specific pathways in a lexical decision task as a function of the interval between successive repetition of a word to which a lexical decision must be made. (After Kirsner & Smith, 1974.)

data are too sparse to provide complete decay functions, but they are sufficient to show that modality-specific information in this task does seem to be lost over time, at least in the presence of interfering items of the same type.

There is no reason to suppose that the loss of modality-specific information as measured by facilitation of lexical decision RTs means that subjects would be completely unable to identify the modality of input. Both recognition memory studies (Hintzman, Block, & Inskeep, 1972) and studies using reaction time methods (Hintzman & Summers, 1973) give evidence that some residual sensory-specific information remains at longer delays. Additional studies using methods similar to the Kirsner and Smith method should allow us to plot the loss of information in automatic pathways.

Higher-Level Primes

So far I have sought to establish that the presentation of a prime may automatically activate a set of codes that can speed the processing of a subsequently presented item. To maximize the possibility of obtaining automatic effects, the prime has been identical with the array items. Under these circumstances, the prime does seem to activate pathways even when subjects do not intend for it to do so. However, our data also show objective effects of the subject's active attention toward the prime both in boosting the extent of the benefit obtained and in providing cost through the commitment of the limited capacity system.

Many interesting results occur when the prime is not physically identical to the array. Such studies provide evidence on a form of automatic activation that results from a spread of activation from the prime to the later task-related items (Collins & Loftus, 1975; Meyer & Schvaneveldt, 1976). Such spread is frequently intermixed with active attention to the prime, and the two are difficult to disentangle.

Lexical decisions. A distinction between automatic activation and conscious attention is useful in understanding the lexical decision task (Rubenstein, Lewis, & Rubenstein, 1971). These experiments show that when subjects are asked to judge whether a string of letters is a word, judgments occur more rapidly following a semantically related item than an unrelated item (Schvaneveldt & Meyer, 1973).

Two mechanisms might produce this effect. The first is based on the concept of automatic activation. According to this view, activation of a particular memory location spreads to nearby locations. The increase in activity in these locations makes it easier to access information stored there. The second model assumes a limited-capacity system that can read out of only one memory location at a time. Time is required to shift from one location to another, and the shifting time increases with the distance between locations. Thus the association effect occurs because shifting to nearby locations is faster than shifting to more distant locations.

To test these two models, Schvaneveldt and Meyer (1973) presented three words in a simultaneous vertical array. The first and third words were associatively related. They examined whether improvement in the processing of the third word was reduced when the middle word was unrelated. The location-shifting model predicts that an intervening item will abolish the advantage of the association between the first and third items, whereas the automatic activation model does not. Their initial results conform to the automatic activation model; but the materials were presented simultaneously, and there was little real control over the order in which the subject examined them.

Subsequently, work by Meyer, Schvaneveldt, and Ruddy (Note 9) presents evidence somewhat more favorable to the location-shifting view. In this study they found evidence that the advantage of an association between two words is reduced by an unrelated intervening item, particularly when it is a nonword and thus uses a different output, as well as input, pathway.

The evidence used to choose between automatic activation and location shifting is biased. If both are true, as I believe results cited from other paradigms suggest, one will expect to find facilitation when the items are separated by an unrelated item, and the experimenter will conclude that the effects are due only to automatic activation. In order to separate the automatic from the conscious effects, one may examine what happens to a nonword or unrelated word that occurs following a priming word as compared to one following a neutral warning signal. If the facilitation of a word by another word is accompanied by an increase in reaction time to unrelated items, one might argue for an attentional explanation. If the benefit for an associated word is not accompanied by a cost to the unrelated word, a more automatic process seems required.

Neely (1977) sought to separate the two mechanisms by directing the subject's attention deliberately toward a particular category associated to the prime stimulus. The prime was either neutral (XXX) or a word. The subject was instructed in various conditions either to expect the target word to come from the same category as the prime (nonshift) or from another category (shift) that had been associated with the prime. The experiment manipulated whether the target was from the same category as the prime or whether it was from the category that the subject had been led to expect. Based on the dual model presented above, one would expect both automatic and attended benefit for words in the category of the prime when no attention shift occurred. These benefits should occur rapidly and be accompanied by more slowly developing costs when the target was not from the expected category. This effect is illustrated by the solid lines in Figure 4.9 for the nonshift condition. Benefits arising from a word in the category to which attention is shifted should accrue more slowly with symmetric costs when the target is not from the expected category. Finally, when subjects are instructed to shift attention to a new category but the target is unexpectedly from the original category of the prime word, an initial benefit should switch to cost as the expectancy builds up. The results of this study are shown in Figure 4.9. All of these predictions were confirmed by the data.

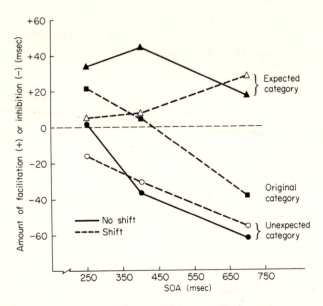

FIG. 4.9. Amount of facilitation and inhibition in the lexical decision task as a function of whether the word comes from the expected category and whether subjects are instructed to shift attention to a new category. (From Neely, 1977. Copyright 1977 by the American Psychological Association. Reprinted by permission.)

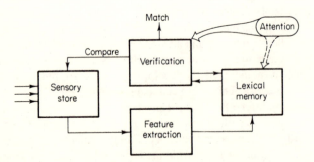

FIG. 4.10. An activation verification model of lexical decisions involving passive processes (feature extraction) and active (verification) components. (After Becker, 1976.)

One would also expect that the extent of attention to the prime would increase with the probability of the target being an associate of the prime. This has been found to be true under some conditions (Tweedy, Lapinski, & Schvaneveldt, 1977) but not always (Fischler, 1977).

Recent models for the lexical decision task (Becker, 1976) have sought to combine the idea of automatic activation of features and lexical items with verification endogenously driven from hypotheses concerning what might occur on a given trial. Figure 4.10 indicates a flow diagram from Becker (1976) outlining such a model. Becker sees the verification process as involving active attention while the activation of feature occurs outside of attention. Either process may succeed in producing a correct response. When the set of possible hypotheses is small, verification will usually provide the basis for the response; when subjects know little about what might occur, a more passive process would be expected. The Becker model involves the combination of psychological pathways and active attention being advocated here in more general form. Becker's view places more emphasis upon expectancy in the form of a specific hypothesis about what will occur rather than in terms of commitment of a central processing system. In many cases attention is directed toward a specific hypothesis about the nature of the input. This is probably true both in the primed letter-match studies and in the lexical decision experiment. My own interest, however, is more in obtaining evidence concerning the system that controls the hypothesis formation than in dealing with the hypotheses themselves. In Chapter 6, I turn to methods that seek to measure attention without the need to invoke specific hypotheses about the input.

There is little doubt that a word will activate not only its own internal representation but its associates in an automatic way. We have seen such evidence accumulate throughout this chapter in studies of Stroop interference, priming, repetition, and lexical decisions. I turn now to the limitations to this spread of activation.

Limitations.   One limitation involves studies in which no use is required of the form pathways that relate the prime and the imperative stimulus. Consider the following situation. Subjects are asked to concentrate their attention on a central fixation point that is a letter of the alphabet. They are then told to move their eyes to any position at which another letter appears. The latency of saccadic eye movements is measured as a function of the position in the visual field at which the target letter appears and the identity between the fixation and target letters. The results of such an experiment indicate no difference in latency of the saccade depending on whether the target letter was identical to the fixation (see Figure 4.11). It is not the response system (saccadic eye movements) that causes this result. If in some blocks of trials the subjects are told to move their eyes only when the imperative stimulus matches the fixation and in other blocks only when it does not match, there is a significant difference in latency between matching blocks and mismatching blocks. This shows that the initiation of saccadic eye movements can be influenced by physical identity between fixation and test letter.

Why doesn't pathway activation occur in the condition when the subject moves to all stimuli in the visual field? One possible reason for this is that the subject relies upon detection of energy rather than form and thus facilitation of the passage of the form information would not affect the response. In order to investigate this possibility, two new conditions were created. In these conditions, the subject either did or did not have to respond on the basis of form information. In one condition, the subject moved to all upper-case letters regardless of whether they matched the fixation letter or not. To determine whether a letter was upper-case, the subject clearly had to consult form pathways. In another condition, the subject moved to all letters occurring at some positions in space but not at other positions. In this case, the reliance on form information was not necessary. Both these conditions gave highly similar reaction times (see Figure 4.12). However, the former condition showed the effect of pathway priming (e.g., target letters that matched the fixation gave faster reaction times), but the latter condition did not. This result seemed to confirm the notion that subjects will show automatic pathway effects only in those cases when the task makes it necessary for them to deal with form information.

There may also be limitations to the downward spread of activation from a superordinate to systems coding the physical form and name of its members. Rosch (1975a) has investigated this question using a priming technique. She found that presenting a superordinate color name will facilitate processing of good instances of the name but inhibit poor instances. The cost for poor instances and the nearly symmetric time course of cost and benefit over the first .5 sec suggest that this effect is basically attentional and not due to an automatic spread. There is, however, also some evidence of benefit without cost at longer intervals that may indicate an automatic effect as well.

How does this effect occur? Since color categories have been shown to be represented by a best instance (Rosch, 1975a), one might expect the instruction *red* to lead subjects to expect (generate) a typical instance. If such an instance is presented, performance is facilitated; but if a noncentral instance appears, it is inhibited. Thus Rosch's data are quite consistent with the type of representation of the color categories that she has obtained in other studies, together with the idea that the prime word *red* does not automatically excite the physical form but does so if the subject is led to attend to it. Rosch's finding that attention can affect color matching seems to fit with the ability of subjects to couple attention closely to color information, as suggested in Chapter 3 (p. 69). Rosch also finds that when subjects are required to match two colors within the same category regardless of their physical identity, priming helps reaction time both for good and bad instances.

There is some evidence that a higher-level semantic category prime can activate processing of its physical form when subjects choose to do so. Rosch (1975b) studied physical matching of word pairs following a semantic prime

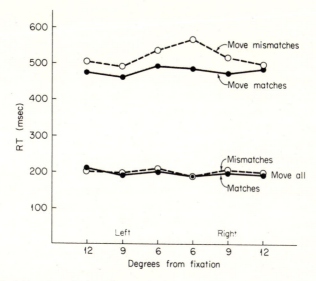

FIG. 4.11. Saccadic latencies to a letter, occurring at a distance from visual fixation, which either matches the central fixation (solid lines) or not (dotted lines) for conditions in which subjects are instructed to move only to matches or only to mismatches (top curves) or instructed to move to all letters (bottom curves).

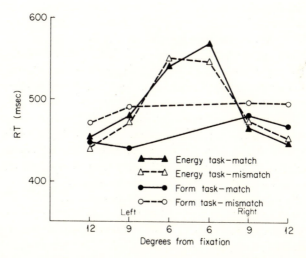

FIG. 4.12. Saccadic latencies in a task requiring subjects to attend to form pathways (circles) or allowing energy decisions (triangles) for both match and mismatch stimuli.

indicating their category. She found that semantically related primes facilitate good instances of the category only when semantic match instructions were used and not when the task involved only physical matching. This suggests that there is no automatic improvement of the physical codes following a semantic prime. Nissen (1976) tackled this question directly by studying repetition of the same semantic category across independent trials. There was little or no incentive for subjects to attend to the semantic category of the previous trial in her paradigm. She found that repetition of the semantic category facilitated semantic and phonetic matches but found no evidence of facilitation for physical matches.

These data seem to deny that spreading activation automatically improves physical matches in any paradigm using a semantic prime or repetition of the semantic categories over trials. The strongest exception to this generalization arises from Rosch's finding that a semantic category can improve instances of reaction time to physical matches of good instances of the category and retard it to poor instances. Unlike the color category results, however, this occurs only when subjects are instructed to do semantic matching. There are a number of ways to conceptualize Rosch's results, but the interaction between instruction condition and benefit probably argues against an automatic spread explanation.

We need also to consider the direction of attention. When subjects are instructed to make semantic level judgments, they presumably are in a horse race between physical match of the two array items and a match of these items to the category. As we have seen in letter matching, this race is likely to be rather close when there is only one semantic category that needs to be considered (as occurs in the prime condition). Note that good instances not only match each other but readily match the prime, whereas poor instances do not readily match the prime and may give rise to an implicit "no" response (e.g., alligator is not a good match to "animal"). These concepts could be put together in a way that would give the kind of results obtained by Rosch.

The problem of deliberate strategies is a particularly difficult one for all studies of priming. Much evidence on priming comes from studies in which the subject is instructed to respond based upon whether array items match. There is a strong tendency for subjects to include the prime in the match. This strategy will produce fast reaction times to arrays that match the prime and slow reaction times to those that mismatch. Thus such strategies can account for many of the cost–benefit results. Moreover, if subjects tend to use the prime less when it is invalid, this strategy can also account for differences between high- and low-validity conditions. This strategy is apparent in much of our priming data (Posner & Snyder, 1975a). However, it does not seem to provide a reason for the asymmetry in the time course of cost and benefit. Moreover, studies using lexical decisions (Kirsner & Smith, 1974; Neely, 1977), naming latencies (Eichelman, 1970b), and stimulus repetition (Hinrich & Craft, 1971) argue that the benefits of priming are not limited to matching tasks.

TABLE 4.1
Costs and Benefits in RT and Errors for Physical and Name Matches
with Valid and Invalid Primes[a]

	Cost		Benefit	
	RT	Error	RT	Error
Invalid (20–80)				
Physical	3	1.4	51[b]	.4
Name	34[b]	11.2[b]	47[b]	7.2[b]
Valid (80–20)				
Physical	14	16.2[b]	48[b]	−.9
Name	44[b]	35.7[b]	77[b]	15.1[b]

[a]From Snyder & Posner (Note 10).
[b]Significant .05 or less.

Another qualification of the cost–benefit analysis arises in unpublished studies by Snyder and Posner (Note 10). In these studies, subjects were asked to make matches based on whether pairs of letters had the same name. A priming manipulation similar to that described in physical match studies was used. For pairs of letters that were physically identical, priming had the usual effect (see Table 4.1). However, both the high- and low-validity conditions showed costs and benefits for the name match pairs. The sizes of costs and benefits were greater for the valid condition, but they were not eliminated even when the prime matched the array on only .2 of the trials. A similar inability to obtain benefit without cost was found by Posner and Snyder (1975b) for the task of reporting whether or not a digit was present in an array of letters. Priming by a single digit only produced benefit when subjects were instructed to deliberately use the prime, and in this case cost was also obtained. Clearly we are not yet in a position to know the conditions under which automatic pathway activation effects will be obtained.

Summary

Priming provides evidence to support the concept of psychological pathways that show orderly facilitation and decay over time. It is a difficult inferential process to be sure that the facilitation and decay studied in any particular experiment are of the automatic type rather than products of the subject's conscious attention. However, the bulk of the studies seem to provide evidence that psychological experiments can examine automatic activation of pathways and their loss over time.

To continue the argument, we turn now to another manipulation that might be thought of as affecting automatic pathway activation.

INTENSITY EFFECTS

Few generalizations in the study of mental chronometry are more firmly established than the decrease in reaction time with increases in stimulus intensity. Teichner and Krebs (1972) have provided a summary showing the orderly reduction in latency with increasing visual intensity for simple reaction time. This summary is illustrated in Figure 4.13.

It has been shown that single cells in the striate cortex of the monkey increase in firing rate with increases in intensity (Bartlett & Doty, 1974). As intensity increases, the rate of firing of these luxotonic cells is speeded within the first 100 msec after input. This increased electrical activity also shows up in larger amplitudes of the visually evoked potentials within this latency range (Regan, 1972). Subjective intensity judgments and backward masking functions indicate that the effective intensity of a visual stimulus can be altered either by changes in stimulus duration or by masking from other stimuli within the first 100 msec after a stimulus occurs.

How are these changes in electrical activity at the level of the cortex converted into reaction-time differences? There is controversy as to whether intensity effects of reaction times are primarily sensory, whether they are more central, or whether they combine both central and sensory components. One way of illustrating these views may be clearer by reference to Figure 1.2. Intensity manipulations may change the response criterion, the time at which information

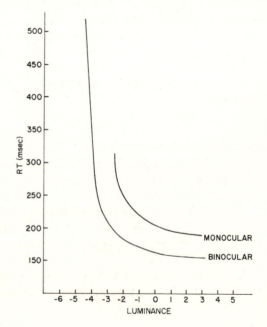

FIG. 4.13. General reductions in RT as a function of visual intensity summarized from many studies. (From Teichner & Krebs, 1972. Copyright 1972 by the American Psychological Association. Reprinted by permission.)

starts to accrue (i.e., leaves the x-axis), the rate at which information grows, or any combination of these.

Since intensity affects retinal processing, there is a reason for supposing that intensity ought to affect the rate of accumulation of information in automatic pathways. On the other hand, several results available in the psychological literature suggest that more efficient pathway activation cannot by itself account for results obtained with changes in intensity. For example, Grice and Hunter (1964) and Grice (1968) have suggested that the size of the intensity effect is dependent on the experimental design used. They found a much smaller effect of intensity on auditory simple reaction time when the stimuli were presented in pure blocks than when they were mixed in a single block. This, together with the influences of warning signal intensity and sequential effects found in mixed blocks, led Grice to propose that subjects raised their criteria following intensity stimuli and lowered them following weak stimuli. Grice's view of criterion setting stresses the role of prior stimulation, alternative stimuli, and habits in establishing the criterion.

Another view of criterion effects stresses changes in the state of alertness of the organism (see also Chapter 5). If an imperative signal is preceded by a warning signal, reaction time to the imperative signal is reduced but errors tend to increase (Posner, 1975a). This type of speed–accuracy tradeoff can be considered as a reduction of the criterion illustrated in Figure 1.2. Such a criterion effect can also be obtained if a noninformative auditory accessory signal is presented coincident with or slightly after the presentation of an imperative visual stimulus. This "intersensory facilitation" is due to alerting and produces an increase in speed and a reduction in accuracy (Nickerson, 1973). The ability of an accessory stimulus to produce alerting even when coincident with the imperative signal raises the question of whether intensity manipulations of the imperative signal might operate by a similar mechanism. Thus a more intense imperative signal could activate the perceptual pathways leading to identification and/or simultaneously produce an alerting change. Since there is evidence that alerting changes the availability of the central processor (Posner, 1975a), this would provide another mechanism for the operation of intensity. This view predicts that the effect of intensity will interact with the degree of alertness of the organism. An organism that is at a low level of alertness when the signal arrives will receive a large alerting effect from the more intense stimulus and thus respond more quickly. It also predicts that improvements due to intensity of the signal will be primarily speed–accuracy tradeoffs just as are improvements due to alerting. The alerting theory of intensity is similar to that used by Grice, but it does not predict sequential dependencies in mixed blocks or differences between mixed and pure blocks.

There is no complete resolution to the effect of intensity upon criterion and pathway activation processes. However, a number of experimental investigations suggest that there is an asymmetry in the effects of visual and auditory signals upon the processing system (Sanders, 1975). There is evidence that with visual input, the intensity of a stimulus is additive with the effect of a warning signal (Bernstein, Chu, Briggs, & Schurman, 1973). Thus the effect of intensity on performance is independent of the level of alertness at the time the stimulus occurs. This appears not to be true of auditory signals. Rather, auditory signals frequently show an interaction between warning signal and intensity manipulations (Murray, 1970). Niemi (in press) has shown direct evidence favoring additivity between foreperiod duration and signal intensity for visual signals and interaction for auditory signals. The difference between visual and auditory signals is probably not absolute. It is likely that very intense visual signals will also produce automatic alerting effects (Sanders, 1975); but within a reasonable range of stimuli most often used, auditory signals are more likely to do so.

A second distinction may be necessary to account for some of the complex literature on the effects of intensity (Sanders, 1975). Simple reaction time may be viewed as a task requiring deliberate detection of energy. More complex tasks, such as naming the stimulus or matching one stimulus to another, cannot be based on the presence of energy alone. Grice has found consistently that simple reaction time (particularly with auditory signals) differs between pure and mixed blocks and shows strong sequential effects of intensity in mixed blocks.

A major point of this chapter is to indicate that the selection of a stimulus dimension for conscious attention can influence its processing. Thus it would be no surprise that instructing subjects to attend to intensity even obliquely by giving them an intensity-detection task might influence the mechanisms through which intensity operates. Much of the psychophysics of intensity is based on the requirement that subjects judge intensity directly. These findings may not generalize to situations where the intensity is not selectively processed. Indeed the effects of intensity may turn out to fit simpler models such as those based on counting neural spikes or interspike intervals (Luce & Green, 1972) better when the subject is not deliberately set to judge intensity.

For this reason, work in our laboratory has mainly involved the study of visual choice reaction time (see also Sanders, 1975) and may not be generalized beyond that domain. However, it is illustrative in showing the important effects intensity manipulations can have on pathway activation. One study compared blocks of mixed intensities with pure blocks of strong and weak stimuli as Grice (1968) had done for simple auditory reaction time. No differences were found between the two kinds of blocks (see Figure 4.14). Moreover, within mixed blocks there were no sequential dependency effects involving intensity (see Figure 4.15). These findings ruled out a criterion effect of the type studied by Grice in audition.

The idea that each signal has both an alerting and a pathway effect on the organism has been advocated by many psychological theories. In the next chapter, I will outline in more detail the internal consequences of alerting. It seems appealing that the intensity effect on reaction time for visual signals might be

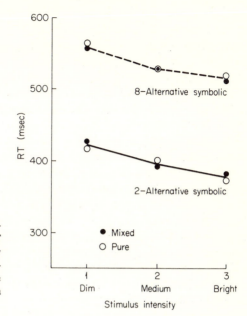

FIG. 4.14. Effects of visual intensity and number of alternatives on RT in pure blocks differing in intensity and in mixed blocks of differing intensities. The effect of intensity is the same regardless of block and over a wide range of task difficulty.

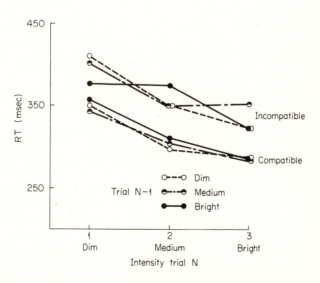

FIG. 4.15. RT to visual stimuli of varying intensities that follow a bright, medium, or dim trial for spatially compatible and incompatible tasks.

115

mediated through its alerting effect. To test this idea, we added a visual stimulus with no task-relevant information (accessory) to a visual imperative stimulus requiring a choice response. Intensity of both the imperative and accessory signal was varied. The results showed quite clearly that an intense accessory did not compensate for a dim imperative; indeed no improvement in the reaction time to the imperative was found due to the accessory. This result seemed to show that the effects of intensity on visual reaction time were not due to general alerting.

There is some direct evidence that intensity effects in visual choice tasks are due to the time at which information begins to accrue, or its accrual rate. Pachella and Fisher (1969) found contrast to affect the intercept of the speed–accuracy tradeoff function, whereas Lappin and Disch (1972) found effects both on the intercept and slope of such functions. My results show that the effect of visual intensity appears to be additive with task difficulty over a wide variety of choice reaction-time tasks. Figure 4.14 indicates the effect of intensity manipulation on performance in a two- or eight-alternative digit classification task. Despite large differences in the mean reaction time for the tasks, the effects of intensity are always about 40 msec over the range studied.[4]

If manipulations of visual intensity affect pathway activation, one would expect them to interact with priming. There is evidence that this is the case. Much of the evidence on this comes from the lexical decision task. Recall that the presentation of a word on trial n reduces the time to classify a related word on trial $n + 1$, an effect that was previously shown to result from a combination of automatic and attended pathway effects. One study varied the signal–to–noise ratio of the test word by imposing a checkerboard noise pattern over it (Meyer, Schvaneveldt, & Ruddy, 1975). The noise mask had a large effect on time to classify a target word following an unrelated word and a much smaller effect following a related word, thus showing an interaction between signal–to–noise ratio and priming by an associated word. More recently it has been shown (Becker & Killion, 1977) that changes in visual intensity also produce the same interaction with priming (see Figure 4.16). The same interaction was found when subjects were required to name the test word rather than to classify it. Moreover, there was little evidence of an interaction between the task (naming vs. classifying) used and intensity, nor did the word frequency of the test word interact with intensity. These data support the view that visual intensity and priming from an associated word affect the same internal pathway activation process at some stage. They also suggest that the intensity effects are cortical rather than merely involving conduction time to the cortex.

Studies that vary visual intensity give evidence in favor of the proposition that psychological pathways can be activated more quickly by more intense

---

[4]Unfortunately, the literature on the effect of intensity on RT performance has not been very consistent. There are reports both of additivity as I have found and also of interaction (Becker & Killion, 1977; Shwartz, Pomerantz, & Egeth, 1977; Stanovich & Pachella, 1977).

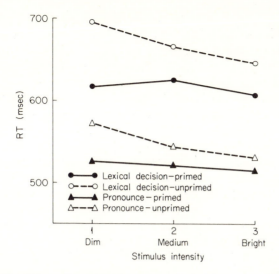

FIG. 4.16.   Effects of intensity and expectancy for lexical decision and pronunciation tasks. (After Becker & Killion, 1977.)

input, as suggested also by the evidence from single, cortical-cell discharge rates. However, intensity appears to involve other mechanisms as well. What seems to me most hopeful is the ability of chronometric studies to tease apart effects of intensity that involve pathway activation, alerting, and criterion setting. The results warn us that manipulation of one independent variable cannot be thought to mean the change in only one internal mechanism. Rather a single external change may have widespread internal effects. Despite these difficulties, Chapter 5 does provide model situations in which alerting and pathway activation effects can be dissected (see p. 131).

INHIBITION OF PATHWAYS

The cost–benefit analysis I have developed suggests that it is possible to inhibit or retard the latency of responses by calling the subject's attention to a competing stimulus. Such inhibition is at the level of the central attentional system and does not affect the automatic accrual of information along habitual pathways. Another kind of inhibition might occur due to the repetitive activation of a pathway. If a pathway was activated continuously, one might suspect inhibition due to fatigue of the pathway itself. This idea has been prominent in the visual literature (Sekuler, 1974). It has also been discussed for semantic systems (Esposito & Pelton, 1971). Of first importance, in my view, is an effort to determine whether the adaptation that is obtained is due to changes in the pathways that mediate input information or to an aspect of central attentional mechanisms. Second, we must consider the level of processing (isolable subsystems) at which inhibition has been demonstrated.

Visual System

Evidence for pathway inhibition due to fatigue in the visual system has depended upon adaptation to spatial gratings. If one presents a subject with a sinusoidal grating for a long period of time, allowing the visual system to adapt to that grating, there are systematic elevations in the detection threshold for other related gratings. In addition, visual evoked potentials also are systematically reduced in amplitude. What needs to be understood is the location specificity of this result. Sekuler (1974) cited results showing that when adaptation and test occupy different positions in space, there is not threshold elevation. The concept of psychological pathways connecting visual analyzers for letters to letter names clearly cannot involve fixed positions on the retina.

There is little evidence that pathways defined as we have done can be adapted by continual visual presentation.[5] Efforts in our laboratory to obtain such adaptation by presenting subjects with matrices consisting of a single letter (for example a capital "A") flashed on and off over and over again and then examining luminance estimates, responses to matching tasks, short-term memory, etc., using the "satiated letter" versus other letters, have turned up no important effects. Although few studies have been published discussing the difficulty of fatiguing pathways at nonoverlapping spatial positions, consultation with other colleagues suggests that other people have also had difficulty obtaining such inhibitory effects. This should by no means be taken as evidence that such inhibitory effects are impossible in the visual system; but there is not yet any convincing evidence that spatially distinct material that produces facilitation in priming also causes inhibition following continued presentation. On the other hand, this effect has been widely reported in audition.

Auditory System

A reliable finding in audition is that the repetition of a single item will cause a change in verbal reports of what the subject hears (Warren & Warren, 1970). This has been called the *verbal transformation effect*. The occurrence of the verbal transformation effect is not in doubt and gives assurance that at some level the repetition of an item causes changes in perception. At this point, the same problems arise in audition that we just discussed for vision. First, what evidence is there that this effect is due to adaptation of the input pathway and not of central

---

[5]One study has shown adaptation for letters in the sense that clarity ratings declined with successive exposures, but this has not been found for performance measures (Pomerantz, Kaplan, & Kaplan, 1969).

attentional mechanisms? Second, if some or all of the adaptation can be attributed to pathway effects, at what level does the adaptation occur?

The former question has really not been satisfactorily addressed in any of the literature using auditory adaptation. The reasons that visual grating evidence appears to implicate sensory adaptation rather than more central attentional mechanisms are:

1. There are changes in *detection* threshold.
2. The effect is closely locked to the physical features of the input grating.
3. The adaptation effects occur in visual evoked potentials.

These points are less clear in audition. The most systematic investigations have used artificial speech stimuli and examined the ability of subjects to identify stimuli before and after adaptation. It has been shown repeatedly (Eimas & Corbit, 1973) that following adaptation to a stopped consonant, such as "BA" or "PA," the phonetic boundary representing the voice onset time at which the subject begins to hear the distinction between "BA" and "PA" is shifted in the direction of the repeated or adapted stimulus. One interpretation is that adaptation produced fatigue of the neural analyzer of the repeated consonant. This idea has been developed by results suggesting that the adaptation occurs across different acoustic realizations of the same phonetic feature. All the studies that have been reported so far have used adaptation at the phonetic boundary as a sign of the fatigue of the pathway. Obviously other interpretations are also possible. For example, one might suppose that repeating a stimulus over and over again simply redefines the nature of the target more precisely, thus getting the subjects to reject stimuli that they previously thought were perfectly acceptable realizations of that phonetic class.

A chronometric framework allows investigation of the locus of the adaptation effect. Studies that examine errors of identification usually yield close to 100% performance with the stimuli used to produce adaptation, since these are well removed from the phonetic boundary and thus easy to identify. It is possible to determine whether the input pathway of the exact stimulus actually undergoing adaptation is changed in efficiency by use of the same chronometric techniques that underlie priming. One study (Cole, Cooper, Singer, & Allard, 1975) found no support for the idea that the adapted phoneme itself was identified less efficiently in terms of errors or reaction time, although there was a clear shift at the phonetic boundary. Other chronometric techniques such as speed–accuracy tradeoffs or evoked-potential changes have not been applied following adaptation. Moreover, there has not yet been any effort to link priming with adaptation, although in theory they are two points on what should be a continuous curve relating prior pathway activation to performance.

It has been difficult to determine whether such adaptation effects as occur with auditory phonemes are acoustic or phonetic in character. Some experiments appear to favor a phonetic component, but the effect does not appear confined to the phonetic code. The difficulty in separation between acoustic and phonetic codes of auditory stimuli should be no surprise, given the similar problem that we have found in determining whether they behave as isolable systems (see p. 34).

Memory

There is a great deal of evidence that suggests that presentation of the same item twice in succession will reduce the probability of a subject recalling or recognizing that item (Hintzman, 1976) in comparison with spaced repetition. This finding is obtained over a large range of human memory studies that use a variety of materials and methods of measuring retention. Moreover, it is known that the effect is produced by a failure to store the repeated event, not by a disruption of the first trace (Hintzman, 1976). This finding suggests that retention rests upon the operation of a mechanism that is different from the automatic pathway activation, since activation is made more efficient by repetition within this range. There is much evidence that retention depends upon an active process of rehearsal and is interfered with by any mental operation that requires attention (Posner & Rossman, 1965). These points lead to the notion that there is a reciprocal relationship between the ease with which a stimulus activates its internal codes and the degree of active attention one will pay to that stimulus.

Similar evidence favoring this proposition comes from the study of conditioning with nonhuman organisms. A stimulus that has been presented often so that it no longer produces an orienting reflex is quite difficult to condition. A stronger example favoring a reciprocal relationship between pathway activation and learning is the finding that a primed stimulus does not accrue as much habit strength from being followed by an unconditioned stimulus as does the same stimulus when it has not been primed (Pfautz & Wagner, 1976). Somewhat more distant is evidence that the presence of a cue with a strong predictive relationship to the reinforcing event prevents other cues from becoming conditioned (Rescorla & Wagner, 1972). The "blocking" effect suggests that unless some central mechanism is committed to processing a cue, it does not become conditioned. The "blocking" that occurs is clearly central, since a shift in the unconditioned stimulus will produce conditioning. Finally, there is evidence that subjects will generally attend longer to a stimulus on its first occasion than when it is repeated twice in a row. Unfortunately for the acceptability of the reciprocal relationship, efforts to reduce the effect of repetition on memory by manipulating the active rehearsal of a repeated item have not been successful (Hintzman, 1976). Nonetheless, it is clear that producing efficient pathway activation by priming does not improve *all* aspects of performance. This empirical fact is a strong argument for the distinction between pathway activation and active attention, which is a theme of this chapter.

The adaptation that takes place following many presentations of an auditory item and the reduction in memory that occurs with repeating a single item are both evidence that repetition causes inhibition at some level. The level of these inhibitory effects is unclear. One possibility is that the system that underlies active attention is designed so that a repeated event becomes increasingly unable to engage it. In the case of acoustic adaptation, competing pathways that are also activated but to a lesser degree by the input phoneme or word would eventually come to control conscious attention. In the case of the memory studies, a repeated event would be given reduced active attention and thus have a lowered memory strength. At first this view might be thought to contradict the position that pathway priming produces no widespread inhibitory effects (see p. 99). It should be born in mind, however, that the memory paradigm involves an implicit instruction to attend to each stimulus event as it occurs. Thus the processing of each item would generally involve attention. The evaluation of this idea concerning attention rests both upon future research and upon a better understanding of the attentional system itself. The latter problem is the theme of the next two chapters.

SUMMARY

Psychological pathways are the set of internal codes automatically activated by a given input item. The term *automatic* connotes the ideas of invariance and separability taken from the reflex views of Sechenov and Sherrington. Evidence suggests that pathways can be activated irrespective of the subjects' intentions and without the necessity of their devoting active attention to them. Study of the costs and benefits from priming a pathway suggests that it is possible to separate the automatic activation of pathways from attentional processing.

Evidence for facilitation and decay of pathway activation from priming is reviewed. The rate of pathway activation for visual stimuli appears to be a function of the intensity of the stimulus. Intensity also has some effects that appear due to more central mechanisms, and these different effects show some promise of being separable by chronometric techniques. Finally, inhibition due to repeated activation occurs. Evidence comes both from studies of recognition following adaptation to acoustic events and from studies of the memory strength for items presented twice in a row. There is some evidence that such inhibitory effects involve central attentional systems either alone or in conjunction with changes in pathway activation patterns.

5 Alertness

ENDOGENOUS CONTROL

There is almost an inevitable bias in research toward the study of processes that can be initiated under the control of the experimenter. A stimulus event may be viewed as initiating a complex of internal activity, and clearly one goal of experimentation is to describe those processes that are the inevitable results of such stimulation. The bias toward such exogenously controlled processes in biology gives reflex activity an edge over the study of endogenous or spontaneous behavior. Similarly in animal psychology, respondents yielded to empirical analysis before the pioneering work of Skinner provided a detailed analysis of operants. In the study of human performance most experiments have concerned responses to external stimuli, as in reading,[1] rather than performances emphasizing control by the subjects, as in writing.

Marler & Hamilton (1967) put the issue in zoology as follows:

It was perhaps inevitable that the fruitful exploration of environmental control of behavior should lead to a neglect of the importance of changes generated from within . . . [p. 6]. Interaction of exogenous and endogenous factors is a major topic of this book. The position we shall try to establish is that both internal and external factors are involved in *any* behavior pattern. No animal is a passive respondent to environmental commands [p. 9].

---

[1]This is not to argue that reading is a passive process but only that in comparison to writing, it is more structured by external stimulus events.

Theories of human performance also oscillate between those in which all performance is seen as driven externally and those in which every action is said to be controlled by internal hypotheses and expectations (Neisser, 1967). The former is sometimes called the "bottom-up" approach and the latter is called "top-down." It was my original intention to divide this book so that the first four lectures were concerned mainly with externally driven processes with little control from endogenous plans and strategies, whereas the next three would deal increasingly with attention and cognitive control over the same activity. I have been thwarted in this pedagogic design by the inability to disentangle completely the passive and active nature of processing within any single task. Marler and Hamilton are clearly right. Human performance, like animal behavior, is always an interaction between endogenous and exogenous factors. The very early work in letter matching led to an examination of subjects' abilities to generate visual codes from letter names if they desired to do so. Efforts to deal with conflicting results in the time course of sequential matching also required reference to active attentional processes. Thus even though it was my intention in the early chapters to provide mainly the passive features of the processing system, it was not possible to eliminate some consideration of attention and cognitive control. In the next three chapters my primary concern will be to develop more complete notions about the mechanisms that subserve central attention and its cognitive control over information processing.

To do this I have not chosen tasks very far in spirit and style from the ones we have been examining. Instead of attempting to examine tasks that employ the full range of human hypotheses and inference capabilities, I have attempted to keep the features of tight time locking that allow for the use of chronometric techniques. The focus, however, shifts to the attentional mechanism. The hope is to reveal basic processes by which people bring their expectations to bear upon the automatic activation processes of the type discussed so far.

In this chapter concern is focused on an important property of the state of the organism: the level of alertness. The next chapter deals with mechanisms responsible for the acts of stimulus detection and recognition. According to my view, both detection and recognition result from the operation of a single limited capacity system.[2] Detection emphasizes contact with energy pathways, and recognition stresses the influence of information stored in memory. Chapter 7 examines the ability of central systems to be summoned (oriented) toward an activated pathway. Alerting, detecting, and orienting become three basic factors in the study of attention.

Attention is not used here as an explanation for selective processing. Rather, I use it as a name of a field that consists of the study of internal mechanisms

---

[2]Limited capacity in this sense refers to the characteristics of an isolable system that is so richly interacting that its efficient utilization for the processing of a signal will usually reduce the efficiency with which it can process any other signal.

relating to our awareness of events. For subjects to attend efficiently at least to external events, they must be in a general state of alertness. This state allows mechanisms that subserve the subjective experience of consciousness to be brought efficiently into contact with sensory information.

The contrast between the sleeping and waking organism is impressive. Although in part, the control of sleep and wakefulness depends on external stimuli, there is clear evidence from neurophysiology that it depends as well on intrinsic rhythms (Kleitman, 1963). The study of the sleep–wake cycle then becomes one area in which both physiologists and psychologists can study a model system of changes in behavior that accompany changes in alertness. Differences between the information-processing capabilities of sleeping and waking organisms are so gross as to require little experimentation for their demonstration. Waking organisms respond readily to a variety of sensory modalities and show a planned integration of complex behaviors that contrast markedly with the performance while asleep. If one were attempting to predict the responses of an organism to a given stimulus event, perhaps no single fact would be more important than whether the organism was awake or asleep. The obviousness of the contrast between sleeping and waking in its effect upon performance should not mask the more subtle changes that occur with less drastic shifts in alertness. Our discussion of changes in alertness will begin with those that can be obtained most easily in the laboratory and that occur at a rapid rate and usually under volitional control. These changes are called *phasic*. After studying the mechanisms that underlie phasic changes in alertness, I turn attention to slower changes that might be called *tonic*. These slower changes can be revealed in vigilance tasks that require long continued performance from the subject and are also apparent in the changes in alertness that accompany diurnal rhythms and changes over the life cycle.

PHASIC ALERTNESS

General State

Suppose a human subject is asked to prepare to process an incoming stimulus. There is widespread agreement from many studies about some of the things that happen. The EEG shows a temporary blocking of rhythmic alpha activity, which is replaced by fast, desynchronized activity (Lansing, Schwartz, & Lindsley, 1959). There is a slow negative drift in the EEG (contingent negative variation or CNV) that begins as rapidly as 100 to 200 msec following a warning signal and that approaches its minimum at a rate that is a function of the warning interval (Walter, 1964). Both the CNV and the alert state itself depend upon both exogenous and endogenous factors. The warning signal provides the occasion but does not force the occurrence of the contingent negative variation. A subject who

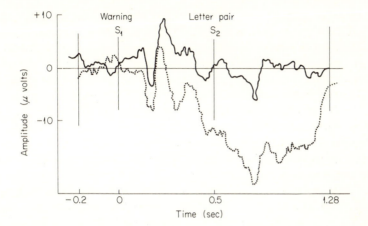

FIG. 5.1.   Electrical activity averaged from the vertex in an experiment in which a warning signal (S_1) is followed after .5 sec by a letter pair (S_2). In the solid line conditions, subjects are instructed to ignore the warning and not respond to the letter pair, whereas in the dotted line, they are to use the warning to prepare for the letter pair. The contingent negative variation (CNV) is the negative shift in the instructed condition with respect to the uninstructed one. It has clearly begun by 200 msec following the warning. (From Posner, 1975a. Copyright 1975 Academic Press.)

receives a warning signal without an instruction to use it to prepare for the oncoming stimulus shows no sustained CNV. There may be a part of the brain change that later becomes the CNV that is automatic in the sense that it follows the warning signal (particularly if it is auditory) irrespective of the instruction.[3] However, the bulk of the CNV changes seem to require the intention of the subject to prepare for the following stimulus. Even without any external stimulus, subjects can of course develop such states of preparation on their own (McAdams, Irwin, Rebert, & Knott, 1969). The stimulus does serve to time lock the activity, allowing more convenient measurement by the experimenter.

The solid curve in Figure 5.1 involves a warning signal followed by a pair of letters where the subject is not instructed to process the letter pair. The evoked potential to the warning signal is not followed by any convincing negative shift in the EEG. On the other hand, the dotted trace shows a condition in which the subject is required to prepare for the processing of the letter pair and to respond to it by pressing one of two keys depending upon whether the letters match or not.

Much of the reason for believing in the relationship between CNV and alerting is the fact that the CNV appears in every paradigm where subjects are

---

[3]The presentation of a warning signal prior to a stimulus to which an animal or human normally shows a startle response reduces the amplitude of the startle activity. This inhibition of unconditioned responses has been shown to occur in as little as 30 msec following the warning (Reiter & Ison, 1977). It is not yet known what effect the instruction to use the warning signal to prepare for some event would have on this inhibition.

told to get ready to attend closely to an external event. Thus it appears to be closely related to the process by which subjects prepare for external events. Similar surface changes in the EEG also accompany the transition from sleep to wakefulness (Caspers, 1963). As I have already pointed out, the CNV emitted by the subject under the intention to process a signal is not elicited by the warning signal without such an intention.

The time relationship between the warning signal and the CNV bears considerable resemblance to the time course of changes in reaction time. When I began to investigate CNV, it was thought that the negative shift did not occur prior to .5 sec following a warning signal. These studies used foreperiods longer than a second and provided little incentive for more rapid preparation. When we (Posner & Wilkinson, Note 2) began to use shorter foreperiods such as are optimal in reaction time tasks, a different picture emerged. The top panel of Figure 5.2 indicates the time course of preparation in a visual letter-matching task when the foreperiod is varied between blocks. For this task, the optimal foreperiod is about .5 sec, although the increase in reaction time with longer foreperiods is slight. The lower panel shows a study of CNV depth as a function of foreperiod (Gaillard & Näätänen, 1973). The CNV clearly is present even with foreperiods as brief as .2 sec. With short foreperiods, the CNV is superimposed on the evoked potential to the warning signal. It is best defined by that difference in the negative shift in a condition where subjects are instructed to use the warning signal and where they are not so instructed. With short foreperiods, the CNV may actually start prior to the warning signal as though subjects were anticipating—as they surely do in such situations. With brief foreperiods, the CNV continues after the presentation of the imperative signal and remains present until after the decision is made. For this reason, even though Figure 5.2 indicates the deepest CNV is with a 1,000-msec foreperiod at the moment of presentation of the imperative stimulus, it is likely that the depth is actually as great or greater at a foreperiod corresponding to the optimal reaction time (e.g., 400–500 msec). In any case, both reaction time and CNV are optimal in about the same range of foreperiods.

Although CNV depth is correlated with reaction time in some situations (Hillyard & Picton, in press), the relationship is not too high, and the CNV is probably one of many physiological indicants of the alert state. The CNV is accompanied by a constellation of changes in autonomic activity, many of which are related to the general state of sympathetic dominance that accompanies nearly any difficult mental activity (Kahneman, 1973). However, it also includes an inhibitory component that is related specifically to states of high alertness for external signals. It involves both cardiac deceleration and fairly widespread inhibition of spinal reflexes. This alert state has a marked reduction in irrelevant movement and a steady, unblinking eye (Webb & Obrist, 1970). The state of preparation for external signals is also marked by specific inhibition of spinal reflexes associated with the muscle that is to eventually respond (Requin, 1969).

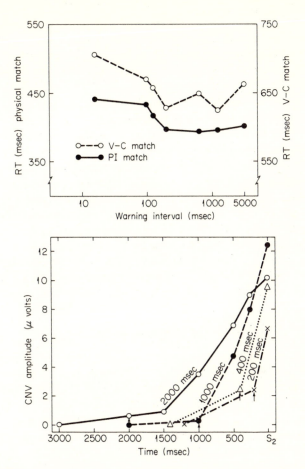

FIG. 5.2.   Upper panel shows changes in RT for two letter-matching tasks as a function of foreperiod. (From Posner & Boies, 1971. Copyright 1971 by the American Psychological Association. Reprinted by permission.) Lower panel shows amplitude of CNV for differing foreperiod between warning and imperative signals varying from 200 to 2,000 msec. Arrows represent the time when the warning signal is presented. (From Gaillard & Näätänen, 1973. Copyright 1973 North-Holland Publishing Company.)

Thus the constellation of bodily changes in a high state of phasic alertness has some of the components of general arousal or excitability and also changes that involve inhibition or suspension of activity.

There is some evidence that the CNV and the preparation process itself can be divided into at least two phases. An early phase of the CNV is more pronounced for auditory signals than for visual warning signals (Gaillard & Näätänen, 1973) and is strongest in the frontal areas of the brain (Loveless & Sanford, 1974; Rohrbaugh, Syndulko, & Lindsley, 1976). A second phase appears to be more closely locked to the difficulty of the response required and is mainly motor in character (Kornhuber & Deecke, 1965). A long warning interval gives rise to feelings of strain in maintaining alertness. Even with constant foreperiod signals, there is usually some difficulty in maintaining peak performance for longer than about .5 sec.

The use of the CNV as an index of the alert state gives us a method of dealing with the recruitment of brain systems following a warning signal. That CNV topography changes during the foreperiod provides hope that we will eventually come to understand in more detail how systems are brought into play as the person mobilizes to take in and then respond to a signal. Although these preparatory developments are likely to be complex and differ with task, the details of their time course and organization may be most helpful in fostering an increased understanding of brain localization within a functional context.

Much of the work on the CNV has been concerned primarily in providing a psychological name for its function. Although I feel that the CNV does serve as a good index of the alert state, the most important issue for our purposes is to determine the detailed changes in information processing that accompany the state induced by a warning signal. I turn to this question in the next section.

Information-Processing Effects of Phasic Alertness

Results of studies of the effects of phasic alertness upon performance can best be understood with reference to the build-up of information in automatic pathways. Consider the presentation of a visual letter. When the letter is left present until the subject is ready to respond, there is a build-up of information over time that must eventually reach an asymptote. The rate of build-up is related to signal intensity as we have seen previously (see p. 112). Since foreperiod does not

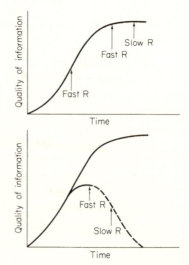

FIG. 5.3.   Hypothetical build-up of information about a signal as a function of time. Upper panel is when the signal remains present until a response. Faster RT is associated with equal or poorer quality. Lower panel also includes the condition (dotted line) when the stimulus is presented briefly and then removed. Faster RTs may be associated with increased or reduced quality of information. (From Posner, 1975a. Copyright 1975 Academic Press.)

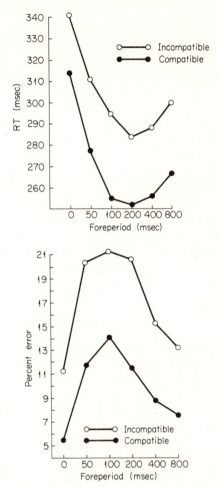

FIG. 5.4.   RT (upper panel) and errors (lower panel) as a function of foreperiod for a two-choice compatible and incompatible spatial task. (From Posner, Klein, Summers, & Buggie, 1973. Copyright 1973 by the Psychonomic Society.)

interact with intensity for visual signals (see p. 114), it is reasonable to expect that a warning signal will not influence the rate of build-up of information but rather the time that subjects can respond to that build-up. What is the consequence of this? If the signal is one to which information builds up relatively slowly, fast responses will come when information quality is poor and will be accompanied by an increase in errors. When the signal is one to which information builds up quite rapidly, responses will come at an asymptote in quality, and one will not expect an increase in errors to occur. Figure 5.3 illustrates this idea.

To test this idea, subjects were presented with a task of pressing a key when an "X" appeared to the left or right of fixation. In the compatible condition, each key was assigned to the "X" on the corresponding side; in the incompatible conditions, the assignments were reversed. Foreperiod was varied in constant blocks. The results for reaction time and error are shown in Figure 5.4. As in all of the tasks discussed in previous chapters, increasing the difficulty of the task by the compatibility manipulation increased reaction times and errors. However, foreperiod had quite a different effect: It reduced reaction time up to an optimum interval at 200 msec though errors increased. These results fit reasonably well with the assumption that alertness affects not the build-up of information but the rate that some later system can respond to that build-up.[4]

In reviewing the studies of the effect of alertness on reaction time and error, it was found that functions of the type shown in Figure 5.4 were quite frequent. In most studies, low error rates prevented the error function from being significant and thus the authors ignored it.

Even when subjects are given strong incentives to respond as quickly as possible to the input by means of a pay-off matrix, a warning signal still reduces reaction time further (Farrar, Note 11). When a pay-off matrix stressing speed was imposed on the task above, reaction time was reduced by 20–30 msec; but the effect of a warning signal remained about the same. Thus voluntary effort on the part of the subject seems unable to compensate for the absence of a warning signal. An ability to compensate would be expected if the warning operated to produce a voluntary shift in criterion (beta) of the same sort as an incentive.

The problem with viewing alerting changes simply as criterion (beta) shifts becomes more clear when one uses a brief or dim imperative signal followed by a mask. This situation is illustrated in terms of the build-up of information in the lower portion of Figure 5.3. If alertness affects the time at which the subject can respond, it is clearly possible for a faster response to be based upon a higher quality of sensory information. This constellation of results (faster reaction time and fewer errors) was first reported by Fuster (1958). He presented monkeys with brief visual signals and varied alertness by reticular stimulation prior to the signal. Improvements in both errors and reaction time following a warning signal have also been found in letter matching when the letter pair is rapidly masked (Posner et al., 1973). Under these circumstances, measurements of d' and beta show a strong improvement in d' following the presentation of a warning signal (Klein & Kerr, 1974).

The data are clearly inconsistent with the idea that alertness is simply a change in beta. Rather, alertness affects the ability of subjects to respond to the build-up of information about the task signal. This may be measured as a ''sensitivity'' or ''bias'' change depending upon aspects of the physical situation.

The beta parameter of signal detection theory is generally supposed to be the bias of a single-state system. When we talk about the subject's criterion in

---

[4]The spatial RT task described above is one that reaches its optimal with foreperiods of about 200 msec, whereas letter-matching tasks reach optimal at about 500 msec. The latter task usually shows no change in errors with changes in alerting rather than the sharp increase found in the spatial task. Both no change and increase in error with alerting are consistent with Figure 5.3. However, at present there is no a priori reason why the spatial task should show one effect (regardless of compatibility) while the letter match shows another.

detecting a dim input, we are concerned with conscious or unconscious strategies that change the probability of saying a signal is present. However, we are dealing with a system that involves multiple subsystems—for example, the physical, phonetic, and semantic codes of letters and words. Subjects can activate different codes of a stimulus, thus biasing the activation of that code by input. Bias at one level of the system affects the input available at some other level. Thus d' and beta are complexly related to the processing operations of the human nervous system. There is a strong tendency in psychology to define internal processes in terms of a particular statistical parameter or empirical technique. Thus d' comes to define what is meant by the sensitivity of the system, or magnitude estimation is taken as the direct method of measuring psychological intensity. Such definitions can blind the investigator to the changes in what a given technique might be measuring as the physical situation or strategy of the subject changes. The method of converging operations through different chronometric techniques may serve as a useful counter to that tendency.

One might ask whether the concept of a central attentional mechanism is useful or whether it might not be best to suggest that alertness operates directly upon the motor output. I do not feel that the motor view as used in psychology[5] can be a correct one. On the behavioral side, similar foreperiod functions have been shown in number estimation tasks that require no speeded response (Leavitt, 1969) as are found in reaction time tasks. Moreover, the CNV and EEG desynchronization occur in roughly the same way regardless of whether or not an overt motor response is required. Finally, there is evidence that a warning signal affects the time between stimulus and the first change in the EMG (premotor time), not the time between the EMG and overt response (motor time; Botwinick & Thompson, 1966). The effects of alertness seem to be best described as reducing the time for some central mechanism to respond to the build-up of information about the signal. The central systems of an alert organism react more quickly. If the task requires detection of a transient signal, a warning may improve all aspects of performance. If the signal is steady state, a speed–accuracy tradeoff is usually found.

ALERTNESS AND PATHWAY ACTIVATION

According to the theory of phasic alertness I have outlined, a warning signal improves reaction time but does not affect the build-up of information in automatic pathways. This is an important observation that deserves additional evidence. In order to do so, it is necessary to separate the time for information about an item to activate automatic pathways from nonhabitual, overt responding to that

---

[5]This is not to deny the possibility that the central system may involve motor cortex, but rather to propose that it is not priming of a muscular system that is the major effect of alertness.

information. One way to separate the build-up of information about a letter from the time to develop a response to the letter is to present a single letter followed after a short, variable interval by a second letter. During the interval, information can build up about the first letter, but the response by the subject can not be begun until the second letter has occurred. The task for the subjects is to respond "same" if the letters are identical; otherwise they are to respond "different." This method is obviously similar to the priming technique discussed in the previous chapter, except in this method the first letter is necessary in order to perform the task. I doubt if there would be any important difference in conclusion if priming were used instead. The encoding process introduced by the first letter provides no information about the response to make when the second letter occurs, yet both reaction time and errors to the second letter decline regularly as the time by which the first letter leads the second letter is increased from about 0 to 300 msec. The reduction in reaction time as a function of the time between letters is called an *encoding function*. The encoding function is particularly sharp over the first 150 msec.

Since in these experiments the probability that the second letter will match the first is always .5, one would expect both automatic and attended influences. Automatic effects should be limited to the cases when the two letters match, since only then would the second letter find an already active input pathway. Thus one expects an asymmetry between type of response and the interval. This asymmetry does occur. Figure 5.5 indicates that reaction time improves with interval between the two letters for both matches and mismatches but that there is a significant interaction due to a larger improvement for matches.

To study a combination of phasic alerting and pathway activation, three conditions were used (Posner & Boies, 1971). In one condition (preparation), the subjects are provided with a warning signal following an interval of 150 or 500 msec by a pair of letters to which they are to respond. The top curve in Figure 5.6 shows the results of changes in reaction time in this condition. In the second (encoding) condition, the subject is first given a warning signal followed after a 500-msec delay by a single letter, followed after delays of 150 or 500 msec by a second letter. In this case, the subject is given a 500-msec warning interval and then a variable time for pathway activation prior to the second letter. That subjects do prepare during the 500-msec interval prior to the presentation of the first letter is shown by the finding that with zero delay between the letters, the reaction times are at the appropriate point in the preparation function. Nonetheless, additional improvement is obtained through pathway activation, which is very sharp over the first 150 msec following input. The third (both) condition involves presenting the subject with the first letter not preceded by a warning interval. In this case, the letter may act both as a warning signal and to activate the pathways concerning the form of the letter. If both these processes can go on together without interference, one would expect that the improvement in reaction

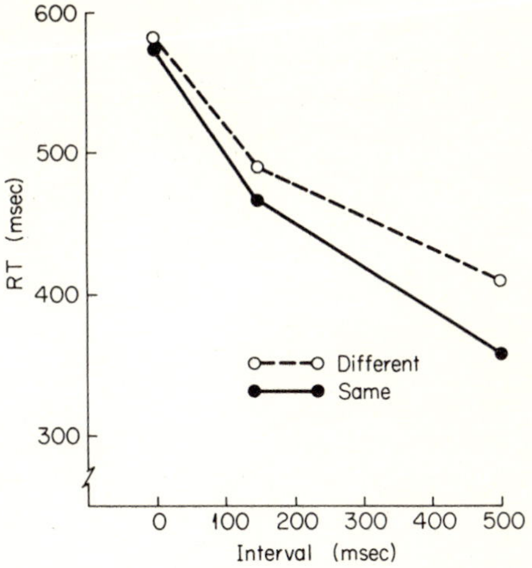

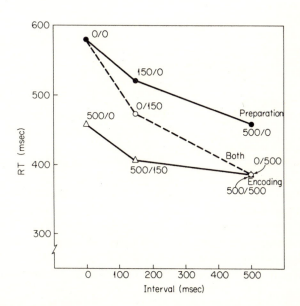

FIG. 5.5. Same versus different match RTs as a function of interval for the condition in which the first letter serves as a warning. (From Posner & Boies, 1971. Copyright 1971 by the American Psychological Association. Reprinted by permission.)

FIG. 5.6. Comparison of improvements in RT due to preparation, encoding, and the two combined. The graph shows curves for the physical match task. Table 5.1 indicates results for physical, phonetic, and vowel-consonant matching. (From Posner & Boies, 1971. Copyright 1971 by the American Psychological Association. Reprinted by permission.)

133

TABLE 5.1
Amount of Improvement in RT from Preparation,
Encoding, and Both[a]

	Interval[b]	
Match	150	500
Physical		
Preparation	58	122
Encoding	53	73
Both	101	195
Name		
Preparation	42	127
Encoding	58	98
Both	111	201
Vowel–Consonant		
Preparation	71	170
Encoding	124	150
Both	157	296

Note: Improvement is measured by subtracting
RT at specified interval from RT at 0/0 for preparation and "both" function and 500/0 for encoding.
[a] From Posner and Boies (1971). Copyright 1971
by the American Psychological Association. Reprinted by permission.
[b] In milliseconds.

time due to a warning signal alone plus the improvement in reaction time due to
pathway activation alone would add to the improvement in reaction time obtained
from both processes together. This is indeed exactly the case that was obtained
for both physical and name-matching tasks (see Table 5.1). This result suggests
both that pathway activation and alerting can go on simultaneously with no
interference and also that the alerting that is obtained prior to the presentation of
the first letter does not change pathway activation in any important way. If it did,
one would not expect exactly the same amount of improvement from the first
letter as was obtained when there is no prior warning signal. These results have
been replicated in an extensive series of experiments by Thomas (1974). Although there were some differences between Thomas' results and those of Posner
and Boies, the main additivity result is identical.

It has been supposed so far that the alerting effect of the warning signal is
totally independent of pathway activation. Put in physiological terms, the input
signal has a cortical pathway that activates relevant stored codes and a subcortical
pathway that produces alerting. Psychologists often refer to the separation between the cue and arousal values of the stimulus event. A strong view of such
separation would argue that there can be no difference in the alerting effects of a
signal depending upon information that is stored about that signal. This view

holds that alerting depends only upon modality, intensity, and other physical features of the event that do not depend upon retrieval of information stored about the stimulus.

This strong theory of separation is probably not correct. A close connection between alerting effects and their pathway activation has been shown by Kraut (1976). It has been known that children respond to familiar signals more slowly than unfamiliar ones. This appears paradoxical, given the strong evidence in adult studies that familiar signals are encoded more readily. Kraut reasoned that the slower responses to these signals were due to their low alerting effects. He found (see Figure 5.7) that when familiar signals were used as warning signals for a task, children responded to that task more slowly than when novel signals served as a warning. With alerting held constant, he was able to show that encoding (pathway activation) of the familiar signals was actually somewhat faster in children than was such activation for unfamiliar signals. Obviously, children placed in reaction time tasks are more critically dependent upon the alerting function, since they tend to be somewhat more easily distracted and perhaps less motivated than adults placed in the same task.

The Kraut results suggest that an analysis of the detailed, internal effects of signals may resolve many results that seem at first quite paradoxical. The use of the same signals as targets in one task and as warning signals in another task provides a powerful method for analysis of factors that affect alerting.

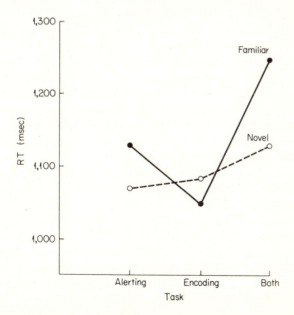

FIG. 5.7.   RT to prefamiliarized and novel signals when they are used as warning signals (alerting), imperative signals (encoding), and have both functions. Data are for children. (After Kraut, 1976.)

So far I have been writing as though a warning signal had no selective effects on information processing but simply changed a general, internal alerting state that affected any following signal. Although I believe that alerting itself is nonselective, it is clear that the warning signal can both alert and activate an internal cortical pathway. The latter effect leads to specific preparation for signals using that pathway. I have already reviewed evidence that an input letter has two effects. It changes alertness and activates its own internal pathway, and the two effects go on together without interference. The two effects can also take place endogenously. Suppose that subjects receive a warning stimulus. If they know that the stimulus is most likely to be followed by a high probability event, they can prepare selectively for that event. For example, Bertelson and Barzeele (1965) found that foreperiod and relative frequency interacted so that a high-probability event was more affected by foreperiod than a low-probability event. Thomas (1974) has also shown that a warning signal leads to specific preparation for a high-probability pair. These results do not lead me to change the view that alerting itself is nonselective; rather, it once again indicates the fact that several different processes accompany the manipulation of a given independent variable.

In some cases simultaneous manipulation of foreperiods and other variables such as number of alternatives (Alegria & Bertelson, 1970; Holender & Bertelson, 1975) have shown additivity between the two factors. The finding that warning interval interacts with relative frequency in some cases (e.g., Bertelson & Barzeele, 1965) and not in others (e.g., Alegria & Bertelson, 1970) suggests an important point about use of the additive factors method for determining processing stages (Sternberg, 1969). If, as I believe, both alerting and pathway activation can occur either automatically or through active attention, the existence of an interaction will probably often have more to do with the employment of attention than with processing stages. When subjects are induced to prepare quite actively during the warning interval for a given item, as in the case where there is one highly frequent alternative, one might well expect this preparation to require capacity and thus interact with foreperiod duration. When no deliberate preparation for a stimulus is involved, as well might happen when subjects are given different numbers of equally likely events, no interaction would be expected. It is not enough to determine that two independent variables interact or are additive. What we actually want to know is which of the many internal processes initiated by an event interact with other processes. This can help us understand the common mechanisms by which they operate.

The widespread nature of the internal state induced by a warning signal, the evidence that its influence is on a general central system, and the tendency for warning sometimes to interact with specific pathway processes and sometimes not—all support the view that alerting mechanisms are separate from those underlying specific pathway activation. In general, the result of our studies is further confirmation of the behavioral view that the build-up of information is unaffected by the level of alertness. It also shows that the mechanism that varies the level of alertness is independent of the mechanisms that gather information in specific automatic pathways. The selective character of pathway activation is indicated by the advantage a matching letter has over a mismatching letter following pre-exposure to the first letter (see Figure 5.5). On the other hand, a warning interval improves reaction time to matching and mismatching letters equally. The data reviewed in Figure 5.6 and Table 5.1 thus indicate that alertness (a state effect) and pathway activation make independent (additive) contributions to the improvement in reaction time.

Of course there are also physiological reasons for viewing alertness and cortical pathway effects as resting upon independent mechanisms (Groves & Thompson, 1970). For example, Gazzaniga and Hillyard (1973) have shown that the contingent negative variation induced by the presentation of a warning signal to one hemisphere of a split-brain organism spreads to the other hemisphere. Their data contrast with the information concerning the identification of the stimulus (such as a letter) that is generally not available to the opposite hemisphere in the split-brain organism. The split-brain work provides additional support for the hypothesis that phasic alertness induced by a warning signal involves a subcortical mechanism, whereas selection based upon activation of units related to identification of the stimulus involves cortical processes.

When the physiological evidence for independent mechanisms is combined with the information-processing account, the sense of independence between pathway activation and alertness is enlarged. The physiological evidence suggests a separation of mechanisms in the brain, e.g., subcortical in the case of phasic alertness versus a cortical pathway. The psychological evidence adds to that independence of function. Phasic alertness operates not in reducing the sensitivity of sensory or memory units but upon a later system, whereas pathway activation involves activation of a specific cortical pathway that improves the build-up of information.

PHASIC ALERTNESS AND SENSORY MODALITY

If subjects are required to process visual stimuli, their reaction times are reduced when an auditory accessory event, which carries no response-relevant information, is presented coincident with or even slightly after the imperative visual event (Nickerson, 1973). This phenomenon has been called *intersensory facilitation*. As can be seen from Figure 5.8, the presence of the auditory accessory signal produces a decrease in reaction time accompanied by an increase in error. The behavioral effects of the accessory make it appear likely that the auditory signal produces an automatic change in the alerting state. This change might be mediated by the same subcortical pathways as are assumed to be involved in warning signal effects. If the auditory alerting effects were not automatic, it would be difficult to understand how a signal that follows the imperative stimulus

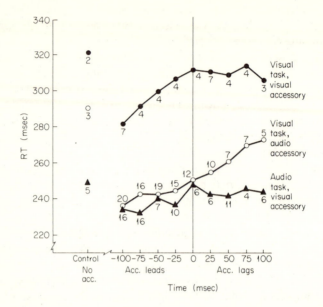

FIG. 5.8.   Performance on visual and auditory choice RT tasks when an accessory stimulus presented in close temporal proximity to the task was in the same or in a different modality. (Numerals indicate the percentage of errors.) (From Posner, Nissen, & Klein, 1976. Copyright 1976 by the American Psychological Association. Reprinted by permission.)

improves reaction time. If the auditory accessory required active attention in order to produce its alerting effects, one would expect it to interfere with rather than to facilitate the visual processing. A visual accessory that follows the imperative stimulus does not produce facilitation of auditory reaction time (see Figure 5.8); at least it is far less easy to obtain a visual accessory effect than the auditory accessory effect. The visual accessory must precede the auditory stimulus before improvements in the auditory reaction time are found. In addition, the last chapter (see p. 116) shows that a visual accessory cannot be used to improve reaction time to a dim, visual imperative signal as might be expected if it had automatic alerting effects.

Standard accounts of intersensory facilitation are of two types (Bernstein, 1970; Nickerson, 1973). One type proposes that intersensory facilitation is due to an integration of visual and auditory energies. This is in fact likely to be the case in a simple reaction time experiment where subjects are required only to detect the presence of energy. In that case, the accessory stimulus and the imperative stimulus can produce a combined effect that may allow the subject to respond to the stimulus faster than with either stimulus alone. Either an increase in the rate of build-up of energy due to the presence of stimulation to both modalities or a statistical effect where either modality may be responded to depending on which one reaches the central processing mechanisms more quickly could account for the simple reaction-time results. However, with choice reaction time, sensory integration would not provide a mechanism to produce faster responding, since the presence of the auditory accessory does not tell the subject which response to make. Here an alerting account of the effect of the accessory stimulus seems to be the one to be preferred.

Why is there asymmetry in the effects of the two sensory modalities? One usual answer supposes that auditory information reaches the central nervous system more rapidly than visual information. Thus the asymmetry in intersensory facilitation is an artifact of the different accrual times of auditory and visual signals. There may be something to this argument, but it is not the entire answer.

The reason for the unsatisfactory nature of the accrual time hypothesis is that even with long foreperiod, a strong asymmetry between visual and auditory warning signals can be shown. Consider the following experiment (Posner, Nissen, & Klein, 1976). The subject is presented with either a visual or an auditory warning signal followed after a fixed foreperiod of 150, 250, 500, or 1,000 msec by a stimulus that may be either a visual "X" appearing to the right or left of the center line or an auditory stimulus to the right or left ear. The right stimulus requires a right-hand response, and the left stimulus requires a left-hand response regardless of modality stimulated. The results of this study are shown in Figure 5.9. Note that the auditory warning signal produces strong speed–accuracy tradeoff regardless of whether the following signal is auditory or visual. The visual warning signal, however, shows a different effect. The visual warning signal produces a change in reaction time for visual stimuli but virtually no effect at all on the auditory task. This peculiar interaction cannot be due to differences in the relative strength of the visual or auditory warning signal or the visual or auditory task. A hypothesis based either on the nature of the warning signal or the nature of the task does not produce the peculiar interaction where only the combination of a visual warning signal followed by an auditory task shows no effect of alerting.

This result coupled with the results obtained from the intersensory facilitation experiment led us (Posner et al., 1976) to suppose that visual stimuli simply are less able to activate alerting mechanisms automatically than are auditory stimuli. This hypothesis helps explain a great deal of data. For one thing, it shows why it is the case that visual intensity effects are primarily pathway effects (see Chapter 4), whereas auditory intensity effects seemed to affect both pathways and alerting. The hypothesis makes a rather unusual prediction. It suggests that if subjects are focused on the auditory modality, it should be rather difficult for them to switch attention to the visual modality but that the reverse should be less of a problem.

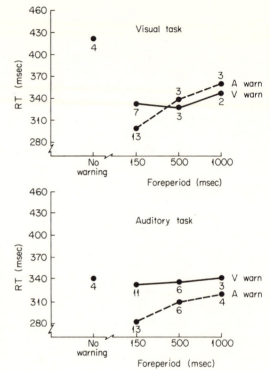

FIG. 5.9. Performance on visual (upper panel) and auditory (lower panel) choice RT tasks following auditory-, visual-, and no-warning signals. Subjects were equally likely to receive a visual or auditory task. (Numerals indicate error percentages.) (From Posner, Nissen, & Klein, 1976. Copyright 1976 by the American Psychological Association. Reprinted by permission.)

Some evidence has already been cited favoring this proposition. Posner and Summers (Note 8; see Chapter 4, p. 98) found that visual signals are affected by modality and uncertainty more than are auditory signals.

A similar result can be found when subjects are warned to attend to an auditory stimulus but on a small proportion of trials they receive an unexpected visual probe. In these circumstances they are quite slow in comparison to when their attention has been called to the visual modality and a low probability auditory probe is presented (Nissen, 1974). In an experiment on switching time, Klein (1974) informed subjects either to attend to the kinesthetic or to the visual modality. In order to assure that their attention was maintained on that modality, the largest percentage of trials was presented to that modality. On a small percentage of the trials, however, a stimulus in an unexpected modality occurred. Klein found a very strong asymmetry. When the subjects were attending to kinesthesis, it took a long time for them to respond to a visual stimulus. On the other hand, if they were attending to vision, there was little delay in their responding to a kinesthetic stimulus.

The results seem closely related to the failure of visual stimuli to produce an automatic alerting effect as do stimuli in other modalities. In the next chapter (see

p. 175) we will see that there are important consequences for attention of the tendency of stimuli in different modalities to have differential access to alerting mechanisms.

TONIC ALERTNESS

Rapid phasic changes in alertness following a warning signal have been discussed above. These can be contrasted with slower diurnal changes that occur over the course of a day. The next section concerns these changes.

Diurnal Rhythm

There is a marked change in many autonomic indicants over the course of the day (Colquhoun, 1971). A simple measure of the time course of these bodily changes is the oral temperature. There is a steady rise of temperature throughout most of the day from early morning to late evening and then a steady fall to reach a low in early morning of the next day. A number of investigators have shown some prominent changes in performance that seem to follow a similar cycle. Most indicants of the efficiency in detecting and responding to external signals show changes that mirror the rise in body temperature during the course of the day. A typical result is that shown in Figure 5.10 for speed of letter processing. Similar

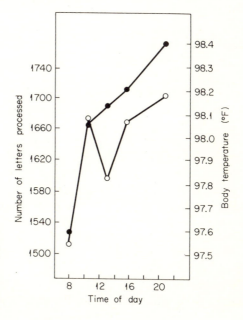

FIG. 5.10. Relationship between time of day and both body temperature (closed circles) and performance (open circles) in a letter-cancellation task. The score represents the number of letters marked in a fixed time. (From Blake, 1971. Copyright 1971 Academic Press.)

results are obtained for vigilance and detection tasks. Although there is much similarity between the temperature and performance curve, the postlunch dip in performance but not temperature serves to illustrate the multiple determination of performance changes.

It is important to emphasize that the improvement in performance over the day is restricted to tasks that emphasize a direct response to external stimulation. Figure 5.11 shows data on the memory span as a function of time of day. This task does not show improvement over the course of the day but instead declines. Whatever mechanism is postulated to improve the reception of external signals is apparently not a general potentiator of all performance. This point provides additional justification for distinguishing between alertness to external signals and other forms of arousal.

One physiological mechanism that might relate to these changes is the level of corticosteroids. There is reason to believe that the level of steroids is related to sensory detection threshold. Patients with an adrenal cortical insufficiency show greatly decreased sensory thresholds (Henkin, 1970). They are more effective in detecting sensory signals in several modalities than are normals. It has also been shown that changes in adrenal cortical steroids have effects upon peripheral and central conduction speed, although the effects are not of the type that would obviously predict the improvement in reaction time that has been observed. Data obtained following replacement therapy suggest that reduced levels of carbohydrate steroids is the main factor in the effects for patients. Of course, changes in patients with adrenal cortical insufficiency are not identical to the changes that are obtained as a function of the time of day during the diurnal cycle. However,

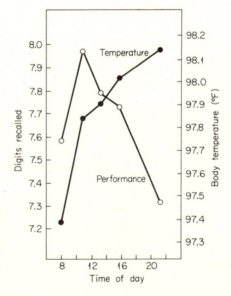

FIG. 5.11. Relation between time of day and both body temperature (closed circles) and memory-span performance (open circles). (From Blake, 1971. Copyright 1971 Academic Press.)

since normal subjects undergo a drop in adrenal cortical levels from early morning until late at night, it is not unreasonable to expect them to show some decrease in sensory threshold over the course of the day.

There has been some effort to test these notions by measuring evoked cortical potentials. Patients suffering from adrenal insufficiency show a decrease in amplitude of evoked-potential components following replacement therapy (Henkin, 1970). Some of the changes occur in components of the evoked potential that are likely to be due to primary cortex activity (Regan, 1972). Latencies and amplitudes of some evoked-potential components have been shown to change in the normal subject over the course of the day as serum steroid levels decline (Heninger, McDonald, Goff, & Sollberger, 1969). These changes are small and variable in direction, however. Efforts to abolish this diurnal variation with drugs that held serum steroid levels constant were not successful (Heninger et al., 1969).

How do tonic processing changes that take place during the diurnal cycle relate to phasic changes that follow a warning signal? Phasic changes in alertness appear to affect the efficiency with which the central processing system can interrogate the input pathways. Some evidence has suggested that the diurnal cycle might affect performance rather differently. Blake (1971) reported significant changes in d' during vigilance tasks and improvements in speed and accuracy of classification reaction time during the afternoon. However, the data were relatively sparse, and—as has been shown before—changes in d' can result from central processing systems or from pathway changes, depending upon the nature of the physical signal (p. 131).

In order to examine the relation of tonic and phasic alertness, a study was undertaken (Gostnell, 1976) in which curves of reaction time as a function of foreperiod (like those shown in Figure 5.4) were obtained during early morning and later afternoon sessions. Normal adults, retarded adults, and children were run as subjects. The phasic curves for all three groups closely resembled those illustrated in Figure 5.4. The effects of time of day were slight. In general, reaction times were faster and less accurate in the afternoon than in the morning, although the differences were very slight and only significant for the retarded adults. One tendency in the data was particularly suggestive, although not significant. It appeared that at intermediate foreperiods where phasic alertness was highest, the difference between morning and afternoon disappeared. This result suggests that subjects compensate for low tonic alertness by high phasic alertness.

Such a compensatory view would fit with the general difficulty of obtaining effects of time of day or of sleep deprivation during short task sessions at which phasic alertness might be quite high (Wilkinson, 1967). The Gostnell results contradict the notion that tonic effects produce improvement in reaction time without compensating increases in error. Instead they are consistent with the idea that phasic and tonic alerting effects operate at least in part through similar mechanisms.

Further experimentation is needed to determine in more detail the relationship between tonic and phasic alerting changes. It is still unclear to what extent they represent independent physiological mechanisms and also how their effects are combined to influence performance. Both of these questions are of particular interest, since there is some evidence that tonic alertness may shift in rhythms faster than the diurnal cycle. The most prominent such rhythm is a 60–90 minute ultraradian rhythm (Globus, 1966). It has been shown that the diurnal cycle of blood cortisol levels is actually mediated by short bouts of active secretion, which themselves show an ultraradian rhythm (Weitzman, Fukushima, Nogeire, Roffwarg, Gallagher, & Hellman, 1971). Little analysis of chronometric performance during these rhythms has been carried out, but one might well expect the same pattern of results as in the diurnal cycle. If similar mechanisms are involved in ultraradian and diurnal rhythms, the former may be much easier to investigate because of the faster changes they would involve.

Vigilance

Studies of vigilance can be divided into two general classes. First are those that use a high rate of sensory signals, and second are those that involve only a few, infrequent signals. Both of these types show clear losses in performance efficiency over time, but the mechanism(s) may be quite different (Broadbent, 1971). Studies with rapidly occurring signals show similar declines in performance with time on task, whether the subjects are actively responding to each signal or whether most signals are nontargets to which they do not respond (Mackworth, 1969). This fact makes it unlikely that a loss in performance can be described as only due to a general reduction in alertness.

There is evidence that the effective brain response to the second of two identical signals is reduced even at the level of primary cortex (Angel, 1969). All components of the vertex potential are remarkably reduced when repeated auditory stimuli occur at intervals of less than 10 sec (Davis, Osterhammel, Wier, & Gjerdingen, 1967). The extent of reduction of evoked potential is related to the similarity of the paired signals but occurs even with pairs in different modalities. This appears to be additional evidence of the reciprocal relationship between the effect of repeating a signal on pathway activation and its effect on the higher-level, central mechanisms upon which alerting acts (see p. 121). If the same signal is presented twice to an organism, one gets improved automatic pathway activation. These results have been documented by priming studies discussed in the last chapter. However, presentation of the same stimulus twice produced a reduction of the tendency of the stimulus to be effective in summoning central processing mechanisms. This shows up in reduced vertex potential and in the effect of prefamiliarization on alerting (see Figure 5.7). The reduction in the alerting effect of stimuli presented repetitively could be an important part of the vigilance decrement at fast rates of presentation. This suggests a mechanism that depends upon the specific pathway by disconnecting it from access to alerting mechanisms (Mackworth, 1969). High-event-rate vigilance tasks generally produce changes in d'. This effect suggests but does not prove that there is some genuine reduction in the efficiency of the input pathways.

Results obtained with a high event rate contrast markedly with those in low-event vigilance tasks. In this latter situation (Broadbent, 1971), changes in performance tend to affect the beta parameter (criterion). Subjects appear to show increased reluctance to respond as the task continues. They appear to be more sluggish or conservative in their performance. This performance change is accompanied by EEG and behavioral signs that are often related to drowsiness. The EEG shows frequent signs of high amplitude sleep spindles, and the evoked potential shows an enlarged, second negative component similar to that which occurs during sleep (Wilkinson, 1967). The results obtained in low-event-rate vigilance tasks appear to be central in character in that they suggest a reduction in the general availability of central processing mechanisms to all input signals because the subject is less alert. In that sense, they resemble states of low phasic alertness.

Recently, the vigilance task has been analyzed using reaction-time techniques similar to those that have been used following warning signals. In one study (Parasuraman & Davies, 1976), rare target events were mixed with nontarget events. Subjects had to report whether each event was a target or not. The latencies for correct detection of signals increased at both fast and slow event rates. However, analysis of nontarget events suggested, in agreement with previous work, that the fast event rate was reducing sensitivity (d'), whereas the slow rate produced a criterion change (beta). According to one way of looking at this result, the fast rate conditions might be slowing reaction time only to signals similar to the targets by reducing the alerting effect of these specific pathways, whereas at slow rates all signals are increased in latency due to a state change in alertness.

To test this notion, Ogden and I (Note 12) adopted a method first suggested by Pushkin (1972). We set up a visual monitoring task in which subjects were required to press a key when a particular target letter occurred. The frequency of events (letters) was either high or low, but the target rate was one event per minute on the average. Superimposed on the primary vigilance task was a task in which subjects had to detect an auditory probe stimulus that also occurred once per minute. The latencies for correct detection of the visual target letter were quite similar to those of Parasuraman and Davies and increased regularly over the 40-minute vigilance interval (see Figure 5.12). The probe detection times, however, show a clear vigilance decrement only in the case of the slow event rate.

These results argue that a major difference between fast- and slow-event-rate vigilance tasks is the degree of specificity of the habituation that has taken place. With slow event rates, the subject's performance reflects the usual pattern of low alertness. At fast rates, the subjects feel alert and indeed do fine in reporting

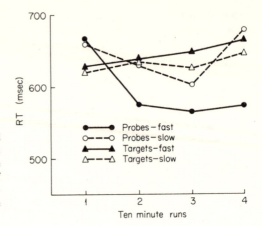

FIG. 5.12. RTs to detect visual targets and infrequent auditory probes for slow and fast event rate vigilance tasks as a function of the length of time subjects are run in the experiment. (From Posner & Ogden, Note 12).

signals other than those of the class that has undergone continual presentation. This effect is much more like those attributed to pathway inhibition in Chapter 4 (p. 117) and may reflect the tendency of repeated items of a certain class to fail to produce activation of the central processing mechanism.

LIFE CYCLE

Because alertness has widespread effects upon the latency of performance of any signal (state effect), it is frequently invoked as an explanation for the large differences in reaction time that occur when comparing studies conducted at different ages. Developmental changes in the rate of information processing are difficult to explore. Longitudinal studies require more patient experimentation than most hypotheses are worth, and cross-sectional studies always run into the difficulties of proper matching of control groups. This is particularly true in ages before and after schooling, where subjects available for experimentation may come from very different populations than those available within public schools or universities. Nonetheless, there is little doubt that reaction time undergoes a developmental change, first improving from early childhood and then undergoing a slow deterioration such that performance late in life is slowed.

Because of the ubiquitous nature of these changes in reaction time, it has often been assumed that they are due to a very general change in state that affects the processing of all signals. Rather than review the large literature on chronometric changes with age (see Botwinick, 1973), I would like to concentrate only on those paradigms closely related to the ones that I have been reviewing. To anticipate the conclusion, there is a certain degree of truth to the supposition that the level of alertness changes over the life course of the organism and also reason to suppose that the observed changes are not due to one factor alone.

Phasic Alertness

The mechanisms of phasic alertness appear to work in pretty much the same way in children and adults and the elderly. One study (Gostnell, 1976), described earlier, examined the changes in phasic alertness for normal adults, children, and retarded adults. Although the reaction times of retarded adults and children were very much longer than those of normal adults, the effects of phasic alertness upon reaction time and errors appear similar.

There are some reports (Botwinick, 1973) that elderly subjects show slower alerting (a longer optimal foreperiod) than younger subjects. However, in the main, there appears relatively little change in the development of phasic alertness over the life course of the organism. In so far as the large main effect differences between children and adults are to be accounted for by differences in tonic arousal or alertness, they would have to be independent of the phasic alerting effects.

Conservatism

One of the main features of a comparison between the elderly and young adults is the remarkable differences that favor the young in speed but the elderly in accuracy. In nearly every paradigm, young adults will operate faster but often less accurately than the elderly (Botwinick, 1973). In part, this appears to be a voluntary characteristic of behavior. Younger subjects without feedback, for example, will tend to slow down and behave somewhat more like older subjects (Hines, Note 13). With incentive—the addition of intersensory facilitation or other factors—older subjects will speed up. However, it has not been found that elderly subjects can voluntarily operate as quickly as the young subjects do. Thus it is not clear that the speed–accuracy differences in the old and young can be considered as due purely to differences in voluntary effort on their part. Indeed, slowing has also been found in various reflex activities such as the change in pupil size to light (Kumnick, 1956).

One of the striking features of the comparison of the elderly with young adults is that elderly subjects tend to do much less well as the difficulty of the task is increased. For example, the rate of memory search is increased 2-to-1 in elderly subjects over young adult controls (Anders & Fozard, 1973). Similarly, the time between physical and phonetic matches is increased about 1.6-to-1 between elderly and the young adult controls (Hines & Posner, Note 14). Finally, the slopes relating reaction time to information are also higher in the elderly subjects than in their young adult controls (Welford, 1962). In part, these differences between old and young may be somewhat of an artifact of the conservatism the older subjects display.

If older subjects are very resistant to making errors, in more difficult conditions they will probably tend to slow down relatively more in order to keep error rates at a constant level. This tendency does not always explain the differences between elderly and young adults found in experimental results. For example, Anders and Fozard (1973) showed that even with the same error rate, older subjects tended to do memory search more slowly than young subjects. Indeed the finding that rate of memory search is slowed in the elderly and the rate of retrieval of phonetic information is also slowed may suggest that elderly subjects have a specific problem with information retrieval (memory). This notion may fit with a general observation that memory processes are often more difficult for older subjects than they are for young adults (Botwinick, 1973).

In an effort to separate automatic pathway activation from active attention effects, Hines and I (Note 14) applied the priming technique and cost–benefit analysis to the study of the performance of young adults and elderly subjects. The results generally conformed both to the slowing and conservative principles that are mentioned above. The benefits due to a matching prime and the costs due to a mismatch were not significantly different between young and elderly subjects. There was a tendency for elderly subjects to show less benefit and more cost than the younger subjects, but neither of these trends was significant. Thus our effort to pinpoint in more detail the locus of effects in the elderly was not successful. Similar changes in costs and benefits with age were also found by Rabbitt (1964).

Given the problems of sampling mentioned above and the few studies that have been analytic in the attempt to locate the deficits, it appears that only the generalization that performance is slower and more accurate in the elderly seems justified at this time. These generalizations become more interesting when differences between children and adults and between retardates and normals are examined in the same way.

Developmental Performance

Both the slope of the function relating size of the positive set to reaction time and the difference between physical and phonetic matches have been compared for children and adults. The interesting result is that although reaction time is much slower in children, neither the slope with set size (Hoving, Morin, & Konick, 1970) nor the difference between physical and phonetic matches is increased (Hoving, Morin, & Konick, 1974). Indeed the difference between physical and phonetic matches remains about 100 msec from kindergarten to college. These effects are particularly interesting in light of the increase found between adulthood and old age. Nor do the children appear to show the conservatism that characterizes elderly performance. Generally children tend to be slow and less accurate than adults and show no specific problem of memory retrieval as do the elderly.

Performance over the life cycle goes through changes that might be characterized in terms of an increase in alertness from childhood to adulthood and then a decrease in old age. One factor that implicates alertness is the general nature of the slowing. When looked at in more detail, changes in alertness do not seem adequate to account for the results. Elderly subjects depart from young adults in being slower but more accurate. Moreover, they tend to show differential slowing when the task is made more complex, particularly when it involves the retrieval of phonetic or other stored information. On the other hand, children are slower and less accurate and show no differential effects with increased difficulty.

In some ways, retardates who are also quite slow seem to resemble elderly adults more than they do children. One way to view this is to suppose that the chronometric effect of brain damage (retardation and aging) is quite different than the effects of development per se. This contrasts with an idea sometimes advanced that retardates are simply developmentally younger.

Although the techniques of mental chronometry seem to be useful ones for understanding changes in nervous system activity that accompany age changes, they are fraught with great difficulty because of the problem of getting adequate control groups. At every age, individuals differ dramatically in the speed with which they respond to external stimuli. If selective effects are occurring in the samples of the different age groups studied, these could greatly damage the accuracy of a detailed chronometric analysis.

SUMMARY

Changes in phasic alertness due to the presentation of a warning signal and in low-event-rate vigilance tasks have in common a speed–accuracy tradeoff by the subjects. Subjects perform more rapidly and less accurately when in a higher state of alertness. A somewhat similar change appears to occur during tonic biological rhythms during the course of the day. While these latter changes seem less under voluntary control and might be expected to produce changes in the rate of pathway activation, there is little evidence that the effects on performance are different than those found in phasic experiments. Auditory signals appear to be able to produce changes in alertness more easily than visual signals. The common feature of alertness in all of these situations appears to involve changes in the rate at which the central processing system can interrogate sensory–memory pathways.

Vigilance tasks in which signals occur very rapidly seem to produce a reduction in the ability of a specific pathway to activate central systems. This result together with the finding that prefamiliarized signals produce more efficient pathway activation but less efficient alerting suggest once again a reciprocal relationship between the efficiency of pathway activation and activation of central systems. In any case, there must be connections from pathways in the cortex that subserve identification to the subcortical mechanisms underlying alertness.

Changes in performance over the life span can be attributed in part to state changes that relate to the level of alertness. However, the detailed differences between childhood performance and that of adults on one hand and young and elderly adults on the other seem to require more complex explanations.

6 Conscious Attention

HOMUNCULUS

A ghost haunts experimental psychology and many of our demonstrations and results. The ghost is homunculus, the little man inside. What use is a psychological theory that postulates a man in the head whose behavior must itself be explained by psychological theory? To some extent the inhibitions associated with the homunculus problem have been reduced by the existence of computers that simulate human behavior. Computer programs can execute plans that pass control from one subroutine to another. The plan that controls the various subroutines has sometimes been called an *executive routine;* its role is one often given to homunculus. The fact that such computer programs exist within purely mechanical systems gives some assurance that the overall idea of the executive routine is not foreign to scientific analysis. Attneave (1960) has suggested that homunculus might not be a fatal aspect of psychological theory. If some processes go on outside the homunculus, then at least they may be accounted for separately; and what remains for homunculus consists of a simpler problem than existed before. In some sense, one could view the task of psychological theory to reduce as far as possible the scope of activities for which homunculus need be postulated.

The effort made in Chapter 4 to outline various kinds of "automatic" processes that presumably do not require central processing mechanisms, and thus do not evoke the homunculus notion, is one effort to follow Attneave's suggestion.

The main reason that I feel justified in discussing homunculus in the form of central processing systems is that the goal of these lectures is not so much to use homunculus to explain behavior as to discuss the constraints upon homunculus. The goal is to locate the homunculus both within the temporal stream of information processing and as a brain system. Even if we are as yet unable to understand the operation of homunculus, we still might be able to deal with such questions.

The basically introspective terms "detection," "recognition," and "identification" are used to indicate aspects of our awareness of a signal. Detection refers to being aware of an energy change. Recognition implies a feeling of familiarity based upon the contact of the input event with some form of stored information. Identification usually involves our awareness of a relevant category to which the stimulus belongs. Although the terms involve awareness of different aspects of the process of pathway activation, they all imply an interaction between the stimulus and the central processing system. Since this chapter's theme is the common system that underlies the experience of detection, recognition, and identification, the terms will not be differentiated in what follows.

When a subject detects a stimulus in a way that would be called effortful or conscious, there are clear behavioral and physiological changes. Both information processing and physiological studies can be used to trace the time course of entry of a signal into this system.[1] Such tracings have the virtue of linking the processor chronometrically to the sequence of input and allow us to investigate the consequences of a signal's involvement with the mechanisms that subserve active attention. There is little doubt that this approach is limited in what it can tell us about the nature of consciousness. Nonetheless, it seems possible to answer a number of interesting questions. This chapter seeks to examine evidence that the central processor can be viewed as an isolable system[2] related both to specific, physiological indicants and to the ability to provide introspective reports of the type so commonly used in psychological research (see Chapter 1).

The next section will deal with purely behavioral techniques that serve to separate pathway activation from active attention. A variety of dual tasks and probe techniques are reviewed. The third section examines a number of psychophysiological indicants of active attention such as changes in evoked potentials, pupil size, etc. These methods have the long-term potential to deal both with the temporal location of conscious attention within the stream of information processing and with the physical location of attentive mechanisms

---

[1]The assumption is that psychological processes take place in real time. The assumption is supported by the experiments outlined in Chapters 2, 3, and 4. It is true that experiments based upon subjective reports may not show isomorphism between real time and psychological processes. For example, subjects ascribe apparent motion to events that take place following the first of two events when in fact they clearly occur as a result of the presentation of the second event. Subjective reports cannot be relied upon as providing the order of occurrence of psychological processes, because the systems that underlie our awareness are not at a fixed point in the activation of psychological pathways as is pointed out in this chapter.

[2]The claim for isolability of the central processor means that the experimenter can manipulate its time course (e.g., by use of a warning signal) independently of the time for the activation of psychological pathways (see Chapter 4).

within the brain. The fourth section examines the relation between this central processing system and subjective reports. Situations in which one code of a given signal dominates over other codes of the same signal show that powerful, subjective consequences can be related to the relative speeds at which codes enter the central system. The final section examines possible roles of the mechanisms that subserve consciousness. Taken as a whole, the chapter attempts to relate attention as a unified, central system to the operations of pathway activation already discussed.

LIMITED CAPACITY

The key to understanding the nature of conscious attention is its limited capacity. The relatively parallel systems of information processing that allow simultaneous coding of physical, phonetic, and semantic codes of words have been examined. In contrast to these automatic systems, on occasion we have encountered the remarkably limited capacity of the subject's conscious attention to items. Limited capacity is meant to suggest a system that is so richly interacting that its efficient utilization for the processing of a signal or code will usually reduce the efficiency with which it can process any other signal or code. This corresponds both to the findings of reduced performance that accompany dual tasks and to the narrow range of current conscious experience to which William James referred. In Chapters 2 and 3 it was shown that when a subject's attention is diverted to the phonetic code of a letter or word, information about the physical code of that same item becomes less available within 1 or 2 sec. Although subjects show clear evidence of being able to generate visual images, they do not do so with more than one or two items, when time is short, or when external visual stimuli are present. When items are presented successively and subjects have chosen one code on which to concentrate, matching is done entirely on that code as though the other code were no longer available. In Chapter 4, the cost–benefit analysis led to a contrast between the parallel operations of the habitual pathways and the limited capacity effects when subjects choose to attend to an item. All theories of attention seem to focus upon the relatively limited capacity of the systems that underlie attention (Broadbent, 1971; Kahneman, 1973; Treisman, 1969).

The priming studies outlined in Chapter 4 provide one means of studying the commitment of this central processing system to an input pathway. The method depends upon a task in which a prime may be either ignored by the subjects or used by them actively to plan for other items. Thus the method may place more emphasis on the operation of planning for the array than upon a system involved generally in all conscious mental operations. As a symptom of this problem, the priming approach outlined in Chapter 4 was frequently confounded with a particular strategy on the part of the subject to match the prime against the array. It would be useful to have a more general method for examination of task interference than the priming method.

Dual Tasks

There is a long history of examining limited capacity mechanisms through interference between tasks. Two signals that occupy the same limited capacity system might be expected to interfere with one another. This idea was first proposed by the biologist Loeb (cited in Welch, 1898) and was exposed to empirical test by his student, Jeannette Welch, in the very first issue of the *American Journal of Physiology*. She introduced the idea of a coefficient of attention. The idea was that attending to any difficult task would produce interference with other tasks. If one used a standard secondary task, it would be possible to use the degree of interference with the standard task as a measure of attention demands of the primary task. She chose maximal hand grip as the standard task and examined the interference obtained from such other tasks as reading and calculation. This idea of examining the attention to one task by its effect on other tasks has been used in many psychological literatures. The psychological refractory period (Bertelson, 1967), the dual-task technique (Brown, 1962), expended processing capacity (Johnston, Wagstaff, & Griffith, 1972), and the probe technique (Posner & Boies, 1971) are but four descriptions of the same, general idea. The secondary task can be either continuous, as in tracking, or discrete, as in a reaction-time task. It can be either confined to the period of time following the primary task item (psychological refractory period studies), or it may occur sometimes prior to the introduction of the primary task (probe technique). Finally, the secondary task might require an overt response, or it might require merely a detection and later report.

My reading of these literatures suggests that none of these factors makes a great deal of difference and that regardless of the method one uses to examine the relation between primary and secondary tasks, the results are similar. What does matter is whether the experimenter measures those aspects of the primary and secondary task that are likely to require the central processor. Bear in mind that much of the habitual activation that a signal produces occurs regardless of whether the subject attends or not. Thus one would not expect that the encoding of an item when the subject has little incentive to attend would produce interference. When one examines aspects of tasks that use the central processor, there is evidence for interference and clear indications that dual-task techniques of nearly every variety work in much the same way.

There have been many objections to the use of dual tasks as a measure of attention; some of them clearly are justified and others more problematic. One objection is that a primary task will not interfere with a secondary task unless their joint difficulty exceeds the capacity of the system (Norman & Bobrow, 1975). This is the kind of point that appears justified in principle yet unwarranted in practice. Even the simplest of secondary tasks will show a surprising amount of interference with quite simple primary task processing. Moreover, increasing task difficulty does not necessarily increase the amount of interference (see p. 165). Another objection is that subjects may set up deliberate expectancies that might affect the interference obtained. This objection is well taken, but it is possible to guard against it by varying the percentage of the trials on which probes occur and changing their distribution. In what follows, I will try to confine the argument to studies that have attempted to do this. It is often argued that the response requirements of the secondary task rather than its internal processing are what produce interference. Though this point is important, in what follows it is often possible to show that response processes alone cannot account for probe performance. Kahneman (1973) suggests that it is better to confine arguments to points that have been explored by more than one dual-task method. I have also tried to observe this caution in what follows. This will become more clear as the literature below is examined.

Probes in Matching

The letter-matching sequence has been used in earlier chapters to examine the development of processing codes. To be concrete, consider an experiment in which the subject is required to process visual letters. The processing is divided into stages as follows:

1. The subject receives a warning signal.
2. A single letter is presented .5 sec later.
3. A second letter that may or may not match the first occurs 1 sec later.
4. The subject's response indicates whether the two letters are the same or not.

According to the views that we have outlined previously, the warning signal allows a generalized change in alertness, such as discussed in Chapter 5. The first letter activates pathways corresponding to its physical, phonetic, and semantic codes. Only when the second letter occurs are the subjects allowed to choose a response, because only then can they determine whether the second letter is the same as or different from the first.

On some trials an auditory probe stimulus is presented at varying points in the sequence. In the experiment illustrated in Figure 6.1 (Posner & Boies, 1971) the probe stimulus is a low-intensity, short-duration, white-noise burst to which the subject must respond by tapping a key. The figure displays reaction time to the noise burst as a function of its position in the primary task.

During the warning phase, response time to the probe tends to improve slightly, presumably due to a general increase in alertness. This agrees with a nonselective view of alertness that I outlined in Chapter 5.[3]

The reaction time to the relevant probe stimulus continues to improve for some period of time after the presentation of the first letter. In this particular experiment, that turns out to be between .3 and .5 sec following the first letter. At that time the reaction time to the probe stimulus begins to increase dramatically.

---

[3]A problem with this account is that the visual warning signal should produce a strong visual bias (see p. 175), but in this study RT improvement to the auditory probe is still present.

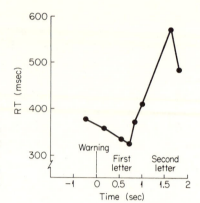

FIG. 6.1. Probe RTs to a white-noise burst during a letter-matching task. (From Posner & Boies, 1971. Copyright 1971 by the American Psychological Association. Reprinted by permission.)

This increase in reaction time to the probe occurs well before the second letter is presented. It is not due to the actual presentation of the second letter; because even when all probe responses that actually occur after the second letter are eliminated, the interference in reaction time is still obtained. After the response selection phase, the reaction time to the irrelevant probe improves until it comes down to approximately the same baseline as would be obtained if it were presented prior to the warning signal.

Dual-task techniques almost always show interference between a primary task to which a rapid response is needed and a secondary task such as is used here. To illustrate this point, consider the effect on the probe once the second letter is presented. These results are shown in an expanded way in Figure 6.2, which shows reaction time to a white-noise probe in a simultaneous letter-matching experiment (both letters presented simultaneously following a warning

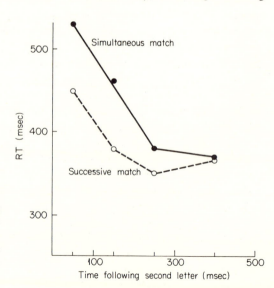

FIG. 6.2. Probe RTs following both letters in a simultaneous matching task or the second letter in a successive matching task. The results show how task difficulty affects probe times.

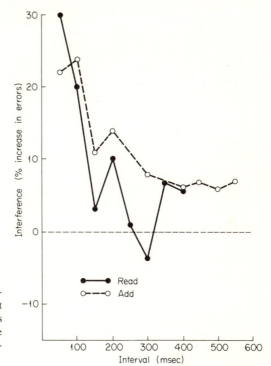

FIG. 6.3. Interference with detection of a Landolt C following a digit that a subject either must name as quickly as possible or to which the subject adds 1, naming the sum (dotted line). (From Ninio, 1974.)

signal) and in a successive letter-matching experiment of the type that we have described above. Compare this figure with Figure 6.3 (Ninio, 1974). In Ninio's experiment a single digit is presented at time 0. The subject is required to read it aloud or to add 1 to it and pronounce the sum. Figure 6.3 shows the increase in percent errors to detect a figure that is presented at varying times following the item that is to be read or transformed. The interference with reaction time in the probe technique and the interference with the detection task as measured by percent errors are quite similar. In both cases, interference is greater, the more difficult the primary task, either because the primary task lasts longer or because it requires more processing capacity during the time that it lasts. In both experiments probe performance is poorest when the probe stimulus occurs immediately after the critical event and improves as the time increases to about 300 msec following the primary task event.

As far as I know, no experiments using probe techniques have failed to find a result similar to those shown in Figures 6.2 and 6.3.[4] Indeed, these two experi-

---

[4]One possible exception to this finding is an experiment by McLeod (in press). He found the usual effect when a manual response to the secondary probe task was used but little or no interference when a vocal response was needed. The vocal probe response did appear to show interference at positions prior to the presentation of the second letter.

ments are extreme ones in the sense that in one the probe is a reaction-time task and in the other a detection task that requires no immediate response to the probe. Yet the results are nearly identical.

One point that has been considered surprising by some people is the fact that interference with the probe is most severe close to time 0. If the primary task stimulus has to go through an encoding phase that is automatic or nonattentive, why shouldn't there be a very low level of interference with the probe when it occurs during this automatic encoding phase? The reason should be clear from the theoretical position presented in Chapter 4. If the subject is required to shift attention as rapidly as possible to the primary item in order to respond to it, there is no evidence of a dead time or automatic activation time because attention is there right from the beginning of the task.

The Relation Between Pathway Activation and Interference

Next we examine probe effects that follow the first letter in a successive match-ing experiment. Before doing so, it is first necessary to examine again the nature of pathway activation functions. Several times previously in these lectures I have had occasion to refer to such functions. In Chapter 4 the nature of activation of physical, phonetic, and semantic codes of items was studied using a cue item to which the subject might or might not attend. The focus was on the relationship between the activation of a pathway and the subject's conscious attention to that activation. Chapter 5 showed that for letters, such pathway activation could be time shared with alerting without interference. It remains to examine the time course of such encoding functions.

To do so, subjects were presented with a single letter that remained present in the visual field until joined by a second letter after varying intervals (Posner & Boies, 1971). In this experiment, the time between the onset of the first and second letter is always fixed for a given block of trials, so the subject is not surprised at the occurrence of the second letter. Moreover, a warning signal is presented 500 msec before the first letter to provide a high level of alerting. The results of experiments in which physical, name, and vowel–consonant matching were used are shown in Figure 6.4. In all cases the reaction time to the first letter is longest when the two letters are presented simultaneously and declines sys-tematically until a minimum is reached at around 500 msec. Note that the encod-ing function does not seem to vary with the level of match required of the subject. This was a surprising result. I had hoped that the time necessary to reach the optimal level of encoding would vary as a function of the kind of code necessary in the matching process. Instead, it was found that the time to reach an optimal performance level was relatively uninfluenced by the codes involved. Figure 6.5 shows a number of encoding functions for words (Sabol & DeRosa, 1976) in which the task was matching of antonyms, synonyms, and unrelated pairs. These functions are generally similar to those obtained with single letters. Similarly,

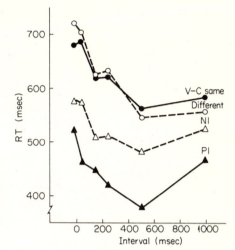

FIG. 6.4. Encoding functions for physical (PI), name (NI), and vowel–consonant (VC) matches and different responses. (From Posner & Boies, 1971. Copyright 1971 by the American Psychological Association. Reprinted by permission.)

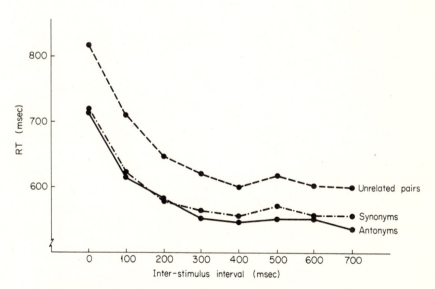

FIG. 6.5. RT as a function of interstimulus interval for antonyms (solid line), synonyms (dashed-dotted line), and unrelated pairs (dashed line). (From Sabol & DeRosa, 1976. Copyright 1976 by the American Psychological Association. Reprinted by permission.)

159

Sternberg, Knoll, and Leuin (Note 15) have examined encoding functions during memory-search tasks. Encoding functions for the intercept changes in this experiment are also similar (see Figure 6.6).

Encoding functions can be influenced to some degree by the warning interval given prior to the stimulus (Thomas, 1974). Figure 6.7 indicates an encoding function for physical matching obtained by Thomas when the warning interval prior to the presentation of the first letter was either 250, 500, or 700 msec. Note that the exact form of the function differs, depending on the prior warning interval; however, given this small difference, the major results obtained by Thomas are similar to those obtained for other encoding functions.

Thus the literature seems quite clear that following a single visual item, the most efficient response will occur with time delays between the occurrence of that item and the test of .2 to .6 sec. This change in reaction time with interval I have called an *encoding function*. Encoding functions seem relatively impervious to the type of task given the subject. It is my belief that encoding reflects the course of automatic pathway activation (see Chapter 4). Thus the presence of encoding would not by necessity produce any interference with a secondary task.

In successive matching, when a 1-sec interval is placed between the first and second letter, probe interference does not begin until .5 sec following the first letter (see Figure 6.1). How should that result be interpreted? One interpretation is that the subject simply does not process the first letter until relatively late in the interval between the first and second letters. Another view is that the encoding goes on in a normal way, even though the subject does not attend to the first letter. Thus, one should find a normal encoding function during the time when the subject shows no probe interference.

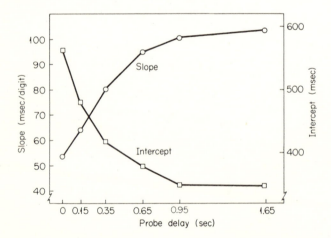

FIG. 6.6. Encoding functions for slope and intercepts in a matching task following an array of varying size. (From Sternberg, Knoll, & Leuin, Note 15. Reproduced by permission of the authors.)

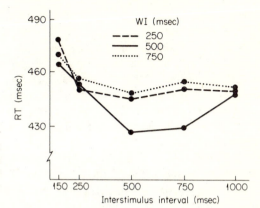

FIG. 6.7. Encoding functions for letter matching following different warning intervals (WI). (From Thomas, 1974. Copyright 1974 by the American Psychological Association. Reprinted by permission.)

The following experiment (Posner & Klein, 1973) examined this question. Subjects were given a successive matching task with Gibson figures. On half of the trials a 1,000-msec interval was used between the two Gibson figures, and auditory probe stimuli were presented on these trials. The probe stimulus occurred at one of the eight positions indicated in Figure 6.8. On the other half of the trials, the time between the first Gibson figure and the second was varied such that subjects had either 50, 150, 250, or 500 msec of pre-exposure to the first

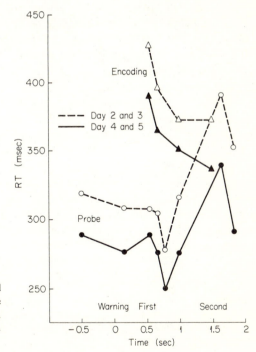

FIG. 6.8. Encoding functions and probe interference during successive matching of Gibson form stimuli. (From Posner & Klein, 1973. Copyright 1973 Academic Press.)

Gibson figure before the arrival of the second. The results in terms of an encoding function and probe interference effects are shown in Figure 6.8. It seems clear that the encoding function is normal, and yet no probe interference effect occurs until after encoding is nearly over. These results are quite consistent with an automatic pathway activation notion that does not require attention, together with the assumption that commitment of a limited capacity system produces probe interference effects.[5]

It might be thought that a fixed time is needed for the limited capacity mechanism to be contacted by input. Indeed in the experiments using the cost–benefit analysis, it was found that the exposure duration of the prime did not influence the onset of the cost function. Thus if only that technique were used, one might conclude that it takes at least 300 msec after an event for the limited capacity mechanism to be committed in such a way as to produce cost.

The probe technique, however, has consistently shown a great deal more flexibility than this in the time for interference to occur. Consider experiments in which the time between the first letter and the second letter is systematically varied. The subject receives the first letter followed by a second letter after .5 sec, 1 sec, or 2 sec. Figure 6.9 indicates the extent of interference of the probe as a function of the interval between letters. In the solid curve, the second letter follows the first letter by .5 sec, in the dashed curve by 1 sec, and in the dashed-dotted curve by 2 sec. The probe interference effect increases both in magnitude and decreases in latency as the time between the first and second letter is reduced. Note that when the time between the two letters is 2 sec, one does not begin to get a probe interference effect until about 1.5 sec following the first letter.

The results show clearly that the start of central processing is a function of the subject's knowledge about the time between the two letters. In no case is the actual occurrence of the second letter necessary for interference, because the few reaction times that occur after the second letter can be ignored and the interference effects remain. These results indicate that probe interference is clearly a function not only of a stimulus event, but also of endogenous plans about when the subject needs to attend to the letter in order to carry out the task to be performed when the second letter appears.

Nor should it be concluded that the first letter has no influence on these plans. In another systematic set of experiments, the time between the first and second letter is kept constant at 1 sec, and the exposure duration of the first letter is varied. The solid and dashed lines in Figure 6.10 (Posner & Klein, 1973) are for first letter exposure duration of either 50 or 500 msec. The dashed-dotted line (Comstock, 1973) is from a study in which the first letter was exposed for only

---

[5]There is some evidence that encoding produces interference with a visual probe task (Shwartz, 1976). This result seems to arise when a visual probe is presented very close to the onset of a visual item. Such results may be due more to a local sensory interaction rather than to the operations of the central processor.

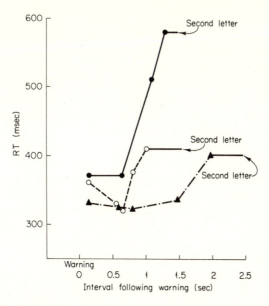

FIG. 6.9. Probe RT as a function of the time from onset of trial warning. Solid line is for .5 sec ISI, dashed line for 1 sec ISI, and dashed-dotted line for 2 sec ISI. The time of presentation of the second letter is marked by an arrow.

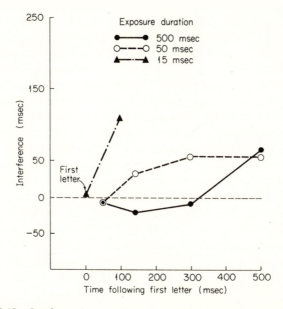

FIG. 6.10. Interference in probe RT as a function of time after first letter and exposure duration of the first letter when the time between letters (ISI) is fixed at 1 sec. Dashed-dotted line is for 15-msec exposure (Comstock, 1973), dashed line for 50 msec (Posner & Klein, 1973), and solid line for 500 msec (Posner & Klein, 1973).

15 msec. With the time between the first and second letter held constant, the exposure duration of the first letter influences the start and the magnitude of the probe interference effect. As that exposure duration is reduced, the magnitude of the probe interference effect increases, and its latency decreases. I interpret this as an indication that when the first letter is turned off, subjects tend to turn their attention to that letter in order to preserve it. If they have a good time cue, it is possible for the attention to be allocated when the first letter is presented and thus for probe interference effects to be observed immediately, just as they are following the second letter (as shown in Figure 6.1). These results indicate that the commitment of the central processor is not forced by an external event but can be influenced by a variety of experimental manipulations that induce the subject to turn attention to the input.

Problems

Several difficult problems in this field remain unexplained by the results that we have observed. First it is difficult to know why the probe technique produces such clear evidence of flexibility of programming of attention, whereas the cost–benefit analysis, regardless of the exposure duration of the cue, produces cost at about 300 msec. Two reasons for this discrepancy present themselves. One might be that the cost–benefit technique depends upon the subject developing a particular hypothesis or expectancy about the second letter. Perhaps this expectancy cannot develop sooner than about 300 msec. The interference that I call cost would then not occur until the hypothesis is developed. A second possibility is that the structure of the prime method does not require that the subjects use the cue stimulus. The task can be done even if the cue stimulus is completely ignored. This might produce a tendency not to turn attention to the cue even when it is removed. McLean (1977) has provided strong evidence that the first hypothesis is the correct one. He compared directly cost and probe interference following a priming stimulus in a letter-matching experiment. His result (see Figure 6.11) showed that cost increased over the 500-msec interval when the prime was present, whereas probe interference was large immediately following the prime and then declined. Since probe interference was present, it seems clear that subjects were actively attending the prime. This result suggests that one may be able to measure both the presence of attention (probe interference) and the hypothesis produced by attention (cost) and that the two are not identical. An ability to measure these two aspects of attention to the prime could result in a large improvement in our ability to examine fine attentional effects that accrue over time.

A second unsolved issue is what it is about the processing of the first letter that produces interference with the probe. It seems clear that the interference is obtained only when subjects are required to process the primary task as quickly as possible, as when they are forced to make an overt response to it. Thus the conclusion that probe interference effects are often related to motor processes is

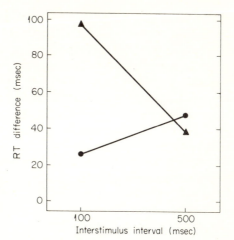

FIG. 6.11.   Time course of cost in letter matching (lower line) and interference with a secondary auditory probe (upper line) as a function of time between the priming stimulus and the two array letters used for matching. (From McLean, 1977.)

true (Keele, 1973). However, the results obtained from the offset of the first letter and the fact that probe interference occurs with reaction time probes and with detection probes in about the same way, suggest that a motor theory would not be completely adequate. All that appears necessary is that the primary and secondary tasks individually require close attention and be time locked. If those things are done, probe interference is found. Thus I feel that no specific mental operation is necessary to produce probe interference. All that is necessary is that the subject be induced to commit conscious attention. This can take the form of an overt response, remembering, transforming, hypothesis formation, or nearly any other mental operation (see Kerr, 1973, for a review).

A third problem with the results outlined above arises when the secondary task is systematically varied in difficulty. This technique was first introduced by Karlin and Kestenbaum (1968) and exploited theoretically by Keele (1973). It has also been employed by Becker (1976), who used it to examine the attention demands of a lexical decision task. In all cases, it has been used following the presentation of an imperative signal. This means that one would expect interference based on the probe results. This technique involves a subtraction of the extent of interference when the probe is of low difficulty from when it is of high difficulty. Comparisons of low- and high-difficulty probes during letter matches have given additivity (Comstock, 1973).[6] Karlin and Kestenbaum found a decrease in the amount of interference by the primary task when the secondary task was made more difficult. Keele used this to argue that some aspects of the secondary task could be carried on at the same time as the primary task was being performed. Becker found a divergence such that there was less overlap between the primary and secondary tasks as the secondary task was made more difficult.

---

[6]There is also some conflict on this issue, because Shwartz (1976) showed quite different functions for simple and choice RT probes, whereas Comstock (1973) showed the same function even though choice RT was longer.

The literature indicates additivity, convergence, and divergence in different situations. The only common result is that all agree that there is some interference with the secondary task.

The secondary task technique can be extended to examine questions about the relative processing capacity involved in different tasks. For example, it has been shown that storage, active rehearsal, and output stages of memory task produce interference with a probe signal (Kerr, 1973). It has also been shown quite clearly (Ells, 1973) that motor responses produce interference with probe signals to the extent that they require active monitoring or correction. It is not the movement itself that produces probe interference but the initiation of the movement and the corrections close to the end point. Surprisingly, probe interference effects have not been shown to be sensitive to modality-specific processes. For example, Griffith and Johnston (1973) compared visual and auditory probes during memory tasks in which the subjects were or were not encouraged to use visual imagery. Though the visual imagery had a clear effect on the ability of the subjects to memorize, it did not differentially affect auditory and visual probes.

Summary

These experiments have shown some techniques that psychologists have available for examining the role of active attention in the processing of information. It is easy to show both that some aspects of information processing can go on outside of attention (i.e., no probe interference effects are obtained) and that other aspects require a large amount of attention. Attentional effects appear to be due to the utilization of a system that can be linked to experimental events such as the time between the first and second letter, exposure duration of the first letter, and requirements for transformation imposed by the experimenter. The most likely way of explaining these facts is to suppose that the subject has a great deal of control over when the attentional system enters the stream of information. The development of methods to study the entry of this mechanism into the stream of information processing may allow further understanding of the brain mechanisms that underlie it. The mechanism involved seems to be relatively independent of the sensory information that is presented, has flexible time locking to input stimulation,[7] is heavily under the control of the experimental conditions, is necessary in order to generate a response, and is selective in terms of the cues that are processed.

---

[7]The view that attentional systems are flexibly time locked to input is not a contradiction of the assumption that psychological processes take place in real time. The activation of codes is assumed to be governed primarily by past learning and input. The control of attention is thought to depend in part upon endogenous processes. Thus input does not control the allocation of attention in the same tight sense that it controls code activation. Nonetheless, the operations of attention will be shown to take place in real time, even though they involve endogenous control and are thus not so tightly dependent upon input. It is this property of endogenous control of attention that may lead to the feeling that psychological time and real time are not isomorphic.

BRAIN PROCESSES AND LIMITED CAPACITY

Association Potentials (P300)

The presentation of a stimulus event produces a variety of time-locked electrical changes that can be amplified, recorded, averaged, and analyzed in the evoked response. Many recent publications have attempted to summarize the result of information-processing studies using the average evoked response as a dependent variable (Regan, 1972). Several components of the evoked response seem to occur in much the same way, regardless of the direction of the subject's attention. In a variety of paradigms that require the subject to detect dim signals, to respond as quickly as possible to the occurrence of events, or to monitor events for the occurrence of some particular target, one finds a positive wave at about 300 msec following the input (P300 or association cortex potential; Donchin & Lindsley, 1969; Hillyard & Picton, in press). This component is of particular interest at this point in our inquiry, because it has many of the characteristics we have been ascribing to systems that produce probe interference. For example, it does not depend upon the sensory modality of input. Indeed, the P300 component can be obtained when, after a repetitive series of stimuli, one event is omitted. The P300 component following an omission resembles the component following an auditory or visual event. Thus the P300 component seems little influenced by input modality, suggesting that it is something developed endogenously rather than being controlled by the specifics of the input.

Hillyard and Picton (in press) indicate that the P300 component occurs:

1. when the stimulus is a cue for a simple, disjunctive, or discriminative reaction-time task;
2. when the cue is a feedback informing the subjects whether their previous guesses or judgments were correct or incorrect;
3. when pairs of cues are to be matched or compared with one another;
4. when subjects are to detect dim or infrequent stimuli particularly near threshold.

In addition to being independent of sensory modality, the P300 component seems flexible in the time of its occurrence. Although the name seems to indicate a strong time-locking to the stimulus event, in fact the P300 component or something like it appears to occur as early as 150–200 msec after input and as late as 500–600 msec after input. Moreover, if no overt response to the stimulus is required, the P300 appears larger when following a novel stimulus than when it follows a highly familiar or overlearned stimulus. This constellation of results has led a number of investigators to suppose that the P300 is closely related to the conscious detection of a signal and/or its sustained information processing once detected.

Hillyard and Picton (in press) have emphasized detection because of their finding of strong P300s in the signal detection paradigm. The P300 is often closely related in time to the act of responding and indeed often follows the motor act itself. It does not seem to depend on an actual response. Indeed the component is somteimes reduced when the subject must respond overtly in comparison to making no overt response. Donchin, Kubovy, Kutas, Johnson, and Herning (1973) found that when subjects were forced to make a motor response to each signal, the P300 was equally large regardless of the predictability of the signal. However, when no motor response was required, the P300 was greater for unpredictable trials. A trial–by–trial analysis of overt key responses found that P300 appeared to be elaborated in parallel with some elements of the P300 preceding the motor response but most of them following it (Ritter, Simpson, & Vaughan, 1972).

The results of studies using P300 as a brain sign reveal that a large number of antecedent conditions will produce it. Moreover, these appear to vary depending upon the task set for the subject. In detection studies, the complex occurs when the subject detects an expected signal, whereas in reaction-time studies it occurs more often to an unexpected or novel event. It seems fair to say that P300 occurs whenever a signal or time interval can reasonably be said to demand close attention in a particular task and when that attention is carefully time locked. This suggests that P300 is the result of the selection of a signal rather than a sign of some particular antecedent condition that invariably leads to its selection.

The P300 sign adds little to our knowledge about the causes of selection. This view might best be interpreted as supporting Goff's (1969) position that P300 should be thought of as being related to our conscious awareness of a stimulus, or Donchin et al.'s suggestion that P300 reflects the activity of a generalized cortical computer.

These statements are rather vacuous taken by themselves. They have meaning only if it is possible to specify some properties of the brain system that appear to be signified by the P300. In other words, it might be a useful strategy to leave aside the effort to specify the stimulus conditions that will produce P300, just as I have not attempted to say what it is exactly about a stimulus event that will cause probe delay or cost. For if the P300 indexes anything like conscious effort, there would have to be a great deal of flexibility in the conditions that will produce it. Rather, one might try instead to see if the existence of the P300 corresponds at all to the development of the limited capacity inhibitory functions that have been related to the central processing mechanism.

Chronometric Studies of P300

To understand the temporal relationship between input and processing as indexed by P300, we can return to the letter-matching task described previously. In this case, the first letter was followed after 1 sec by a letter that either matches it or

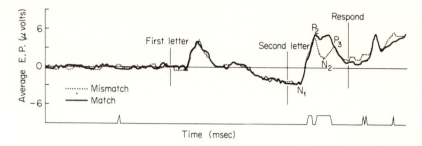

FIG. 6.12. Averaged evoked potential for match and mismatch for 3,072 msec from start of trial through response. Excursions on the x-axis represent significant differences between conditions. The interval between letters is 1,000 msec. (From Posner, Klein, Summers, & Buggie, 1973. Copyright 1973 by the Psychonomic Society.)

not. Response to the second letter is delayed until a signal is presented at .5 sec following the second letter. The subject presses one key for matches and one key for mismatches. The major interest is in the vertex evoked potential to the second item as a function of whether the letter pair matches or not. Our behavioral analysis suggests that the processing of the second letter will be speeded when it matches the first. In this paradigm, the speeding may occur either from automatic pathway activation, conscious attention, or a combination of the two, since they are not separated. Data from vertex electrodes (Posner, Klein, Summers, & Buggie, 1973) indicate that the matching pair differs from the mismatch starting about 160 msec after the second letter (see Figure 6.12). Since matches and mismatches are randomized, there is no possibility that this difference can be due to any difference in prestimulus alert states such as would be shown in the CNV. Moreover, the evidence clearly seems to indicate that the CNV remains negative until after the signal to respond, at which time it is released and superimposed upon an eyeblink artifact that occurs after the signal to respond (see Figure 6.12). The CNV that occurs in this paradigm is weak, because no speeded response is required to the second signal.

The difference between matching pairs and mismatching pairs might well be summarized by suggesting that the late positive wave, P300, that represents the second hump in the response to mismatches occurs faster for the matched pair so that it is superimposed upon the earlier positive wave. If this was the case and if attention affects the amplitude of the late positive wave—as has been suggested by the literature reviewed above—it should follow that when the two stimuli match, the effect of an instruction to attend will influence the evoked potential earlier than when the stimuli do not match. The results of such an experiment are illustrated in Figure 6.13. When subjects are instructed to count matching stimuli (upper panel), the evoked potential size is increased starting at 200 msec after the

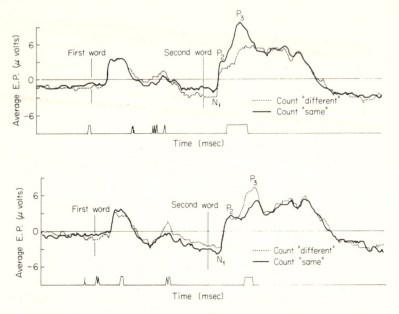

FIG. 6.13.   Upper panel shows average evoked potential for matches when instructed to count "sames" or "differents." Lower panel shows average evoked
potential for mismatches when instructed to count "sames" or "differents."
Excursions on the x-axis of each panel represent significant differences between
conditions. The interval between words is 1,000 msec. (From Posner et al., 1973.
Copyright 1973 by the Psychonomic Society.)

second letter; if they are instructed to count mismatching stimuli (lower panel),
the increase in evoked potential does not occur until after 300 msec.

The method used to examine the evoked potentials in Figures 6.12 and 6.13
was adapted from Wood (1975). It is a chronometric method in the sense that two
conditions are compared, and the departure between these two conditions is used
to define the time at which some influence begins to occur in the evoked potential. This method does not assume that any particular change in the evoked
potential is required by a simple, psychological manipulation. Rather it allows us
to observe the influence of a manipulation that is known to affect behavior upon
the brain's electrical response. Since it is well known that brain responses might
either increase in amplitude with attention (as appears to occur with the P300 in
this experiment) or decrease in amplitude (as happens to EEG background activity following a warning signal), it is difficult to predict a priori which sort of
effect to expect in the brain response to a given manipulation. However, the
chronometric method discussed above does not depend upon assuming either the
direction of an effect or that each wave of the evoked potential is a separate
process. Instead it provides an empirical method of determining how psychologi-

cally relevant manipulations affect brain responses. One advantage of being able to determine the influence of psychological manipulations upon the brain's response is that it may allow us to observe earlier effects than are present in behavior.

In Figures 6.12 and 6.13 the effects of attention appear to occur as early as 150 msec following input. Of course, one would not expect such an early effect in all studies, because behavioral experiments show quite clearly the flexible nature of the time locking of attention to input. The time at which attention has its effect depends upon how the subject uses the information given. One should expect similar discrepancies in the time when an attentional manipulation will begin to affect the evoked potential. In fact, an analysis of the evoked-potential literature appears to confirm this idea.

There is much evidence that the influence of attention is often earlier than 300 msec following input. For example, Sutton, Braren, and Zubin (1965) found that although the late positive wave was the main one to be affected by stimulus uncertainty, a number of earlier components were also affected. In fact, components as early as 100 msec following the stimulus seem to show some effect. However, the effects in their study might be due to differences in preparation prior to the stimulus. The early effect of attention is apparent in an experiment that required subjects to determine which of two letters was later in the alphabet or which of two digits was larger (Chapman, 1973). The subject never knew whether the pair of items would be letters or digits, thus eliminating any possibility of differential preparation prior to the stimulus. In some conditions subjects were required to ignore the letters and classify digits, and in other conditions the reverse. Chapman found that there was an enhancement of the vertex evoked potential as early as 105 msec after input for relevant over irrelevant material.

An additional advantage of the chronometric approach to linking information-processing studies to those using evoked potentials is that the latter can be examined with nonhuman subjects.

Animal studies also suggest that attention can have its influence upon evoked potential much earlier than 300 msec after input. Rudell and Fox (1972) have shown that cats can be conditioned to modify aspects of their evoked potential. The first studies involved modification of components of the evoked potential 180 msec after input; but later they showed a change in evoked-potential components as early as 50 msec after input. Unfortunately, one cannot be certain whether the cat is making adjustments that affect the background EEGs prior to input. Goldberg and Wurtz (1972) have shown modifications of cellular activity in the superior colliculus when a monkey is to attend to the input by making an eye movement to it. These data suggest that this modification can take place within 50 msec after input, long before the start of the eye movement itself. However, it is not clear that the adjustments that take place with respect to eye movements involve attention systems general to information processing or if they are specific to the act of orienting (see Chapter 7).

Stimulus Selection (N100)

The most impressive evidence for early effects of attention upon the evoked-potential components has been obtained in the work of Hillyard and Picton (in press) in situations involving simultaneous presentation of rapid information to the two ears or to eye and ear. Of course, dichotic listening tasks provide strong evidence for selection in behavioral experiments (Broadbent, 1971). There is evidence that subjects are frequently unaware of material coming in on the unattended ear, although material presented to the unattended ear is processed in the sense of producing activation of phonetic (Lyon, 1974) and semantic codes (Lewis, 1970) and perhaps also some autonomic responses (Corteen & Wood, 1972). Hillyard and Picton have found that the N100 component of the vertex evoked potential, about 90 msec after input, was substantially larger to tones presented to an attended ear than to tones presented to an unattended ear. This difference occurred whether the signal on the attended ear was a target signal that the subject was to report or an irrelevant background signal. It was also found, in agreement with studies outlined above, that a target stimulus on the attended ear produced in addition a seemingly independent enhancement of the late positive wave (P300) that did not occur to nontarget signals on either ear, or to target signals on the unattended ear. Hillyard and Picton (in press) have also reported attempts to extend this paradigm to auditory–visual input with good success upon the auditory evoked potential but relatively little success upon the visual evoked potential.

The most interesting aspect of the Hillyard and Picton result is their contention that N100 and P300 reflect two different processing systems; the N100 wave being related to stimulus set (orienting to a stimulus) and P300 related to response set (or selecting an internal pathway). This contention is different than the idea developed in this chapter from the behavioral data of a single internal mechanism that can be committed either early or late in processing.

There is some evidence in the behavioral literature that seems against the dual mechanism outlined by Hillyard and Picton. Kahneman (1973, p. 144) has reported that when subjects are asked to report all information on one ear and only targets on the other ear, they are unable to carry out this instruction. If there were different mechanisms to select ears and to select targets, one might expect this instruction to be easy. However, it is possible that although mechanisms involving stimulus and response set are in some way drawing upon a single capacity, there is also some independence between the two.

Another discrepancy between the Hillyard and Picton result and the behavioral literature (e.g., Ostry, Moray, & Marks, 1976) is that with rapid processing of information to the two ears, behavioral studies have found that subjects can monitor both ears in parallel with no reduction in performance (d') compared to when they are instructed to deal with only one ear. On the other hand, Hillyard and Picton have examined three conditions—a neutral condition in which the subjects are required to divide attention between the two ears as well as both the attended and unattended ear under conditions in which attention is focused on one ear. They find both an amplification of the attended signal (N100) and reduction of the unattended signal (N100) as compared to the neutral condition. The extant behavioral data only examined the benefits when instructed to attend and not the costs in the unattended ear, whereas Hillyard and Picton's technique allows both examination of the costs and benefits. Sometimes it is difficult to show a behavioral effect of selection in terms of benefit that becomes clear when both costs and benefits are examined (see Chapter 7).

Hillyard and Picton's data showing an early N100 effect involve situations in which there is very rapid input of information. There are reports of similar N100 effects in discrete trials reaction-time tasks in which visual signals occur at differing positions in space (Eason, Harter, & White, 1969). Both these lines of research suggest an early brain sign that is specific to the alignment of attention to a particular input pathway (ear or position in space). The idea that the process of orienting to a particular input pathway is in some sense separate from detection of input by a central processing system is discussed in detail in Chapter 7.

Summary

In general the results obtained from evoked-potential studies have established two points. First, there is a brain sign (P300) that is closely related to the act of detecting a stimulus event. The P300 shows many of the same characteristics that have been found to typify probe interference effects. It indexes an endogenously controlled, flexibly time-locked system of limited capacity that can be engaged by different codes activated by an input item. Second, there appears to be another brain sign (N100) more closely related to sustained orienting toward a particular input pathway. The evidence from evoked potentials seems to suggest this sign is in some sense independent of the P300 sign. The balance of this chapter considers the first point further; Chapter 7 deals with the second.

SUSTAINED EFFORT AND AUTONOMIC EFFECTS

Both widespread inhibition effects in behavioral data and the P300 seem to relate to the entry of a signal into a central processing system. If the central processing of the signal is sustained, there is evidence of large behavioral and physiological shifts. Consider a task where subjects are instructed to count forward three letters from the input letter and match the result against a test letter. Probe effects obtained early in practice in such situations are large, as shown in Figure 6.14. A similar result has been reported by Kahneman (1973) when subjects are required to add 1 to each of a set of four digits (e.g., 1, 3, 5, 6). In this case, a detection

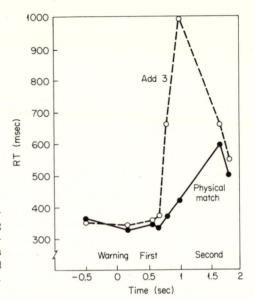

FIG. 6.14. Probe RTs during successive physical letter matching (solid line) and when subjects are required to count forward three letters and match against the result (dotted line). (From Posner & Klein, 1973. Copyright 1973 Academic Press.)

task presented during the time when the subjects are making the transformation produces greatly reduced performance.

During sustained attention there is a broad constellation of changes in the autonomic nervous system, including changes in heart rate, galvanic skin response, vascular dilation, and pupil size. Experimental studies discussed by Kahneman (1973) illustrate these changes. Subjects were presented with a series of four digits. They were required to transform these digits by adding 0, 1, or 3 and to report the result. There was a remarkable similarity in the time course of the various indicators during the listening phase. The striking autonomic changes generally start approximately 1 to 2 sec following stimulation. However, pupil dilation, the fastest of these changes, may start within .5 sec of input.

Thus active attention to a stimulus is detectable in a number of indicants, both behavioral and physiological. The timing of these effects is summarized in Figure 6.15. These data support the supposition that recognition involves a particular brain system whose relationship to processing can be controlled in part by the experimenter and in part by the subject. When the use of this system is extended

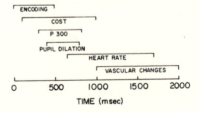

FIG. 6.15. Time course of behavioral, EEG, and autonomic effects that follow the conscious effort subjects invest in a signal.

in time, it is much easier to observe its effects than in some of the more rapid techniques discussed previously. Paradigms using fast indicants are useful in finding early involvement of this system in information processing, but it is difficult to determine whether the occurrence of brain signs in these rapid processing tasks is closely related to the subject's awareness. Paradigms extended in time such as those illustrated in Figure 6.15 make it clear that the mental effort involved in transforming the stimulus is closely related to subjective experience. I believe that the occurrence of P300 and interference with probe reaction time are also closely related to the subject's awareness. In the next section I discuss techniques that indicate the relationships between the chronometric indicants of processing of stimuli and the subject's awareness of them.

MENTAL CHRONOMETRY AND PHENOMENOLOGY

It remains to show convincingly that the chronometric analysis of the central processing system has something to do with the subject's phenomenal experience as indicated by verbal reports. The integration of information processing and phenomenological approaches to perception has been hampered by the tendency to apply them to different problems. Processing models, like the ones we have been discussing so far, have dominated in the field of reading, speech perception, and motor skills; whereas classical perceptual methods have been more widely applied to the study of illusions, depth perception, and distortion of input arrays. In these latter situations, compelling phenomenological experiences occur that are not veridical in terms of the objective input presented to the subject. They thus represent particularly striking ways to manipulate the content of the subject's phenomenal experience. The question remains whether the principles that have been studied chronometrically can be shown to affect these phenomenal experiences. It would aid this argument to have experimental situations involving compelling subjective experiences that would lend themselves to the techniques of mental chronometry. It would then be possible to show whether small chronometric changes in the rate of information processing, which would influence the likelihood that a given code would occupy the conscious processor, lead to predictable phenomenological experience.

Dominance of Visual Input

Chapter 2 discussed aspects of the code specificity of conscious attention. It was argued that attention could be given either to the physical or phonetic code of the stimulus, with matching behavior determined only by the code of which subjects were aware and not by other codes simultaneously active in the nervous system. A perceptual phenomenon where one code has been thought to control awareness and behavior has been called *visual dominance*. A classic case of visual dominance was reported by Gibson (1933), who had subjects wear prism spectacles that made straight edges appear curved. When the subjects watched their hands move along an objectively straight edge, visual information indicated that the edge was curved. Subjects experienced no conflict. They felt the edge curved. Visual input dominated the subject's conscious awareness. Even more striking is the work of Rock and Victor (1964), who reported visual dominance in judgments of size. Their subjects viewed a square object through a minifying lens but were not told of the visual distortion. In one condition, they were asked to grasp the object and then to reproduce or match its visual or felt size. The striking result was that both judgments depend on the perceived visual size of the object and not upon its actual size. Similarly, Pick, Warren, and Hay (1969) showed the dominance of visual input on the perceived location of an object. Subjects were asked to point, with a hand hidden from their view, at a finger of the other hand that was viewed through an 11-degree displacing lens. The subjects pointed very near to the correct optical position.

Similarly, work on memory for movements shows evidence of visual dominance. One series of studies (Posner, 1967) compared the reproduction of blind and visually guided positioning movements. Visual information was greatly affected by an interpolated attention-demanding task, but proprioceptive information was unaffected. When both sorts of information were present, subjects behaved as they would have if only visual information were present. Klein and Posner (1974, Experiment II) asked subjects to reproduce a movement pattern that was either visual (dot on a screen), proprioceptive (passive movement of the finger), or both. They found that subjects could quite easily ignore the proprioceptive information if instructed to reproduce on the basis of vision alone. The presence of proprioceptive information had an effect only when subjects were not informed during presentation about what kind of information they would have to reproduce. On the other hand, proprioceptive reproductions were affected in the same manner by visual information, whether or not the visual information had to be attended. Even when subjects knew at the time of presentation that only kinesthetic information was to be used, they appeared to be unable to ignore the visual information present.

These reports suggest that the presence of visual information can, under some circumstances, dominate information arising from other modalities. Evidence for visual dominance is also present in chronometric studies. These studies provide additional leads as to the source of the effect. Colavita (1974) published a series of experiments showing that simultaneous auditory and visual signals may lead to visual dominance. He first asked his subjects to match a visual and auditory stimulus in subjective intensity. These matched stimuli were then used in choice reaction-time tasks. Subjects were instructed to press one key whenever the light came on and another key whenever the tone occurred. Each of the 10 subjects received 30 trials. On 5 of these trials, both light and tone were presented simultaneously. On 49 out of 50 conflict trials, subjects responded only to the

light. When the subjects knew that dual presentation could occur, visual dominance was still present, although reduced.

Why is it that visual information tends to dominate over the equally intense
auditory information? To understand this effect, it is necessary to review the way
in which alertness affects the direction of attention.

When an auditory signal is presented to the subject, there is a rapid automatic
tendency to respond more rapidly to any following signal regardless of modality
(see p. 140). This appears to be due in part to an automatic rise in alertness that
makes central processing mechanisms more available to input information (see p.
128). Alertness thus produces a shift in criterion. Visual signals are less able to
bring about this alerting as we have seen previously (see p. 137). A visual signal
can be used as a warning signal; but in order for subjects to use it, they must
process the signal actively, thus turning their attention strongly to the modality of
the warning.

There is clear evidence that modality uncertainty will affect the rate of processing of a signal. In one study (Posner, Nissen, & Klein, 1976) subjects
received blocks of trials that were either predominantly visual (80%), equally
often visual and auditory, or predominantly auditory (80%). The visual stimulus
was an "X" to the left or right of fixation, and the auditory signal was a tone to
the left or right ear. Regardless of modality, subjects were instructed to make the
compatible response by pressing one of two keys as quickly as possible. The
results indicate costs and benefits of receiving an expected or unexpected signal
in comparison with the neutral block. There is clear evidence that the speed of
processing is increased when subjects expect a signal on either the auditory or
visual modality. Since the same responses are involved in both tasks and the
stimulus–response assignments are highly compatible, the effects on performance would appear to be due to the subject's ability to allocate attention to the
expected modality.[8]

A visual warning signal produces efficient alerting only if the subjects turn
attention toward the stimulus. An auditory warning requires no active attention in
order to produce its alerting effect; thus subjects do not have to attend actively
to it. This asymmetry makes an attention bias toward vision reasonable, since
the direction of attention produces an advantage for the selected modality.
Let us apply this result to the Colavita effect. When subjects get ready, they
attend to the visual modality so that they may respond rapidly if the visual signal
occurs, relying upon the auditory signal to summon their attention via its automatic alerting capability. When simultaneous events occur, the visual signal has

---

[8]We anticipated strong asymmetries in this study, where the cost of an unexpected visual signal
would be stronger than for an unexpected auditory signal due to the relative automatic nature of
auditory alerting. However, this expectation was not met in this study, as the effects were symmetric.
The reasons appear to be due to details of the location response required in this task. The expected
asymmetry has occurred in other paradigms (see Klein, 1977).

more direct access to the central processing mechanisms. If the subjects expect only one signal, once they begin to process the visual input, they have little incentive to turn their attention toward the auditory modality. This view identifies visual dominance with a tendency of attention to be directed to the visual modality. Once the direction of attention is fixed, prior entry (Titchener, 1908) will *tend* to exclude information coming from other modalities from reaching the conscious attention of the subject.

Why does an attention bias toward vision occur? Unfortunately, I have no certain answer. It is possible that vision's deficient alerting capability makes it necessary for subjects to learn to direct their attention to vision. It is also possible that causation goes in the other direction. An attentional bias toward vision would make it unnecessary for vision to develop the strong connections to an alerting mechanism that other modalities have. Our finding that dominance is very labile gives some reason for supposing the causal direction is from the alerting deficit to the attentional bias rather than the reverse.

Microprocesses

In many of the studies of visual dominance there appears to be something of a compromise between two codes. It is as though the visual stimulus did not dominate so completely that subjects were unable to be influenced at all by the proprioceptive code. Chronometric studies can examine these more detailed interactions between codes of the same stimulus. In particular, a more detailed illustration of the bias toward vision is obtained in experiments in which subjects are required to respond by pressing a key in the direction of a perceived movement (Klein, 1974). The movement may be passive motion imposed on the finger or visual movement of a dot on a cathode ray tube. Either type of movement may occur alone (pure condition), they may occur together in the same direction (redundant), or together in opposite directions (conflict). On some trials the subjects are required to attend to the movement and on other trials to the visual dot. Figure 6.16 shows a method of analyzing the combined performance as applied to one individual subject who has been asked to attend to the kinesthetic information and to respond by pressing a key according to the direction of the movement. The reason for illustrating only a single subject is that there appear to be vast differences in the way in which subjects behave in this task, and I am not suggesting that the same result will summarize the kind of tradeoff between attention to the visual and kinesthetic information in other subjects. Instead, subjects seem to show their own characteristics. I only hope to illustrate the technique for examining the tradeoff.

Notice that very fast reaction times are barely affected by the presence of visual information. If the subjects respond rapidly to the kinesthetic information, they show no tendency to be affected by conflicting or redundant visual informa-

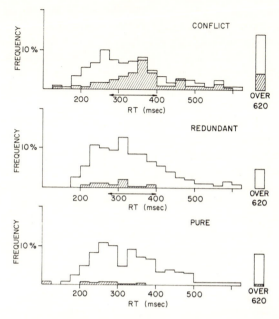

FIG. 6.16.   Frequency histograms of RTs for one subject who was required to report as quickly as possible the direction in which his finger was moved. The three conditions indicate the absence of a visual movement (pure), a visual movement in the same direction (redundant), and a visual movement in the opposite direction (conflict). Hatched areas indicate error percentages. The arrow on the *x*-axis indicates the interquartile range of RT to reporting pure visual movement and hence an estimate of the time by which visual information has developed. Visual dominance is indicated by the large number of errors found in the conflict condition when RTs are long enough for visual information to have accrued. (From Klein, 1974.)

tion. The arrows on the *x*-axis of Figure 6.16 show the interquartile range of visual reaction times in conditions where only visual information was presented. Visual information is processed more slowly than kinesthetic information. The interquartile range provides an estimate of the time during which visual information would be accruing centrally. The estimate is too high, since it involves the response time and movement as well as the central accrual time. Nonetheless, it gives some idea of when the visual information might be available to the central system. In the conflict condition, the particular subject shown in Figure 6.16 performs at far less than chance (hatched areas are errors) when the visual information conflicts and kinesthetic reaction times are delayed. This subject resolves the conflict by following vision once visual codes have developed and thus shows a particularly strong dominance of the visual modality. Other subjects show increases in response time rather than in errors or have other means of adjusting to the conflicting visual information. Figure 6.16 indicates a powerful technique for examining the detailed micropicture of code conflict for a given subject and task.

Summary

What is particularly striking about the results of work on visual dominance is the powerful control that vision generally has over a subject's behavior. The phenomenological investigation of visual dominance via the use of perceptual report indicates that the visual modality may block information occurring in other modalities from the subject's awareness. These reports testify to the power of the effect and to the compelling phenomenal nature. However, a phenomenological study rarely places emphasis on the boundary conditions with which the reports can be obtained. Nor does a study of perceptual report provide any detail to account for the level at which nonattended information arising from other modalities is excluded. The chronometric study of visual dominance not only confirms its existence but has shown in some detail the nature of the conditions under which it occurs. Moreover, chronometric study provides techniques for analytically dealing with the microstructure of such conflict over the course of milliseconds.

Psychology is concerned with the mental content of consciousness and the way in which information flow produces access to consciousness. One difficulty that is common all through the psychological literature is our failure to grasp the idea that conscious awareness is a discrete event that plays a specific role within the stream of information processing. What I have attempted to do in this section is to show that consciousness itself is mediated by a system that can be controlled experimentally. Both the behavioral studies and studies of evoked potentials show the clear, separate nature of this isolable processing system. Its entry into the stream of information processing is heavily controlled both by experimental manipulations and by endogenous strategies employed by the subject. Its presence in the stream of information processing gives rise to indicants, both behavioral and physiological, that can be used to index this system. Physiological studies of the geography of this system (Vaughan & Ritter, 1970), which are currently under way in man, and studies of single-cell activity in lower animals (Olds et al., 1972) may help us understand the evolution and development of the conscious processing system. An effort to tie this system with phenomenological reports seems to be sufficiently successful to indicate that small differences in processing time, such as those obtained in most chronometric studies, under conditions of uncertainty can provide virtually complete dominance of the subject's awareness, memory, and later behavior. This argument greatly enhances the value of chronometric methods by showing that a small effect on processing time can frequently produce control over central processing mechanisms.

SIGNIFICANCE OF CONSCIOUS CONTROL

I have frequently been asked why it is that the nervous system should develop a mechanism for conscious control of the type that I have been postulating in this chapter. At a recent Loyola Symposium meeting, this question was posed by Estes (1975). In a more general way, Broadbent (1973) has raised this issue:

> [It] seems to require a biologically unlikely kind of machinery. . . . It seems to mean that the part of the brain which analyses inputs from the environment, and which is presumably quite complicated, is preceded by another and duplicate part of the brain which carries out the same function, deciding what is there in order to reject or accept items for admission to the machinery which decides what is there [p. 67].

Of course, one has no complete answer as to what the evolutionary significance of consciousness as a mechanism is, but some ideas on the problem are sketched below.

Inhibition

Perhaps the fact that the objective indicants of conscious behavior are primarily inhibitory gives a clue as to the explanation. The basic plan of the nervous system seems to be to provide inhibition from higher levels upon activity occurring at lower levels. This idea was first discovered in the spinal cord at the end of the last century, and it was in fact this discovery that led Sechenov to postulate that thinking was primarily the result of inhibiting motor reflex activity.

This idea has clearly been taken over into the notions that have been discussed in this book. In short, the conscious mechanism is not primarily designed to decide what is there—that has already been done tacitly by lower systems—but to produce integrated actions to often antagonistic habitual responses. Its function, therefore, is not really duplicatory in the sense in which Broadbent intended.

The fact of its limited capacity may itself serve an important controlling function. By giving priority to a particular pathway, it prevents other pathways from having access to any but their most habitual response systems (Shallice, 1972). This has great evolutionary value. Lower organisms tend to have fixed action patterns to stimuli. The crucial role of context in determining human behavior means that only in a relatively minor way can humans afford fixed action patterns to a stimulus. The stickleback may find it safe to attack whatever stimulus is red, because in a stickleback's environment a red stimulus is very likely to mean an enemy; but such a fixed action pattern in human behavior would be clearly untenable. Nonetheless, a basic plan of the nervous system is to produce invariant activation at some level as first outlined by Sechenov. This seems to be confirmed by the studies reviewed in Chapters 2 and 3. If that plan is to be kept, then inhibitory mechanisms at higher levels controlling the output of these systems is necessary. It is for this reason that the interference effects from central processing capacity seem so closely related to output. It is certainly true that the closer the relationship of a mental operation to output, the more likely it is to interfere with other activity. Conscious control of output events insures a degree of coordination in behavior.

Translation

Another role for the central processing system goes back to the understanding developed by Greek psychologists 2,000 years ago. The idea of a central processing mechanism is very close to the ancient Greek notion of *sensus communus* or central sense organ. The notion of a central sense organ arises because of the necessity to coordinate the activity of modality-specific processing systems. Jerison (1973) has argued that auditory and visual information processing have undergone separate evolutionary histories. Moreover, we have found that the phonetic recoding of a visual stimulus places it in a processing system quite different than its origin.

   If, in fact, modalities can be seen as providing basically different languages, it is useful that some central system be able to translate among these languages. One might argue that the language of visual and phonetic codes must be the same in the ultimate sense that they both involve common properties of neural activity. Nonetheless, clear subjective evidence of the difference between visual and auditory stimulation indicates that the neural codes are themselves different in some sense. The idea that each code represents a language is simply a metaphor to capture that difference. It is possible that central mechanisms arise, because the human brain speaks a variety of such languages and needs a central system to coordinate them.

Generalization

Finally, a third role for consciousness of great importance has been discussed by Rozin (1976). He argues that the brain develops very specific patterns for dealing with information. If these patterns are to be used intelligently or flexibly by an organism, they somehow must be abstracted from the very specific context out of which they arise and be applied more generally to new functions. The intelligence of organisms, according to Rozin's argument, depends on their ability to flexibly apply mechanisms designed by evolution for one processing goal into new and different processing goals. Thus Rozin identifies the cognitive conscious that would allow transfer of such skills as those used in navigation to a completely new environment for which they had not evolved. Although the mechanisms to perceive auditory language seem to be innate in the human brain and to be used by every human being regardless of intelligence, they do not easily transfer to the reading of visual language. To do this, one has to bring to awareness mechanisms that are already there tacitly. Once again, the distinction is between tacit knowledge that must be used in a particular stimulus context and knowledge that can be transferred from situation to situation. The latter is a particularly important role for conscious mechanism to play in the processing of information.

It would be presumptuous to suppose that this triple-headed explanation of the significance of conscious control would satisfy those who ask why it is that the brain develops such a mechanism. Yet it does seem to provide some justification in the evolutionary history of the human for the kind of brain organization that one finds in behavioral studies.

SUMMARY

This chapter deals with the operation of a limited capacity central processing system related to acts of attending. The presentation of a signal automatically activates habitual pathways. Such activation has no effect on the ability to handle unrelated probe tones. The commitment of attention, however, produces widespread interference effects that can be traced chronometrically by a variety of dual-task probe procedures. These probe methods show that the central system is not linked closely to any particular mental operation, is relatively independent of modality of input, has flexible time locking, and appears to be necessary prior to the generation of a response.

Chronometric studies using evoked brain potentials suggest a similar attentional system that can be indexed by the occurrence of a late positive wave of the evoked potential (P300). This wave is affected by conditions similar to those that produce interference with probe tasks. Chronometric studies of the late positive wave in letter-matching studies suggest a similar time course to that found with reaction-time studies. An earlier negative component of the evoked potential (N100) appears to index attentional effects when the task allows concentration upon a single input channel. The exact relation of N100 to P300 is not well understood. Continued attention to a signal produces widespread autonomic activity, including changes in heart rate, GSR, pupil size, etc., which appear to index effort produced by concentration over time.

It appears that the same attentional system can be shown to be closely related to phenomenal reports when input gives rise to conflicting codes of the same stimulus event. Studies of visual dominance suggest that under some circumstances the close coupling of the limited attentional system to vision produces control of our subjective report by a visual code to the exclusion of other codes presented simultaneously.

Taken as a whole, this chapter appears to illustrate that attention is not a general property of all information processing but instead involves the operation of a unified central system, the time course of which can be manipulated under experimental control. This point gives hope that the study of this system will allow closer links between the languages of physiology, performance, and phenomenology.

7
Orienting

INTRODUCTION

Psychological studies based upon reflex models begin with a stimulus and end with its detection or with an overt response to it. One of the most important contributions of cybernetics to psychology is the idea that information can be fed back from some higher level or previous output to modify the processing of a new event. Whether called sets, expectancies, hypotheses, or top-down processing, the cognitive control exercised by central mechanisms over new input is of crucial importance to our understanding of human information processing. To a large degree the importance of "cognitive psychology" is in recognizing the degree to which such endogenous control exists as an optional feature of the human processing system.

At various points in this book I have referred to the importance of such cognitive control and to the assumption that it involves the operation of the same limited capacity system described in the previous chapter. Under the title "generation" in Chapter 2, the ability of subjects to develop a visual code of a letter following presentation of its auditory form represents one case where active attention is used flexibly to produce an expectancy. In examining the costs of receiving an unexpected letter following a valid prime, there was clear evidence that an active expectancy was involved (see p. 165). The use of linguistic material with its complex input pathways and multiple codes often made it difficult to observe the effects of such expectancies independent of the exogenous processes that result from the prime. In order to study such endogenously controlled expectancies in their simplest form, it would be useful to have model tasks in which the input is as simple as possible so that little in the way of associated information

185

stored in memory is involved. This is particularly necessary if one hopes to discover whether expectancies arising from endogenous sources affect the simplest cognitive acts such as the detection of visual energy. Some authors have felt that expectancies or sets can operate only upon stored information in memory (Shiffrin & Gardner, 1972). To test this view, it would be helpful to use tasks where the very minimum of stored information is involved. This chapter is specifically devoted to the study of model situations in which central control is exercised to select high-priority inputs.

Set

The term *set* is one of the oldest and most widely used concepts in psychology (Gibson, 1941). Although the term has been used in many ways, I will employ it in this chapter to signify hypotheses resulting from action by the central attentive mechanism, which in turn influence the processing of input information. So viewed, set is an active process that arises from the subjects' knowledge about the nature of the input they will receive. The active nature of set is quite important. In previous chapters, I have dealt with those biases that occur automatically—for example, the bias toward the visual modality (discussed in Chapter 6) and the bias introduced by pathway activation (discussed in Chapter 4). According to this usage, *set* is produced only through the deliberate turning of attention toward some expected event. Studies of *set* should tell us something about the limits of attentional control of the processing of input items.

Orienting

As in many of the previous chapters, I shall examine particular experimental situations that appear to be good model situations for the study of the phenomena being investigated. The most useful experimental situation in which to study set is one closely related to those processes that control the direction of the subject's attention. This line of investigation has generally been called *orienting* or *orienting reflexes* (Sokolov, 1963).[1] The systematic study of orienting, either through the passive activation of input pathways that summon attention or through set, represents an effort to summarize how it is that the central processing system

---

[1]The study of orienting using conditioning procedures has the same general problems as were discussed in Chapter 4 for pathway analyses based on conditioning. The orienting reflex as defined by Sokolov consists of indicants that involve changes in sense organs and undoubtedly mirror early stages in processing, but they also include autonomic changes that follow only after the subject has detected the signal and begun to expend mental effort in processing it. Chronometric techniques can serve to separate orienting in the sense of an alignment of peripheral or central systems to the input pathway of the item from detection of the signal. The latter process involves the commitment of the central system to its processing as outlined in Chapter 6.

comes to be controlled by one item or code rather than another. The consequences of one code or item dominating attention have been examined in Chapters 2, 3, and 6, but little has been said of which item or code will gain control. Clearly, priming, intensity, modality, and novelty are factors that affect the balance of the system leading to selective advantages for one signal or code over another. The control of such selection is probably one of the main options that central systems have in directing processing. It is thus a fruitful place to examine experimentally the role of hypotheses in influencing our awareness of the world around us and our behavior toward it.

The most fundamental question one can ask about *set* is how one prepares to take in information from a particular place in the world. Each stimulus with which an organism interacts appears to occupy a position in external space. Thus we frequently refer to turning our attention toward some source of signals, and this is usually accompanied by motor activity addressed to that source. This chapter will concern the time course of such sets, the mechanisms that are required in order to produce them, and whether they are directed to all stimuli arising from a given position in the environment or only to stimuli in a particular modality.

A fundamental aspect of perception is that the world seems to us to be occupied by objects. Our visual world is experienced as colored objects arising some place in the environment and not from within our heads. When we experience a person, we experience not visual stimuli and a disembodied voice but a unified object that seems to consist of integral auditory and visual components. Spelke (1976) puts it quite well:

> Information from one object or event usually reaches us through several modalities. A falling glass is both seen to break into pieces and heard to crash. A fire is seen to glow, heard to crackle, and felt to radiate heat. To an adult, this information specifies unified objects and events [p. 553].

Neisser (1976) uses this introspective evidence to propose that the perception of objects is primary. This is certainly true at a phenomenological level. However, phenomenological reports must be viewed with caution; for it should be remembered that the experience of a single visual letter is unified, and yet the letter's physical form and its name exist as separate codes within the nervous system, though they often appear introspectively to be apprehended as a unit. In the same way, watching the movement of one's hand through space seems like a unified visual and kinesthetic experience. Yet the data on visual dominance and memory for visual and kinesthetic codes indicate that these codes are sufficiently separate so that either of them may control behavior. It may also be true that objects that seem unified to our phenomenological experience are assembled from separate processing systems. If this were the case, one might expect to be able to disassemble them by chronometric studies. In this view the perception of objects could be studied as the outcome of a psychological process integrating separate codes that arise from a given position in space.

Organization

To examine these questions, the current chapter is divided into five topic areas. It starts with an examination of the temporal dynamics of set without much regard to the way in which set is mediated. The second topic is a comparison of exogenous and endogenous control over set for different stimulus–response combinations. Movement of the eyes toward a visual stimulus appears to be an automatic process in much the same way as the look-up of the name of a letter might be said to be automatic. The movement of the hand in the direction of an object may be thought to be somewhat less automatic in the sense that it would be less under the control of the stimulus event and more under the control of the internal set. Through an examination of control of hand and eye movements, an effort is made to determine the tradeoff between external and internal control. In these sections the argument is confined to overt processes of orientation.

If the argument presented in Chapter 6 is correct, one ought to be able to move attention around independently of overt sensory and motor orientation. The third topic is an examination of this question where new evidence in support of the existence of a central attentional mechanism independent of overt stimulus–response orientation is provided. The fourth topic is an attempt to deal with the way in which particular modalities produce orientation of the central processing system. These results are an extension of the differences between auditory and visual alerting that have been discussed in Chapters 5 and 6.

The fifth topic deals with the relationship between external positions in space and internal pathways as sources of signal selection. By comparing orientation to stimuli arising at the sensory surface with orientation toward events activated in the memory system, I attempt to develop a more general approach to the problem of how the central processing system becomes controlled by stimuli, whether arising either in the external world or in the memory system.

TEMPORAL DYNAMICS OF SET

The time course of the ability of subjects to set themselves may be illustrated by comparing a spatial and a symbolic experiment. In the spatial experiment subjects are required to tell whether an ''X'' is presented to the left or right of the central fixation point by pressing either a left or right key. In the symbolic experiment, subjects are asked to determine whether a digit presented to them is odd or even. At a short interval before the presentation of the imperative stimulus in either experiment, a cue is given that tells the subject either that one of the two responses has a probability of .8 (and the other one of .2) or that the two responses are equally likely. If the subject receives the cue indicating that one response has a probability of .8 and if the imperative stimulus on that trial is one requiring that response, the trial is called valid because the expected response is correct. An invalid trial is one in which the unexpected (.2) response is correct. When the cue gives no information as to the probability of a response, it is called neutral. Time between the cue and the stimulus event is systematically varied in fixed blocks of either no cue or intervals between cue and imperative of 50, 150, 300, 500, or 1,000 msec.

The results of these experiments are illustrated in Figures 7.1 and 7.2. The use of a neutral cue allows us to separate the results into benefits (neutral RT minus valid RT) and costs (invalid RT minus neutral RT). There are two important aspects of these data. The first is that highly significant costs and benefits (as compared to the neutral control) are found even when a cue leads a stimulus by only 50 msec. These effects are most striking in the errors and tend to grow in the first 150 msec following input and then decline. If an unexpected stimulus follows the arrow by as little as 150 msec, performance approaches chance. Most of the subjects in Experiment 1 showed very strong peaks in error or reaction time at some intermediate value of foreperiod. These results suggest strongly that the process of set is an active one. During the time that the subjects are developing sets, they are very susceptible to making errors if the wrong stimulus occurs. Once they have achieved a set, their error rates subside somewhat; although very significant costs and benefits are still present.

Second, the costs and benefits found in this task are nearly symmetric, a fact that differs from the results reported in Chapter 4 (see p. 101). The reason for this is related to the active nature of the set. If the set is caused by the subjects turning their active attention to a particular stimulus and/or response event, then one would expect symmetric costs and benefits rather than the asymmetry caused by a combination of automatic and attended processes discussed in Chapter 4.[2]

The neutral condition in both experiments shows improvement in RT and an increase in error when a warning cue is present in comparison to the no-warning cue trials. This speed–accuracy tradeoff is a usual result of changes in phasic alertness that accompany noninformative warning signals (see p. 130).

The results show very striking effects of costs and benefits, but the reasons for this result are unclear. Four mechanisms that could produce the results in the two experiments are outlined below. They are neither exhaustive nor mutually exclusive, however.

First, one might expect a preparatory eye movement from the fixation stimulus toward the expected event. If such eye movements were effective, one

---

[2]The symmetric costs and benefits found with cues in this condition are related to similar results (p. 106) with linguistic material when a subject uses the prime to switch categories. Following the switch of attention, the build-up of costs and benefits appears to be symmetric (see Figure 4.9).

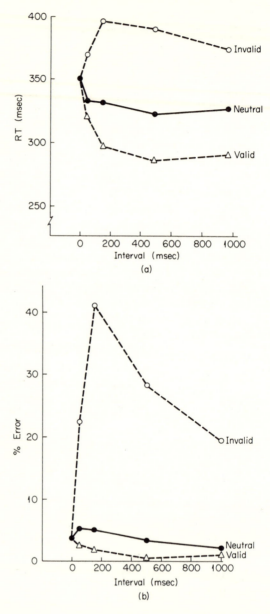

FIG. 7.1.   Time course of *set* in a spatial choice RT task as a function of cue to imperative signal interval. (a) indicates changes in RT; (b) indicates changes in errors. Valid, invalid, and neutral trials are discussed in the text. (From Posner, Nissen, & Ogden, 1978. Copyright 1978 Lawrence Erlbaum Associates.)

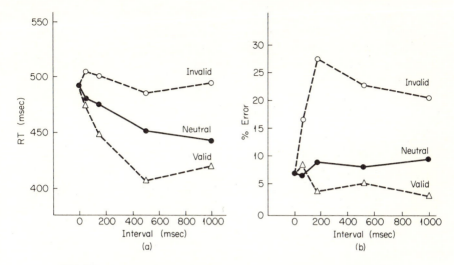

FIG. 7.2.   Time course of *set* following a cue in a symbolic choice RT task as a function of cue to imperative signal interval. (a) indicates shifts in RT; (b) indicates shifts in errors. Valid, invalid, and neutral trials are discussed in the text. (From Posner, Snyder, & Nissen, Note 16.)

would expect better processing of the expected stimulus. In this experiment we did not monitor the subject's eyes.

Second, the subjects may shift their attention to a position corresponding to the likely input without actual changes in fixation. This would be a set mediated not by a direct change in the sense organ but by a change in the commitment of the central attentional system. The attention view would suggest facilitation of any stimulus arising from the position in space to which the subjects move their attention.

This second mechanism could in principle be differentiated from a third mechanism that suggests that set is mediated by a shift in attention to a location in the brain that would be contacted by the external event. To differentiate these views requires the use of multimodal stimulation arising from a common position in the external world but involving different input pathways.[3]

Fourth, the set might be mediated by specific motor tendencies that have nothing to do with enhancement of the stimulus input. In both the location and

_____

[3]If we assume that visual and tactile input arising from the same position in physical space have their primary input to different primary projection areas, then it is possible to discriminate set directed toward a position in the external world from set toward a modality-specific sensory area. However, it is also possible to consider multimodal cells as the primary physiological sites, in which case the two kinds of set cannot be distinguished in this way.

odd–even experiments, the subjects could simply prime the muscles involved in the left or right index finger and obtain the set in this way.

The next section reports experiments that are designed to help to discriminate among these accounts of set toward location.

CONTROL OF REFLEXIVE RESPONSES

Eye Movements

There is little question but that the direction of the eyes is closely associated with a subject's attention. This fact has led to an enormous interest in the study of eye movements as a way of investigating attention (Kahneman, 1973). However, the fundamental question of the relation of eye movements and eye position to *set* has not been settled. The aspect of this issue that concerns how much attention is required to redirect the eyes will be dealt with in this section.

Saccades seem to be forced upon us reflexively without the need for a conscious decision. On the other hand, we may choose to inhibit saccades or to make them voluntarily even without an external stimulus. There are experimental reasons for believing that changes in eye position to visual stimuli are more automatic (reflexive) than other performances studied in the laboratory such as hand movements. First, eye movements are ballistic or nearly so (Komoda, Festinger, Phillips, Duckman, & Young, 1973; Westheimer, 1954). Ballistic movements are defined as being less susceptible to control during the movement than are other nonballistic movements. Second, the movement of the eyes is not much affected by the number of alternative stimuli to which one might move (Saslow, 1967). Although there is dispute on whether stimulus uncertainty affects eye movements at all, there is little question that reaction time to move the eyes to positions in space shows a small increase with stimulus uncertainty. This is usually symptomatic of a highly automatic system. Third, the time between input and firing of collicular cells related to movement of the eyes is very short (Goldberg & Wurtz, 1972).

None of these three results is unique to eye movements. Other types of movement may also be ballistic, show little or no uncertainty effects, and involve rapid responses of motor cells. However, these all are properties of reflexive behavior (see p. 86); thus one might view the eye movement system as one that requires minimal attention but that can be brought under conscious control if so desired.

It is often assumed that the initiation of eye movements is quite separate from the system that can control other kinds of movements. This is undoubtedly true in a physiological sense, but it is less clear functionally. Megaw and Armstrong (1973) found some evidence for functional separation of the two systems. They show that although both hand and eye were affected by stimulus uncertainty, there was little change in reaction time when the two responses were combined.

They also report that directional errors were more frequent for the hand than the eye, and thus a common error resulted in movement of the eye and hand in opposite directions. In this section, we use methods similar to those used by Megaw and Armstrong to determine the degree to which anticipatory eye movements are required for the set effect obtained in the last section and also to understand the degree of independence of the response systems that control hand and eye.

Cost–Benefit Analysis

To study this question we (Posner, Nissen, & Ogden, 1978) used a cost–benefit analysis of hand and eye movements to a target 6.9 degrees to the left or right of fixation. Two separate experiments were run, differing only in whether or not they provided feedback to the subject. Each experiment involved three conditions. In one condition subjects moved eyes alone; in a second condition they moved hand alone; and in the third condition they moved hand and eyes together.

The results of the experiment in terms of reaction time for hand and eye movements are combined in Figure 7.3. All anticipation and direction errors have been removed from the analysis. It should be noted first that both hand and

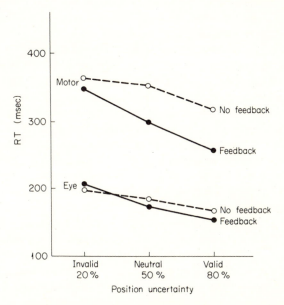

FIG. 7.3.   RT for hand (motor) and eye movements toward a light-stimulus event with and without feedback provided after each trial as a function of position uncertainty as varied by cue validity. (From Posner, Nissen, & Ogden, 1978. Copyright 1978 Lawrence Erlbaum Associates.)

eye movements show costs and benefits, indicating that the effects of set cannot be entirely mediated by changes in eye position since our hand movement experiment was conducted under conditions of no eye movements.

The effect of set on the eye system is about half of its effect on the hand system. The difference in reaction times between movements to expected and unexpected stimuli (costs + benefits) are 90 msec for hand and 45 msec for eye. These differences are systematic across subjects at about the same magnitude as were obtained by Megaw and Armstrong (1973).

There are a number of interesting differences between the ways in which the eye system and the hand system are affected by the imperative stimulus and by the subject's set. Prior to the occurrence of the imperative stimulus, the eye system is very much more affected by the expectancy manipulation than is the hand system. Visual anticipation errors occurred quite frequently, but hand anticipation errors almost never occurred. On the other hand, once the stimulus occurred, the eyes were much more heavily under the control of the stimulus and less under the control of set than were the hands. This is most striking when it results in the kinds of directional error reported by Megaw and Armstrong in which the eyes move to the target while the hand moves in the direction of the set. This occurred on 12% of the trials under the feedback condition. In summary, it appears that both hand and eye can be influenced by the subject's conscious attention but that the visual stimulus exerts a much stronger control over the eye than over the hand. Thus set seems to dominate the eye system only in the absence of an imperative stimulus; but it frequently dominates the hand, even in the presence of the stimulus event.

One effort to examine the role of eye movements in visual attention is to separate the stationary field, the eye field, and the head field (Sanders, 1972). A certain portion of the visual field can be examined even without moving the head and eyes to a stimulus. If the stimulus appears further in distance from the fixation, eye movements to that stimulus become very frequent. As the stimulus gets further moved into the periphery, head movements also become extremely important. Thus one might expect changes in the relative automaticity of eye movements as the eccentricity of a stimulus event is increased. With this in mind, we repeated the experiment described at 25 degrees eccentricity and obtained a somewhat different result.

These results are shown in Figure 7.4. Since the 6.9-degree and 25-degree experiments were done separately using different stimuli and subjects, the two experiments should not be compared directly. Although, as one would expect, the 25-degree eccentricity experiment showed longer reaction times for both hand and eye than did the 6.9-degree experiment. An important point, however, is that at 25 degrees the eye movement appears to show the same costs and benefits as the hand movement toward the same light (cost + benefit = 70 msec, in both cases).

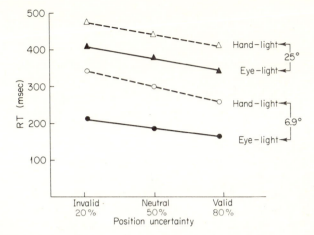

FIG. 7.4.   RT for hand and eye movements to light situated either 25 or 6.9 degrees from fixation as a function of position uncertainty. (From Posner & Davidson, 1976. From the Official Proceedings of the International Congress of Physical Activity Sciences, Quebec City, July 1976, Monograph No. 5.)

I do not know why the 25-degree eye movements seem to be less controlled by the stimulus event and more in control of the subject than the 6.9-degree movements. However, it does correspond rather well to one's subjective experience that for the longer movements it is necessary to voluntarily move the eyes to the stimulus when orienting to it, rather than having movement forced as it seems to happen at 6.9 degrees.

These results might relate to differences in the input of peripheral and foveal regions into systems responsible for eye movements. For example, single-cell recordings from the superior colliculus of the cat suggest that direct input to collicular cells is reduced from the periphery (Stein, Magalhães–Castro, & Kruger, 1975). The behavioral experiments certainly indicate ways in which the relative automaticity of a given stimulus–response combination may depend upon not only the stimulus and response movement but also upon the details of the position in space at which the stimulus occurs.

Compatibility

Another way of examining the control by the stimulus over a pathway is to require the subject to make an incompatible movement—that is, one in a direction opposite to the stimulus. A variety of experimenters have attempted this in both simple and choice reaction-time experiments. Figure 7.5 shows the results of a number of experiments from different sources that have examined hand and eye movement to visual and auditory stimuli using both simple and choice

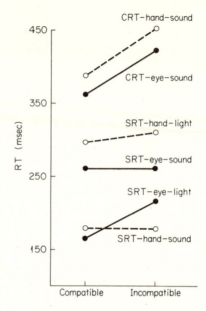

FIG. 7.5.   RT for movements in the direction of the stimulus event (compatible) and in the direction away from the stimulus event (incompatible) for various combinations of stimulus (sound and light) and response (hand and eye). SRT = simple reaction time; CRT = choice reaction time.

reaction time.[4] The results may be summarized rather quickly. For simple reaction time, only when the eye responds to a light is there a significantly larger reaction time when it moves opposite to the direction of the target than if it moves in the direction of the target. No other combination (hand–sound, eye–sound, or hand–light) produces a similar result on simple reaction time. In choice reaction time, only hand–light and eye–sound have been run, to my knowledge. Both show a highly significant increase in reaction time when run under incompatible conditions.

This work seems to indicate that it is easier for subjects to respond in the direction of the stimulus, a point that has been made by J. R. Simon (1969). However, when a very powerful set is present, such as in the case when the response is always made in the same direction regardless of the stimulus, only the eye–light pathway seems to exercise a sufficiently strong stimulus effect to make the incompatible response longer.

Figure 7.5 also illustrates an important control not present in previous studies. In the case of Figure 7.4, the reaction time of the eyes to light is much faster than that of the hand to light, and consequently a smaller effect of costs and benefits may be interpreted as simply occurring because of the faster nature of the response. However, in the case of Figure 7.5, although the eye–light combina-

---

[4]For simple reaction time only a single response is allowed, but in separate blocks it is to be made either in the direction of the imperative event (compatible) or in the opposite direction (incompatible).

tion is still much faster than the hand–light, it shows a larger effect than the hand–light combination, indicating that these results are not artifacts of the mean reaction time.

Summary

This section has shown that sets exercise powerful control over the overt movements of the subject. When subjects prepare to take in information from a visual location, they tend to move their eyes and/or head in that direction. In the absence of a visual stimulus, set tends to control the eye position. The presentation of a visual stimulus in the parafoveal region exercises powerful reflexive control over the eyes. The influence of set in the presence of the visual input is minimized. Eye movements to light have many of the characteristics of automatic control that are called *reflexive*.

These results provide an answer to one question concerning central control over the eyes. Eye movements are neither entirely driven by the stimulus nor by the set. They represent a delicate balance between attentional and reflex control. The second question is whether or not central attentional mechanisms can be shown to exist in these situations independently of the eye position. This question is examined in the next section.

INTERNAL MECHANISMS

Can visual attention be moved around independently of where one is looking at a given moment? Generally, most of us would probably give the same introspective answer as Wilhelm Wündt (1912):

> In natural vision we are always impelled to direct our line of vision to that point to which our attention is turned. If, however, we practice letting our attention wander over different parts of the field of vision while keeping the same fixation point it will soon be clear to us that the fixation point and the field of vision are by no means identical. They can by practice be separated and the attention directed to a point in indirect vision, i.e. a point lying to this or that side of the line of vision [p. 20].

Despite the compelling phenomenal nature of this observation, it has by no means been easy to demonstrate the possibility of attending to a position other than the fixation point, at least in uncluttered fields. Mowrer (1941) measured simple reaction time to expected and unexpected stimuli. For example, he showed that if the subject receives a series of auditory tones and then a light instead of a tone, reaction time to the light is longer than if the light had been presented in a series of other lights. However, using a similar technique, he found no effect on reaction time of expectancy for the location of a visual stimulus. Using detection measures, Mertens (1956) found that subjects were no better in detecting a flash when they knew its location than when they did not know at which of four locations it would occur. Similar results were obtained by Shiffrin and Gardner (1972) and by Grindley and Townsend (1968) when they used an uncluttered field.

On the other hand, Smith and Blaha (Note 17), in an unpublished study, found clear shifts in d' in some of their conditions when subjects knew where a stimulus would occur, even when careful monitoring insured that subjects did not move their eyes in that direction. Eriksen and Hoffman (1973), using the latency for naming a single letter presented in an otherwise blank field, found that the presentation of an indicator telling where in the field the letter would occur improved naming reaction time.

These conflicting results cannot be accounted for by the use of different dependent measures (e.g., reaction time vs. d') or by any other obvious single factor as far as we can determine. Some things that do seem to be important are distance from the fixation point at which subjects must attend, the intensity of the target signal, and whether the target signal occurs at a position that would be preferred by the subjects if they had a choice among the locations at which the target might occur.

Costs and Benefits

Our first study (Posner, Nissen, & Ogden, 1978) asked whether responses to a luminance change would occur more quickly when subjects knew where the stimulus would occur than when they did not. To insure that the differences in reaction time did not depend upon shifting one's eyes to the stimulus, eye movements were monitored by use of the electro-oculograph (EOG). Only those trials in which the eyes remain fixated by our criterion were used. In order to eliminate overt response priming as a contributor, Mowrer's technique of using simple reaction time as the dependent variable was adopted. Thus regardless of what the subjects received as the stimulus, their task was always the same—to press a single key. In order to separate the facilitation due to the subject's knowledge of where the stimulus would occur from the retardation or inhibition to signals that occur at unexpected locations, we used a cost–benefit approach.

Subjects received either a plus sign, which indicated that with equal probability a stimulus could come on to the left or right of fixation, or an arrow, which pointed to the left or right. The arrow was valid on 80% of the trials and invalid on 20%. Regardless of the cuing condition, the task was to press a key under the right index finger when any test stimulus appeared. The stimulus always occurred 1 sec following the cue. All trials in which the subjects responded prior to the occurrence of the stimulus (anticipations) and those in which they moved their eyes were removed from the analysis.

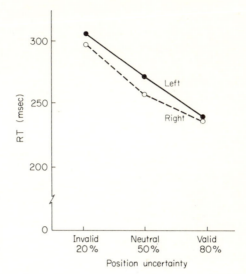

FIG. 7.6. Simple RT to a visual stimulus as a function of position uncertainty as varied by cue validity. (From Posner, Nissen, & Ogden, 1978. Copyright 1978 Lawrence Erlbaum Associates.)

Results are shown in Figure 7.6. The costs and benefits obtained from the knowledge of where the stimulus occurred are both significant and roughly symmetric, the benefit being approximately 25 msec and the cost approximately 40 msec. Very slight differences occurred depending on whether the stimulus occurred to the left or right of fixation.

Approximately 4% of all trials in this experiment produced an anticipatory eye movement. These trials were marked and the reaction times accumulated separately. Generally, when the subjects moved their eyes the reaction time to the target stimulus was somewhat longer than when they did not move their eyes. Thus anticipatory eye movements, even those too small for us to measure by the EOG, are unlikely to produce faster RTs to the expected event.

Figure 7.7 indicates the practice functions over the 100 trial blocks on successive days. Although the RTs to valid and invalid signals maintain their relative positions over the 2-day period, the neutral condition does show some change over that period. One would have more confidence in the sum of cost plus benefit than in the separation of a benefit and a cost. Much previous work has only measured benefits over a neutral condition. Although there are advantages to separate functions since both facilitatory and inhibitory effects are measured, there is also some problem because subjects may tend to work harder when the cue is an arrow than when it is a neutral stimulus. Thus it is difficult to be sure whether the neutral stimulus is in fact the correct baseline for measuring costs and benefits. The use of combined costs and benefits avoids this problem.

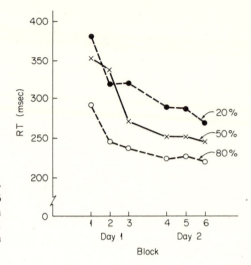

FIG. 7.7.   RTs for the three cue-va-
lidity conditions shown in Figure 7.6
over successive blocks. (From
Posner, Nissen, & Ogden, in 1978.
Copyright 1978 Lawrence Erlbaum
Associates.)

Distance

The results of the last experiment show clearly that the latency of response to a
stimulus is affected by the subject's knowledge of where the stimulus will occur.
Since eye and hand movements occur more rapidly to an expected position in
space than to an unexpected one, a possible method of combining these results
concerning knowledge of spatial position supposes that the size of the expectancy
effects are related to the probability that subjects would in the real world move
their eyes to the input event. Thus one might expect that effects of expectancy
would be greater for distant stimuli, which would normally occasion an eye
movement for careful fixation. It seemed to us that events very close to fixation,
well within the fovea, may not be so greatly affected by expectancy.

To study this, stimuli occurring 6.9 or .5 degrees from fixation were used.
The pure-far block was a replication of Experiment 1. The pure-near blocks were
identical, except that the stimulus was only .5 degrees from fixation. In the
mixed blocks, subjects were equally likely to get the near or far position as either
the expected or unexpected event. Position was randomized within a block.

The results for pure and mixed, near and far blocks are shown in Figures 7.8a
and 7.8b. The pure-far block is an exact replication of the previous experiment.
The pure-near block shows about the same cost and benefit as the far block,
although reaction time is somewhat but not significantly faster. In the mixed
blocks, the far condition was essentially unaffected; but the cost and benefit for
the near condition were substantially reduced in size. In particular, both the 80%
and 50% points were elevated in mixed blocks.

The results clearly disconfirm our notion that the size of set effects is closely
related to the eye movement system and thus to the distance from the fixation. On

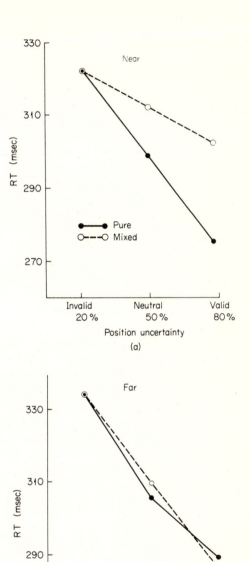

FIG. 7.8. Simple RT as a function of position uncertainty for a visual stimulus that occurs either .5 degrees (a) or 6.9 degrees (b) from fixation. (From Posner, Nissen, & Ogden, Note 18.)

the other hand, they confirm that subjects tend to behave as though they believe in this theory. In the mixed condition, they appear to choose to attend to the far stimulus at the expense of the near stimulus. Mixed blocks increase the times for the expected and neutral near trials only. It is as though subjects believe that attending to the far position is more critical, even though the pure blocks suggest that it is not.

An additional experiment was run with stimuli 25 degrees from fixation. In other respects this experiment was identical to the pure-far blocks. Figure 7.9 summarizes data from three experiments comparing .5-degree, 6.9-degree, and 25-degree positions. The results suggest that distance from the fixation point does not matter, even though the eye movements are summoned more automatically for parafoveal stimuli than for more distant stimuli (see p. 195). This finding suggests that reflexive control of eye position is very dependent upon the spatial position of the event that summons the eyes. On the other hand, voluntary movements of central attentional mechanisms are unaffected by the distance from the fovea of the expected event. Costs and benefits from a voluntary shift of visual attention are the same, regardless of the eccentricity of the events.

The similarity of costs and benefits for foveal and peripheral stimuli are both surprising and important. The result suggests that when attention is moved to a peripheral location, the area of most efficient detection is moved so that it is symmetric around the expected location. This result contrasts rather markedly to effects found when the task demands high acuity (Engle, 1971). In high-acuity

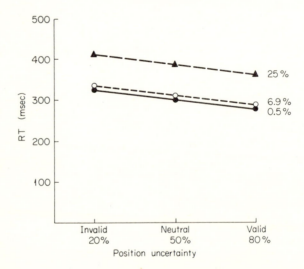

FIG. 7.9.   Simple RT as a function of position uncertainty for a visual stimulus of differing distances from fixation. (From Posner & Davidson, 1976. From the Official Proceedings of the International Congress of Physical Activity Sciences, Quebec City, July 1976, Monograph No. 5.)

situations, the area of efficient detection always includes the fovea, though it is extended in the direction of the point of maximal attention. Attention does not appear to depend upon the fine structure of the fovea, but attention cannot compensate for the acuity limits implicit in the organization of the retina. Since acuity cannot be moved freely over the visual field, it should not be too surprising that subjects behave as though they will have less trouble in detecting foveal signals that occur at unexpected positions even though for detection this is a false belief. The ability to measure this inappropriate bias on the part of subjects is one example of where laboratory studies appear to be able to pick up strategies carried over from the normal habits of the subjects. Though humans are adaptable organisms, they do not always compensate for the contingencies of a new laboratory environment. This sometimes serves to reveal their natural strategies. In this case, subjects seem to invoke a natural strategy that implies that they expect foveal stimuli to suffer less from expectancy than do peripheral stimuli.

Summary

In this section the second question concerning set and eye position has been answered. The internal mechanisms subserving attention are not directly dependent upon the eye movement system. Rather, attention can be moved independently of eye position. In most real behavior, attention moves with the fovea. This produces a strong correlation between the location of attention and the fovea. For this reason subjects tend to behave as though foveal information has a more direct access to central attention, but studies show that they are wrong about this. The retina appears (roughly speaking) equipotential with respect to the role of attention in luminance detection. This result is strong confirmation of the existence of a central attentional mechanism that is related to input pathways but that can also be viewed as isolable in the sense that it can be oriented toward a potential pathway endogenously.

So far, all studies of orientation in space have been visual. A visual stimulus that comes from a given position in space also has a particular internal pathway. By using stimuli of differing modalities, it is possible to disassociate position in external space from internal pathways. The next section develops this theme.

INPUT MODALITY AND ORIENTING

The same methods that have been applied to the study of visual orienting can be used with other modalities. In separate experiments, the effectiveness of cues for spatial location of visual, auditory, and tactile stimuli were examined.

Perhaps the best overall comparison of the results is given in Figure 7.10. The auditory reaction times are uniformly faster than are the visual and tactile reaction times. Of course the absolute levels are greatly influenced by the overall

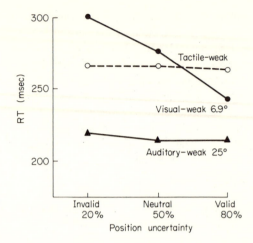

FIG. 7.10. Simple RT as a function of position uncertainty for visual, tactile, and auditory stimuli.

intensity of the stimulus. No systematic relationship between the overall reaction times and the size of the costs and benefits in these studies has been found. For example, the size of the costs and benefits for visual stimuli are identical, whether the stimuli are .5 degrees or 25 degrees from the fovea (see Figure 7.9). Thus it seems doubtful that the differences between modalities can be attributed to their overall reaction times. Instead, the differences shown in Figure 7.10 appear to reflect fundamental differences between modalities in terms of their mechanisms for activating attentional mechanisms.

Alerting, Orienting, and Detecting as Component Processes

Before proceeding further with a discussion of the results of orienting experiments conducted within the different sensory modalities, it will be well to call to mind certain definitions that have been developed in each of the last three chapters. Chapter 5 dealt with the change in internal state called *alerting*. Alertness is defined as the overall activation level of the central processing system. The higher the activation level, the more readily mechanisms could be brought to bear on any new stimulus event.

   In Chapter 6 the entry of the signal into the central processing system was examined. Such entry was traced by a combination of probe and EEG effects. The entry of a signal into the central mechanism is given the term *detecting* when energy pathways are the focus of the investigation (see p. 152). The key-press simple reaction-time task used in the last section is taken as representative of any number of ways that subjects could be asked to report that they are now aware of a signal. Different responses might produce different reaction times; but once a signal is available to the central processor, it has access to any response system that might have been specified.

Finally in this chapter I have introduced the term *orienting* to signify a particular response that may be made to a signal. That response is to turn peripheral or central mechanisms in the direction of the target. The ability to orient internally is signified by changes in the simple reaction-time response (detecting) produced by a cue as to the location of the signal in the external environment. If all stimuli benefited equally from the precue or if none did, it might be thought useless to distinguish between orienting and detecting. As can be seen in Figure 7.10, only visual stimuli seem to benefit from such a precue, and not stimuli in other modalities.[5]

Comparing Input Modalities

Why is it that detection of visual stimuli benefits from the precue about its location? Perhaps it is best to examine this question by first supposing that an overt orientation or movement of the eyes in the direction of the stimulus is a necessary precondition for detection of a visual stimulus. Suppose that only the fovea had access to a subject's conscious attention and that other places in the visual field could only produce an eye movement so that the fovea would be centered on the object. If this were the case, the stimulus falling outside the fovea would produce overt orienting toward the stimulus before the subject could detect the stimulus. Since the location of a signal is highly uncertain, this means that a choice reaction time for orienting could be as fast as the simple reaction time involved in reporting that a stimulus has occurred. A comparison of Figures 7.3 and 7.6 suggests that orienting the eyes toward a visual stimulus occurring 6.9 degrees to the left or right of fixation is faster than the simple reaction time involved in tapping a key. The choice RT for moving the hand in the direction of a stimulus is about as fast as the simple detection response in this condition.

Of course it is false that only the fovea has access to attention. Our results suggest that with respect to orienting produced by precues, the retina is equipotential. One can detect and report stimuli that occur away from the fovea with too brief a presentation for subjects to move their eyes in that direction. One can reject the view that *overt* orienting is necessary for detection. It is still possible to suppose that covert orienting is necessary for detection of visual stimuli.

If this were the case, one would expect that a precue telling the subjects where in space the stimulus will occur would uniformly improve the detection of stimuli that occur from that position in space and retard processing stimuli that

---

[5]The failure to find any effects of precues on auditory and tactile stimuli also helps to provide an answer to the view that visual cues may improve performance only because subjects are somehow reluctant to respond to information arising from an unexpected position in space. If this were so, all modalities should show a similar reluctance or bias. That they do not suggests that the costs and benefits found in vision represent genuine advantages from orienting internal attentional mechanisms toward the input signal.

occur elsewhere in space (see Figure 7.6). Moreover, one would also expect that the relative magnitude of the precuing effect would depend upon how successful the imperative stimulus is in achieving orienting. Imperative stimuli that are very good in bringing the subject's attention to a position in space would not benefit as much from a precue, but those that were poor in producing orienting toward a position in space would benefit a great deal from a precue. Work by Beck and Ambler (1973) and by Shiffrin and Gardner (1972) can be viewed in these terms. Beck and Ambler found that precues work very well in the detection of a shift in stimulus arrangement (e.g., L vs. T), a relatively poor attention-summoning change; but precues are relatively useless in detection of slope (e.g., T vs. ⟩), which is a very good stimulus for orienting attention. Shiffrin and Gardner likewise found that highly confusable stimulus arrays benefit more from location cues than do arrays where one of the stimuli is clearly distinguishable from the others. In their theoretical framework, Shiffrin and Gardner used this as support for the idea that attention has no effect on the selection of a position in space but does have an effect upon selection from among confusable items in the memory system. However, an equally plausible view that is also in line with the cost–benefit results reported above is to suppose that the nonconfusable visual stimulus is simply a good cue for the summoning of attention. Thus it would be expected to benefit less from a location cue. In short, for visual stimuli, orienting (i.e., the change in the direction of central attentional mechanisms toward a stimulus) is necessary for detection. Cues that provide the subject with information about orienting will be helpful in improving the detectability of the signal.

Nothing in this account has discussed the alerting effects of visual stimuli. The bulk of the literature suggests that alerting simply is not a strong feature of visual stimulation unless subjects deliberately attempt through an active process to use the visual stimulus as a way of raising activation of the central mechanism (see Chapter 5). To do so is to turn attention, or orient, toward that visual stimulus. I believe that although orienting and detecting are processes that occur automatically following the occurrence of a visual stimulus, alerting is something that will only occur if subjects make a deliberate effort to produce it.

Why should the effects of orienting be so powerful within the visual modality? In many ways, this should be no surprise to anyone who has considered the nature of vision as a sensory modality. Most books on vision concentrate on the spatial character of the visual system. The visual cortex is itself organized as a spatial system with more or less point–to–point projection from certain parts of the retina to the visual projection areas of the cortex.

Orienting to Touch

Figure 7.11 shows that simple reaction time to a tactile stimulus is unaffected by a cue that tells the subject whether the stimulus will occur to the left or right hand. In our experiment, the subjects examined a central fixation point on a

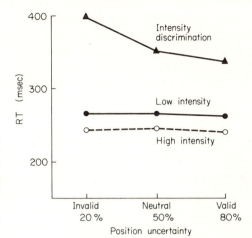

FIG. 7.11.   RT as a function of position uncertainty for high- and low-intensity tactile stimuli in a simple RT task (lower two lines) and in an intensity discrimination task (respond only to weak event; upper line). (From Posner, Davidson, & Nissen, Note 19.)

cathode ray tube, and their index fingers rested on rings. Following a precue, which could be a neutral plus sign or an arrow pointing to the left or right, subjects were given either a weak or an intense tap on the finger. Their task was to press the pair of keys that rested underneath the thumbs. Although a bimanual response was used, either key press was accepted as a detection.

The strength of the tactile stimulus was systematically varied. The results are shown in the lower two curves of Figure 7.11. No significant costs or benefits were found. The low-intensity tactile stimulus was an above-threshold light tap on the finger for which close attention was required for detection. Efforts to reduce the intensity still further did not seem to produce any evidence that costs or benefits could be obtained.

The tactile modality has properties that might classify it as a spatial modality. Like vision, one can image different positions on the body, and our body image itself appears to be extended in space. The tactile modality has nearly point–to-point projections from some areas of the body to the cortex. At first I thought the results with taps to index fingers were somewhat unique and that if the tactile stimulus was moved to other places on the body, costs and benefits would occur. No such effects were found, however.

Why should it be that tactile stimuli do not show the advantage of a cue signifying the position where the stimulus will occur? One idea is to suppose that orienting in the direction of the stimulus was simply not fast enough to precede detection. Unlike vision, in which the central processor appears first to orient in the direction of the stimulus in order to detect, tactile detection appears to precede orienting. In support of this view is evidence that an unattended tactile stimulus tends to summon the subject's attention rapidly. This result was obtained by Klein (1974), who compared the time to switch from the tactile and visual modalities with time to switch to them. He found that tactile stimuli showed a smaller decrement from the subject's attention to a visual stimulus than the reverse. Moreover, tactile stimuli, like auditory but unlike visual, seem to have automatic alerting effects.

In order to explore the relation of orienting and detection, I wished to slow down the tactile RTs and examine the effects on costs and benefits for location cues. To do this, the subjects were required to perform a tactile discrimination. In this task the subjects were to tap the key whenever the weaker of the two possible tactile intensities occurred. Weak events occurred on two-thirds of the trials and strong events on the other third. Thus subjects had to avoid tapping the key to energy alone. Instead they had to process the input in a more complex way in order to determine that it was the weak event. This raised tactile reaction time from 250 to 350 msec. It also produced significant costs and benefits. The size of the costs and benefits for tactile stimuli were small (see Figure 7.11) but within the range of those found for vision. It appears that when tactile processing is slowed by requiring a discrimination, orienting does have an effect. Strictly speaking, the effect may not be on detection itself but on the extra processes required by the discrimination. Nonetheless, it seems to suggest that orienting is an automatic feature of tactile processing but one that occurs more slowly than detecting and thus generally follows, rather than precedes, detection.

Since tactile stimuli produce strong alerting effects, it is altogether possible that the detection response is based on the pathways that produce alerting. This information would be sufficient to perform a detection task but may not allow one to perform a discrimination. It is possible that *detection* precedes orienting because energy pathways can be used for detection, but that tactile *discrimination* would follow orienting. Further work involving tactile discrimination would be needed in order to be certain.

Orienting to Sound

Tactile and visual cortical projection areas both are strongly organized on the basis of spatial position. On the other hand, the auditory projection area is not organized by spatial location but by frequency. Nonetheless, extremely efficient auditory localization mechanisms exist at subcortical levels.

Psychophysical studies are uniformly conducted under conditions in which the subject's attention is directed to the task of localization. Under such conditions, auditory localization is impressive. Introspective evidence suggests that one tends to orient in the direction of a sound. Introspections do not tell us, however, whether such orientations occur following detection (in the sense we have used it) of the auditory event or before it. Auditory events might interrupt ongoing behavior and lead to a decision to orient rather than the reverse.

When attention to auditory localization is reduced by the presence of visual information, some interesting effects occur. One of them is the so-called ventriloquism effect and indicates that it is fairly easy to distort the location of an auditory input in the direction of visual information about where it might have arisen (Radeau & Bertelson, 1974). Auditory localization is superior when visual structure is present in the field and when subjects have their eyes open, indicating that visual cues may aid as well as harm localization (Warren & Warren, 1970). Eye position also seems to play an important role in auditory localization (Jones & Kabanoff, 1975). There are also a number of illusions involving auditory localization (Cutting, 1976; Deutsch & Roll, 1976). All of these results suggest that localization depends heavily upon visual input as a frame of reference. This suggests that auditory localization, though often quite accurate, is not necessarily automatic. Otherwise, it would be difficult to know how vision could so easily distort it.

Chronometric experiments using auditory localization seem to provide new evidence of these questions. The experiments involved localization of a sound played over speakers 25 degrees to the left or right of fixation. The sound used produced rapid and accurate localization when subjects are asked to press a key indicating the side the sound was on. Simple reaction-time experiments were conducted that involved the same precues as discussed previously for visual and tactile stimuli. The subjects pressed a single key when they detected the sound.

An inspection of Figure 7.12 indicates no significant costs and benefits for audition in this situation. For ease of comparison, visual cost and benefit

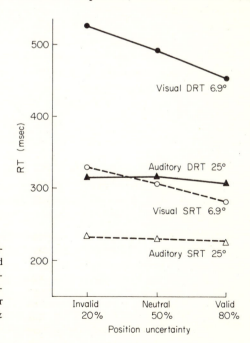

FIG. 7.12.   RT as a function of position uncertainty in auditory and visual simple RT tasks and in auditory and visual intensity discrimination reaction (respond only to weaker event. (From Posner, Davidson, & Nissen, Note 19.)

functions are included in the same graph. Auditory RT is very much faster than visual RT. To eliminate this problem, an auditory discrimination task in which subjects were required to respond only to the weaker of the two stimuli was run. With this procedure the auditory responses are about the same speed as visual simple reaction time at 6.9 degrees, yet there is still no evidence of costs or benefits.

Additional studies should be run to get the auditory reaction times near the visual discriminative reaction time shown in the upper curve of Figure 7.12. But the difference between visual simple reaction time and visual discriminative reaction time in costs and benefits is relatively small, despite an enormous increase in the overall reaction time. Thus there seems little evidence that audition differs only because of its faster RT.

These results suggest two interpretations. One is that the localization of auditory stimuli requires deliberate effort so that it does not occur automatically. A second possibility is that the time course of the influence on auditory localization at higher levels of the system is slow, so that discrimination occurs prior to localization. The latter idea is favored by the frequent finding that choice RT tasks benefit when the stimuli are in the same direction as the response, even when location is irrelevant to the task (J. R. Simon, 1969). On the other hand, simple RT to auditory stimuli by hand and eye do not show such effects of spatial compatibility, arguing that the auditory localization information does not influence rapid detection responses.

Auditory, tactile, and visual tasks show roughly similar costs and benefits when the subject is required to make a localization response by responding with one of two keys in the direction of the stimulus. In this case, the cue allows response preparation as well as orienting to a position in space. More work will be needed to explore these asymmetries in the way input on different modalities is accessed by central attentional systems.

Conclusion

The work on orienting, detecting, and alerting in the different stimulus modalities has not proceeded far enough to be entirely sure about the details of the internal processing. Our results and some of the findings in the literature can be reconciled by supposing that the different stimulus modalities connect central mechanisms in different ways.

In particular, three internal functions of a stimulus seem to be separable and differently organized in the three modalities. These ideas are summarized in Figure 7.13. The first function is the general change in the activation of the central processing system. Both tactile and auditory stimuli produce rapid and automatic changes in this activation level. Thus they serve as good warning signals and produce clear intersensory facilitation. On the other hand, visual stimuli do not seem to be as efficient in producing alerting unless the subject makes a deliberate effort to do so.

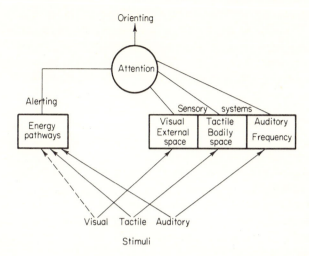

FIG. 7.13.   A proposed view of sensory input to alerting and identification systems and their roles in accessing attention. (From Posner, Davidson, & Nissen, Note 19.)

Visual stimuli produce rapid, efficient orienting. Orienting appears to be a necessary condition for subjects to detect a visual signal. This is not true in either the tactile or auditory modalities.

In the tactile modality, orienting seems to occur more slowly although still automatically to the occurrence of the stimulus. In the auditory modality, orienting either requires a more deliberate decision on the part of the subject rather than occurring automatically or occurs automatically but more slowly than the discriminations so far required.

The process of signal detection as we have defined it in Chapter 6 appears quite different for the three modalities. Even though a general, mathematical theory of signal detection (Tanner & Swets, 1954) can be developed irrespective of the modality involved, it appears to be necessary to bear in mind differences due to input modality. In some sense, viewing signal detection in terms of the specific ways in which an external signal accesses attention may seem like an unnecessary complication to simpler models that rely upon internal counters or hypothetical activity levels. Nonetheless, the results appear far more in line with suggested principles of nervous system organization. It is known that signals do produce general phasic changes in ongoing brain states and that connections of visual signals to collicular eye movement systems appear to be somewhat independent of connections to the cortical systems that lead to identification. It seems to me that the model examined in Figure 7.13 gives promise that appropriate chronometric paradigms can be developed to provide ways of examining these different functions of a sensory event.

ORIENTING TO SENSORY AND MEMORY SYSTEMS

Much of the material introduced in Chapters 2, 3, and 4 involves the processing of visual letters and words. Because of the arbitrary nature of reading, it is clear that their processing depends upon information stored in memory. In Chapters 5, 6, and 7 many of the experiments involve the processing of tones and light flashes. In what ways is orienting to codes in the memory system (e.g., physical, phonetic) similar to orienting to a flash of light or tone? In this section I want to review evidence that suggests similarities between the two situations.

It is important to ask whether the sensory studies discussed above tell us anything about orienting as it takes place in real-world situations. In the last section of this chapter, emphasis was on separate characteristics of orienting toward events in the visual, auditory, and tactile modalities. This emphasis may be puzzling, because if one examines the world from a phenomenological viewpoint, it seems to consist of objects that occupy positions outside of us. Neisser (1976) has put it very well:

> Most events, at least those that interest us and to which we attend, stimulate more than one sensory system. We see someone walk and hear his footsteps, or hear him talk as we watch his face. We look at the things we handle, and experience our own body movements both kinesthetically and visually. In our mouths we feel what we taste, and sense the movements of the organs of speech as we hear the sound of the words we are speaking. In driving a car we feel its responsiveness to the controls as we watch its movement along the road; in observing an argument we see the gestures and attitudes of the participants as we hear their words and tones of voice [p. 29].

The world does not seem to be divided into modalities like audition, vision, touch, smell, etc., but into discrete objects holding their positions as we move around. At first blush, this unity of object perception is in strong contrast with the known physiology of the nervous system. Consider a conversation with a person sitting in your living room. This person appears to occupy a position in the world, and voice and face movements seem to occur as a unit. Nonetheless, sensory physiology tells us that the visual input is processed by different systems and in different places in the brain than is information from the voice.

Sensory physiology is not decisive here, because in addition to the sensory-specific pathways, we also have many multimodal cells that accept input from different sense receptors. There is the physiology present to emphasize either separation by modality or integration across modalities. The psychological question is: To what extent are we able to commit attention or response systems directly to modality-specific input as opposed to input already integrated across modalities? Based upon phenomenological observations, one of the strongest principles for selection of information should be its position in external space. Our perception seems to be of objects, and the common aspect of an object is that it occupies a position in the external world. In the next section I present studies that compare directly orienting to a sensory modality with orienting toward a common external location from which multimodal signals arise.

Modalities Versus Locations

There is evidence that subjects can selectively tune information coming from one modality. This was shown by LaBerge (1973) and by Klein (1974), both of whom examined the time to switch from an expected to an unexpected modality. The same result was obtained via the cost–benefit analysis for auditory and visual signals.

It has been shown that subjects can be instructed to attend to the visual or to the tactile modality. Both visual and tactile modalities show significant costs and benefits when subjects are cued as to where in space the stimulus will occur (at least when a discriminative task is used). It should be possible to compare a modality cue (which gives information on location of the item in the brain) with a spatial cue (which tells the subject where in external space it is most likely to occur). In our experiment we had the subjects rest their index fingers upon vibrators. Above the vibrator was a light. Thus the two positions in space were left and right. The stimuli were strong or weak visual or strong or weak tactile events. Before each stimulus the subjects were given information either about the modality of the stimulus or about whether it would come from their left or right. Subjects indicated a weak stimulus by pressing their two little fingers and a strong stimulus by pressing their two thumbs. Reaction times and errors were measured.

We know from previous work that if subjects are given information about both modality and location, they can take advantage of it to improve performance (see Figures 7.3 and 7.11). Although this result is much stronger in the visual modality, it seems also to occur in the tactile modality for discrimination tasks.

The results of our experiment are shown in Figure 7.14. There is little or no evidence of benefit from knowing where in space the stimulus will occur, but there are clear costs and benefits when the subjects know the modality of input. These experiments should be taken as illustrative rather than definitive, because we do not know the conditions under which these results occur. However, at least for the present method there is some reason for supposing that subjects are better off when they know where the stimulus will occur in the brain than when they know where in space it will occur.[6] These results must be put together with the

---

[6]There are also other reasons for being cautious about our result in addition to the fact that it is so far a single result found in only one chronometric paradigm and should be replicated. More important, the assumption that a light and vibration that arise from the same spatial position should serve as an object depends upon the assumption that the basic common characteristic of objects is that they occupy positions in external space. Familiar objects such as people and cars undoubtedly have perceptual and memorial characteristics other than occupying positions in space. Finally, Spelke (1976) has shown that infants look in the direction of an object that corresponds to a sound arising from another position in space as though they had a natural (perhaps innate) correspondence.

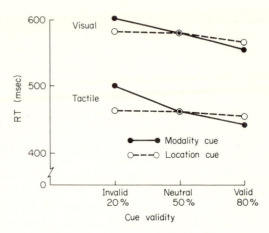

FIG. 7.14. Choice RT for intensity judgments of visual and tactile stimuli as a function of cue validity and whether subjects are given a cue to the modality or to the spatial location of the imperative event. (From Posner, Nissen, & Ogden, 1978. Copyright 1978 Lawrence Erlbaum Associates.)

failure to get faster detection of auditory or tactile stimuli when the subject's attention is called to a position in space. If orienting toward position in space were a unified act across sensory modalities, it is very unlikely that one would get clear results for one modality and not for another. Orienting appears to be different, depending on the modality of input. The overall thrust of our results suggests that the phenomenological unity of objects in space is imposed relatively late in the nervous system, and it is possible by psychological experiments to decompose that unity into the individual pathways of stimulation that are represented by the object.

Intensity Effects Revisited

The previous section emphasized the importance of orientation toward the internal modality-specific pathways activated by an object rather than to multimodal systems representing its position in the external world. If sensory orienting depends primarily upon the internal pathway, there should be a close analogy between orienting to a sensory event and to a memorial code activated by a word or letter.

In Chapter 4 it was found that in a lexical decision task, an increase in visual intensity had a smaller effect upon a primed pathway than on an unprimed one. When a pathway was activated by a previous related word, the effect of making the current word brighter was greatly reduced over when it followed an unrelated word (Becker & Killion, 1977). In the context of visual luminance detection, such an interaction would be unsurprising. What would be more reasonable is that a bright stimulus should be efficient in producing orienting and that intensity should accordingly have larger effects when the subject's attention is elsewhere in the field.[7] The same finding is more surprising in the context of the lexical decision task. Why should a brighter word produce a smaller advantage when the pathway has been primed? No orientation to location needs to take place, because subjects are already attending the correct position for the word. However, carrying forward the analogy with physical location, one might consider a pathway as similar to a position in space. A bright stimulus would be expected to produce a strong tendency to orient toward the pathway. If a primed stimulus has already produced an orientation of attention, increasing its intensity will not have as large an effect on performance.

Unfortunately, studies that pursue the analogy between orienting toward a sensory event in detection studies and orienting toward an internal memory code in studies of matching, lexical decisions, or other cognitive tasks are not very well advanced. It is not presently known whether common principles of the relation between the activation pattern of an internal code and orienting can be developed irrespective of the kind of information that is presented. The importance of sensory modality in determining the relationship between orienting and detecting for sensory signals suggests that the principles that related sensory detection to processing of higher-level linguistic codes may turn out to be complex and rather abstract. Nonetheless, as I hope this chapter illustrates, the chronometric methods used to explore linguistic codes in Chapters 2, 3, and 4 have also turned out to be fruitful in the examination of the components of relatively simple, sensory detection tasks.

SUMMARY

Central processing mechanisms (*set*) can control the selection of sensory input. The mechanisms of set are varied and include the use of overt eye and hand movements as well as the direction of central attention. Set is an active process that can be time locked to events that cue it. Set for the location of an event in visual space influences motor responses in the direction of the event. The costs and benefits of set toward a position in visual space are greater for hand movements than for eye movements.

One way set can be achieved is by orienting the central systems themselves without any overt response. This can be shown by the existence of costs and

---

[7]Unfortunately, what seems obvious is not always so easy to demonstrate empirically. Using the cost–benefit approach for the detection of a luminance increment, an interaction between the intensity of the signal and expectancy about where in space it will occur has been obtained in some conditions. This interaction when found seems to be in the intuitive direction that costs are less to a bright signal than to a dim signal. In other conditions, additivity between intensity and expectancy was also found, and the major determinants of when an interaction occurs are not known.

benefits from location cues when overt preparation is excluded. The ability to move attention in visual space is somewhat independent of the distance of a target from fixation.

The influences of a sensory event upon the nervous system are viewed in terms of three internal mechanisms: alerting, detecting, and orienting. In the case of visual events, detecting appears to occur as the result of a prior overt or covert orientation toward the event. This effect may account for the evidence against automatic alerting by visual stimuli (see Chapter 5). On the other hand, an auditory event appears to cause detection prior to orienting. Indeed in many cases it is difficult to give a location to an auditory event even after detection. Tactile signals appear to be intermediate, producing slow but automatic orientation, which generally follows detection.

There is a resemblance between orienting to simple sensory events such as the ones studied in this chapter and orienting toward the physical, phonetic, and semantic codes of letters and words. Sensory objects may be viewed as assemblies of sensory-specific codes. The effect of intensity is to produce more efficient orientation toward whatever internal pathways are automatically activated by the event. These findings make it possible to treat the time course of processing of stimuli of different types within a chronometric framework.

8
Implications

INTRODUCTION

Ulric Neisser (1976) argues that cognitive psychology has failed to provide an image of human nature that could produce extensions of its principles beyond the specific paradigms in which they are derived. The criticism could be applied to this book. The book title appears to promise a general analysis of "mind," but the reader of the last seven chapters may well wonder what is implied by the methods and principles that have been so laboriously developed. In this chapter I hope to provide at least a partial answer to this question.

The first section of this chapter consists of a brief summary of the principles and methods developed in the previous seven chapters. It may help the reader to hold in mind the essential concepts. The next section argues that efforts to extend these principles to new questions require some analysis of what it is to apply a principle to a new area, task, or domain. The following three sections review implications in three areas of psychological interest—reading, cognitive development, and personality. Implications in such broad areas are bound to sound somewhat pretentious, but Neisser's point about the importance of examining the potential implications of any point of view convinces me that it is better to try, even if the efforts are bound to fall short of hopes.

Methods

The first seven chapters of this book deal with problems that are both methodological and substantive. Two major methodological points have been developed. First is the use of sets of model tasks that allow us to trace basic psychological

217

operations. The use of model tasks in this book differs rather considerably from the central thrust of much of cognitive psychology. Much of the literature in the field involves the development of a single complex task. The goal of the author is then to provide a detailed model of the task that would allow predictions of performance in that task. In a number of cases, such approaches have led to exquisite models of the psychological processes involved in a given task (e.g., Carpenter & Just, 1975; Clark & Chase, 1972; Sternberg, 1969). Much of the malaise to which Neisser points in his book occurs when one seeks to develop a general view incorporating the individual models appropriate for different tasks.

For example, many psychological tasks show clear evidence of serial processing of information and give linear fits between the number of occurrences of an assumed underlying process and reaction time. It is not appropriate to conclude from such results that the human is always limited to one event at a time or that stages never overlap. The method of model tasks involved in this book is quite different. It does not seek such detailed empirical analysis of any particular task. Rather it takes some assumed underlying psychological process, such as alertness or pathway activation, and attempts to understand its properties in a variety of experimental situations. The task becomes a "preparation" designed to maximize the role of a process. The goal is to understand the assumed psychological process, and the model tasks serve as a method of tracing its operation. The construction of the task is in the service of the study of psychological operations, rather than the reverse.

A second methodological contribution of this book is a catalogue of the techniques of mental chronometry. Reaction time is viewed as one chronometric method that—along with speed–accuracy tradeoffs, encoding functions, evoked potentials, poststimulus histograms of single-cell activity, and other methods—can help one trace the time course of information processing in the human nervous system. The book does not attempt to focus on particular dependent variables but rather upon all methods that serve to trace the time course of psychological operations.

These two methodologies rest upon a number of implicit assumptions that have been faced at various points in the book. The first assumption is the close correspondence between physiology and psychology. The close correspondence is often taken for granted in peripheral, sensory, and motor processes; it has been less seriously held with respect to more central activity. I do not believe that physiology should become a model of psychology (Uttal, 1971) or the reverse, but it does seem to me that there should be a fruitful two-way interaction between the disciplines. For example, physiological studies of attention have given us information about the role of the reticular formation in maintaining cortical tone. Psychological studies, such as those discussed in Chapters 6 and 7, show differences in the functional relation of sensory modalities to alerting. These two findings represent the challenge for psychologists to examine whether the alerting that occurs in behavioral tasks can be attributed to known properties of reticular activation. At the same time, physiologists need to determine whether input to the reticular system from different modalities resembles that which might be supposed from their relative effects upon alerting.

Another basic assumption is that of a close isomorphism between physical and psychological time. At the level of subjective reports, it is quite clear that no such isomorphism exists. Our subjective awareness of time is quite limited and in many cases is not isomorphic to physical time. Nonetheless, I hope the first seven chapters of this book have established the surprisingly strong isomorphism between performance measures of psychological processes and the time that they require. If this assumption were fundamentally wrong, it appears unlikely that the chronometric studies would be as successful as they have been.

Substance

The major substantive contribution of our framework is the idea of an isolable subsystem for processing information. It is, of course, well accepted that the great sensory systems exist as complicated and in some sense independent systems for analyzing the world around us. This plan of independent but interconnected systems for processing information appears to extend well beyond sensory systems. The idea that a letter or word exists in the form of independent physical, phonetic, and semantic codes is a concept with pervasive influence and importance to psychology. The principle of independent internal codes turns out to be as applicable to the detection of a spot of light or tone as it does to the assimilation of the meaning of a word or phrase. The isolable subsystem idea provides a basic level of systems analysis for many psychological tasks. This concept is not as restrictive nor as predictive as a serial stage assumption; rather, it incorporates that idea as a special case.

Within each isolable system, complex processing occurs. The overlapping nature of the processes that occur within isolable subsystems produces the richly parallel processing of which the human is capable. Thus even if the leading edge of activation produces a serial organization to the activation of internal codes, the overlapping nature of the processes that occur within these systems provides ample opportunity for principles of parallel processing.

A second substantive contribution of this book is evidence for the existence of psychological pathways of considerable stability that connect isolable codes. Chapter 4 provides evidence that the basic activation pattern of a given word is stable, even under circumstances where differences in context alter the meanings reaching subjective awareness. These stable activation patterns are the basis of our subjective lexicon. Psychological pathways provide a basis for understanding those aspects of human thought that appear to be most stable or rigid.

A basic feature of the views developed in this book is the contention that subjective awareness requires the entry of a signal into a system that is isolable from the activation patterns produced by input. This allows awareness to reflect the activity of different processing systems depending upon strategies, context, and prior experience. Our subjective awareness is an unreliable guide to the activation patterns that are created by any given event. The ability of attention to produce activation of its own allows us to create codes from endogenous sources that serve to guide the processing of new information. Thus attention provides us with limited cognitive control over the activation patterns that are produced.

The conflicts between the relatively rigid activation patterns produced by input and the cognitive control we exercise via attentional mechanisms serve as a major theme for the understanding of internal information processing. Such factors as past experience, differences between individuals, and moment–to–moment changes in strategy affect information processing via the endogenous nature of the limited-capacity mechanisms that make up the systems underlying subjective awareness. The dual nature of reflex and endogenous mechanisms provides some measure of answer to the long debate between entirely passive and entirely active views of human perception and cognition. Perception is neither entirely rigidly imposed by input nor capriciously developed by our own internal strategies. Rather, through the activation of pre-existing pathways, we produce a modicum of influence over our own subjective awareness of the world around us. Higher levels of the system are more easily reprogrammed under the influence of attention. We can expect a name or face so strongly that we believe it to have occurred. In general, however, images and perception are not confused.

This brief summary reviews the basic features that have been explored through the experimentation in the first seven chapters. Although I have more faith in the techniques and methods developed than I do in the exact answers provided, I believe a combination of the substantive and methodological contributions of this framework produce a number of implications that can aid us in the analysis of important psychological questions. These implications are gentle ones, not ones that produce hard and fast predictions. Can such a relatively general framework provide any help in understanding psychological questions? In the next section I turn to this issue.

THEORY AND APPLICATION

From time to time groups or organizations meet to discuss the relation between research and more practical problems that people face. One such meeting to which I was invited concerned the problems of brain damage and memory. I discussed the relationship between the study of memory codes as it was emerging from our laboratory (see Chapter 2) and problems of their pathology (Posner, 1967). It seemed obvious that the language used to discuss the separation of visual and phonetic codes of letters and words was related to problems resulting from strokes and neurosurgical interventions. Another such invitation was to discuss basic research related to reading instruction (Posner, Lewis, & Conrad, 1972; Posner, in press). It seemed that our results helped those present to grasp the underlying difficulty that dyslexic children might have with the seemingly simple problem of interpreting visual letters.

I have also been asked to comment on the contributions of chronometric analysis and information-processing theory to such issues as how best to select people for jobs that demand high levels of skill and deficits in performance due to aging or retardation. And, as a student of Paul Fitts, I have been consulted on occasion about the training of people for industry and human factors positions and the contributions of cognitive psychology to education in general.

These invitations provide a welcome opportunity to discuss our research. Each invitation also led to some perplexity. Although I felt that the researches reported in the last seven chapters had made progress into the specific nature of human information processing, the very complexity of the results and theory seem to preclude any facile generalizations about performance in any real-life task.

Yet working with Paul Fitts provided the conviction that attempts to develop applications of this type are worthwhile for basic theory as well as for what might be contributed to applied problems. On occasion, my conflict between the desirability of the goal and the weakness of my message surfaced in the chapters written in response to such invitations. One paper on reading (Posner, et al., 1972) concluded with a direct reference to applications of our results: "Perhaps we should be grateful that they are neither very obvious nor very direct. Many errors have been made in the enthusiasm to apply research findings directly to the task of learning to read [p. 186]." In some ways more surprising to me than the weakness of my message was the generosity of the comments that sometimes resulted from these efforts when the audience consisted of teachers, clinicians, neurologists, reading specialists, etc. There often was considerable enthusiasm for what seemed to me to be frustratingly weak arguments on my part. In the end, I was forced to conclude that we are badly in need of a better understanding of how applications might flow from the results of basic research.

Conventional Wisdom

The sense of unease about these attempts at application arises in part because of the conventional wisdom of the relationship between application and theory. Because basic research primarily involves the construction of theories that may be tested only through predictions, one gets the idea that it is necessary to derive specific predictions from a theory in order for that theoretical view to have useful implications. Thus conventional wisdom holds that a theory arising out of basic psychology ought to make specific predictions that will tell us what to do in order to solve the problem. The fact that this almost never occurs produces despair about the potential application of psychology. Instead, it could lead us to question whether the conventional wisdom about the relationship between application and theory is appropriate.

It has also been argued (Neisser, 1976) that cognitive psychology lacks implications, because the tasks it studies are not ecologically valid. This criticism certainly applies to the "model task" approach for tracing psychological process adopted in this book. According to Neisser's viewpoint, applications in psychology come from studying real-world tasks in the laboratory environment. It is true that only if the psychological issues that are selected for study are in fact important can the "model task" approach work. If such issues as "alertness," "activation of pathways," "limited capacity for active attention" are unimportant in the real world, a framework developed in the laboratory for their analysis will not be applicable. Thus it is important to select psychological issues that have real importance for the human. If that is done, it seems to me that there will be useful implications if the principles found even in the tasks used to study these processes are selected for their analytic power rather than their ecological validity. The difficulty in trying to generalize from the study of real-world tasks rather than real-world problems is that natural tasks often prove resistant to analytic tools.

Artificial and Natural Sciences

H. A. Simon (1969) has distinguished between natural sciences and sciences of the artificial. His idea is that sciences of design (artificial sciences) primarily involve synthesis, not analysis. Thus the art of the designer does not result through predictions from models developed by the basic researcher. Instead the basic researcher can hope to foster attitudes and principles that might be useful to a practitioner in synthesizing new designs.

Simon hoped to develop a science of the artificial that would tell people how to proceed in a way that would produce good design. Although I believe Simon's distinction between sciences of the artificial and natural is a most useful one, his suggestions for the development of a science of design are less convincing. This probably indicates that we have not progressed far enough to have developed algorithms that would aid in the creation of a science of design. The difficulty may well rest in the weakness of our understanding of how people conceive and utilize hypotheses in guiding their thoughts.

Search Processes

Chapter 7 dealt with how *set* for the location of an event in the visual field or within the memory system guided our attention. This is a relatively constrained experimental model for the study of the more general issue of how conscious search is guided by prior hypotheses. Newell and Simon (1972) point out that this issue is at the heart of the problem-solving process. Placed in the context of applied psychology, the question becomes how does a search plan arise, and what influence does it have upon the designer? The answer seems to me to reflect the crucial role of theory. The person designing a curriculum, a decision-making system in industry, or a complex organizational structure starts with a view of the nature of people. Psychological theory about how people process information is bound to have strong influences on the direction in which designers choose to search. It is no coincidence that following Freud's brilliant analysis of the nature of mind, clinical psychiatry and psychology were dominated by findings showing the importance of sexual adjustment in human behavior. Though no doubt sexual adjustment is extremely important and early life experiences do shape minds, surely they would not have been so much the focus of discussion if Freud had not pointed a generation of clinicians in that direction. In the same way, early mental chronometry led industrial engineers to search for physical and mental units that might be combined into the maximally efficient performance for a given task (Taylor, 1967). Under the influence of more humanistic approaches to psychology, management began to view the importance of relations among workers as crucial to their efficiency. March and Simon's (1958) theory of people as information processors led to a different view of industrial organizations as being shaped by and shaping the motivations of the managers and workers within these organizations. In few cases did the psychological theory make very specific predictions about industrial design; but the applications were made, because industrial designers were led to view their problems in particular ways by the language of the basic sciences.

The methods of forming and breaking habits have been discussed by philosophers, psychologists, and parents for many generations. Yet it was not until the basic theories underlying behaviorism had been dominant for some time in experimental psychology that clinicians began to practice systematic desensitization as a means of breaking inappropriate habits.

Each psychological theory carries with it implications about where practitioners ought to look in order to find those characteristics of a situation that are most salient to their designs. It would be inconsistent with the kind of psychology I have been discussing not to point out that the benefits involved in examining a human problem in one way are accompanied by costs in our ability to observe the same problem in another way. The psychological theory of Sigmund Freud focuses the mind upon sex as an important determiner of human behavior; it tends to blind one to the everyday work experience and economic structure as possible controllers of human behavior and thought. Marxism emphasizes the crucial importance of economic relationships in shaping the mind and also tends to blind one to the considerable importance of the other factors (e.g., physical environment) in shaping personality. Thus each way of looking at the nature of humans carries with it advantages and disadvantages. These are a form of application of a psychological theory. It is not, of course, impossible for a person to work with more than one theory. Given time and careful notes, a designer may examine the same problem from many points of view, just as any of us may use more than one code to think about an issue. Just as our limited capacity for conscious attention often constrains our thought to a single code that dominates memory and behavior, so too our tendency to examine a problem from one point of view tends to reduce the likelihood of its examination from another point of view. Many psychologists have been impressed with the degree to which one set or hypothesis reduces our likelihood of viewing an issue from another viewpoint (Bruner & Potter, 1964).

This way of looking at the relationship of theory and application also explains why efforts along these lines are so frustrating. One labors hard over the distinctions that might separate one psychological theory from another. The researcher must take very seriously the different predictions that result from explaining an effect by a change in the rate of pathway activation as opposed to explaining it as due to changes in orienting. However, the effects of these distinctions on a designer may be less important than the very general underlying assumptions (e.g., that mental processes take time and that capacity is limited) that tend to be common to almost all theories of internal mental processes. When doing experimental research, one's attention is always on the differences in prediction between theories; when trying to choose what to emphasize to those who may apply psychology, attention must be drawn to those common assumptions that underlie the research enterprise but that only in times of paradigm shifts are themselves the object of research activity.

Tools

Another aspect of the potential application of basic researches of the type discussed in this book is the use of the tools developed by them. Doubtless the use of operant conditioning techniques in drug research has had large implications over and above the applications of the principles of operant theory. Chronometric methods are extremely sensitive and when interpreted carefully can give insight both into the structures and processes in the individual human mind. Applications of such methods to the diagnosis of deficit (e.g., due to brain damage or aging), to understanding and predicting performance of people in new environments (e.g., flying or medical school), and for evaluating the success of a teaching method or course are obvious. What seems to me to be the most exciting possibility is the insight that such methods may give each person into the processes that underlie their own mental performance.

Case Histories

It is apparent that no one could expect to apply the myriad of experimental results obtained in the previous chapters directly to understanding of any practical task or general psychological question. There are too many free parameters, too much overlap between different internal mechanisms that might be combined in too many different ways in any given situation for that strategy to work. Nonetheless, there is much that has emerged from investigations employing mental chronometry that does change the nature of where one should search for the key to important human problems. Perhaps researchers in cognitive psychology will forgive me if what follows is more general and less related to the results of specific experiments than what has been presented in previous chapters. It is not useful merely to enumerate very abstract principles that emerge from laboratory experiments. Instead, I have taken three areas of general psychological interest and tried to indicate both the tools and principles that illustrate how analyses based on the concepts developed in this book might change some of the ways people look at these problems. The issues I have chosen represent applications of the principles employed in this book, because they involve extensions of them to areas different from those in which they were derived. I do not wish to argue that the three areas discussed below are necessarily any more ''applied'' in a general sense than the areas discussed in the first seven chapters. Indeed each of the three areas has a substantial number of basic researches exploring it, sometimes using techniques and frameworks not very distant from those employed in this book. My goals are simply to see if there are implications of the framework used here for the analysis of these areas and to point out places of contact with those working more directly in the area.

The first issue concerns the problem of reading. Our research focuses on the internal codes involved in the process and on automation of the skill so that it takes place outside of active attention. It leads to the examination of possible reasons for the special problems that a small number of dyslexic children have in learning to read.

The problem of deficit in learning to read leads quite naturally in the next section to an examination of the development of intelligence over the early life span. Information-processing approaches to this question stress the continuity in performance between children and adults. They also provide new tools to analyze some theories of development. The issue of development is complex, because each individual mind is likely to contain different structures that allow for superior processing in one domain and deficient processing in another.

In the last section of this chapter, personality is viewed in terms of how relatively ''shallow'' differences in the cognitive structures between people can lead to profound variations in their style. Personality is seen as resulting not alone from the early experiences of childhood and adolescence but from the cognitive structures that are undergoing growth and development over the entire life cycle.

READING

Dyslexia

In 1925 Samuel Orton proposed that certain children had difficulty in reading because of problems with incomplete lateralization of the cerebral hemispheres. Both Orton's observation and his theory were met with a singular lack of interest by psychologists. To a psychology dominated by behaviorism and psychometrics, it hardly seemed credible to suppose that difficulty in a complex task like reading could be conceptualized as a specific deficit rather than a manifestation of general low intelligence. As neurologist Macdonald Critchley (1967) has pointed out, psychologists of the time viewed dyslexia as a mild form of idiocy.

Since behaviorism emphasized the correlation between stimuli and responses, a difficulty in reading was seen as a problem in learning. Since intelligence was viewed as the ability to adapt (i.e., to learn new things), a problem in learning must imply relatively low intelligence.

Although Orton's specific theories and observations would still not be generally accepted, cognitive psychology provides a language in which they can be discussed. In light of work reviewed in Chapter 2, a deficit that specifically affects visual language processing would not be surprising. Educational designers looking at the problem of dyslexia with behaviorism and psychometric theory have no language for discussing the problem they see. Viewed through the eyes of cognitive psychology, the problem becomes an instance of the ability of individuals to deal with the different internal codes produced by a word.

To illustrate further how such a language aids in understanding a deficit, consider findings that dyslexics have much greater difficulty in reading abstract than concrete words, even when efforts are made to equate them for orthographic regularity and frequency (Marshall & Newcombe, 1973; Shallice & Warrington, 1975). Of course it is always possible to attempt to explain away this finding as an artifact of frequency, age of learning, or some other confounded variable. The motivation is very great to do so, if one believes either in a strict S–R approach to mental processing or a serial approach in which phonetic processing must come before semantic processing. These approaches make it paradoxical that an individual should not be able to name a word because of something about its meaning —which should only be available after naming is complete.

The viewpoint of isolable systems outlined in Chapter 2 resolves this difficulty. Suppose the dyslexic does have a special difficulty in the pathways that lead from the visual to the phonetic analysis of a word and that the visual to semantic and semantic to phonetic analyses are unimpaired. This view (see p. 93) would suggest that a word would look up its meaning in the memory system. Since concrete words have only one meaning, the semantic to phonetic links could well provide a sufficient basis for pronunciation. Dyslexics would have relatively little trouble in pronouncing such words. Abstract words would tend to look up meanings in the memory system and would not produce an unambiguous phonetic analysis, and thus the dyslexic might then produce a semantically correct but phonetically wrong interpretation of the word (see Marshall & Newcombe, 1973; Shallice & Warrington, 1975; for a discussion of the model).

Instruction

A major controversy in the field of reading instruction has been between the advocates of phonics training and those who favor the look–say or sight reading view. The controversy has been sufficiently vexed as to produce political ramifications, with phonics training being associated with a more conservative orientation and the look–say method being identified with liberal politics. Does mental chronometry provide any fundamentally different ways of looking at the controversy between look–say and phonics? I believe that it does.

We might first ask what are the fundamental codes involved in reading? Psychologists (as outlined previously in Chapter 3) have made important discoveries about the fundamental codes used in reading. At one level the discovery certainly helps to reconcile the debate between the look–say and phonics methods of reading instruction. Unfortunately, the discovery itself does not necessarily carry any particular lesson with respect to educational use, but it certainly changes the direction in which one would be led to search to produce curricular innovations in reading.

This discovery could be put simply and boldly by saying that the nervous system represents a word as a visually organized chunk of information independently of its pronunciation (see p. 76). Put this way, the existence of a visual code that represents an integrated sequence of letters in a word may not seem surprising. However, its relative independence from a phonetic representation and the indication that this visual code has access to important semantic information makes the understanding of the visual code underlying words of considerable importance.

The existence of a visual code that represents a unified set of letters might arise in two ways. One could talk about the effects being due to visual familiarity with certain letter strings, or one could talk about it being due to rule-governed orthographic regularity. There is evidence in favor of both interpretations. The results obtained with mixed cases show fairly conclusively that visual familiarity is not a necessary condition to get a unified visual chunk. Rather, a skilled reader can chunk items (e.g., GaRbAge) that look unfamiliar but that obey the orthographic regularity of the language. This would be necessary if reading is to transfer to different type fonts and to handwritten script. On the other hand, there is evidence that visual familiarity aids in the identification of words. The evidence comes in part from matching tasks that show that visually familiar but not orthographically regular strings, like "IBM" and "FBI," are matched better than are unfamiliar strings (Egeth & Blecker, 1971; Henderson, 1974). Thus orthographic regularity is not a necessary characteristic for visually meaningful units. It has also been shown that subjects who have learned the meaning of words from oral presentation and have separately learned to recode a string of letters into a particular phonetic representation—but who have never looked up the meaning of the word from its visual presentation—are slow on the first few occasions they are required to do so (Brooks, 1977). If orthographic regularity were the only important thing in obtaining the semantics of a printed word, unfamiliar regular words should not have been slow even on their first presentation, since the words had orthographic regularity and the semantics are available in the memory system.

Two studies have examined the relationship between orthographic regularity and visual familiarity in processing strings (Egeth & Blecker, 1971; McClelland, 1976). They used different methods and materials. The results agree in showing an interaction between the two variables. The occurrence of an interaction between orthography and familiarity suggests a possible reconciliation between the look–say and phonics training methods. In so far as look–say stresses visual familiarity and phonics stresses rules of the orthography, their effects on processing could work through a common mechanism to achieve an integrated visual chunk.

The nature of the interaction is important and is in dispute. Egeth and Blecker find either regularity or familiarity alone to be sufficient to get the highest level of performance, whereas McClelland shows the highest performance only when both are present. What I think is most interesting is that from a cognitive psychology viewpoint, what seem to be different teaching methods could operate on a single underlying mechanism and thus to some extent be compensatory. A conflict between fundamentally different ways of looking at the learning process from the outside may turn out not to be different at all in terms of internal mechanisms.

Of course, the issue between phonics training and look–say methods is not solely one of underlying mechanisms. Teaching children phonics helps them to gain the independence necessary to be able to sound out new words. Teaching children by the look–say method may help them to suppress attention to phonetic codes during normal reading and thus produce more efficient silent reading. Thus both kinds of training may play extremely important roles in the overall reading task. It is only when the curriculum designer's attention has been called to the detailed internal processes that take place in real time that the proper role for both phonics and look–say training can be assessed.

Logical and Psychological Units

One of the most puzzling aspects of the reading task has been the difficulty in getting children to recognize the relationship between a set of visual letters and its corresponding blended pronunciation. It seems natural to view a word as consisting of a set of letter elements that form the units of analysis of the visual word. In the same way, it seems logical to view phonemes as constituent elements in the auditory sequence we call a word. A confusion arises between logical and psychological elements. The difficulty in recognizing that an auditory sequence consists of individual constituents called phonemes is not at all apparent. After all, how is it that we could ever recognize the word unless we knew in some sense that it consisted of elements that constitute the word? Gleitman and Rozin (1977) have argued that the question of awareness is quite separate from the question of the logical elements that allow word recognition. They say:

> The child's natural history of explicit language knowledge proceeds in a sequence similar to the evolution of writing. The young child first becomes explicitly aware of meaning units, and only later becomes aware of the syntactic and phonological substrata of language. Thus it is easy for the young child to learn the principles of a script that tracks meanings directly and hard for him to acquire a script that tracks the sound system. These parallels suggest an approach to teaching reading. . . . It might be useful for the child to be introduced to visual language as a logography. Thereafter we suggest that the syllabic unit, which maintains its shape and sequential integrity in speech perception and production, may be useful for introducing the learner of an alphabet to the general class of phonographic scripts. In this approach, the abstract phonemic (alphabetic) concepts would be introduced to the learner relatively late. Summarizing, we propose that an initial reading curriculum that essentially recapitulates the historical evolution of writing will mirror the metalinguistic development of the child [p. 50].

Gleitman and Rozin also argue that decoding is best taught by taking advantage of the level of processing of which the child is aware rather than first attempting to teach the alphabetic principle itself. Their notion is that the child is most easily aware of the meaning of the word but only with great difficulty can bring to attention its individual phonemic structure. On the other hand, the written language is such that the child is probably most easily aware of the letters and only with difficulty begins to grasp the word as a whole.

Awareness is not particularly related to any level of processing but is independent of level. The separation between awareness and the processing systems involved in transforming the material presented to the subject is of use in coming to understand the overall performance. An auditory word is first of all an organized unit, and only with great difficulty can it be segmented into its constituents. On the other hand, a visual word is first of all a conglomeration of separate elements that slowly becomes an organized unit within the nervous system. Although we are far from understanding the details of the synthesis of written words into an organized visual code, or the analysis of an auditory word into its constituent phonemes, the starting place is to recognize the essential separation between the organization of the items within an isolable processing system and awareness (Mattingly, 1972).

Awareness reflects the operation of a system with its own limited capacity characteristics. A recognition of the difference between our being able to use something and our awareness of it is an important starting place in attempting to understand the kinds of problems a child has in mating the psychological units to the logical ones.

The problem of dyslexia, the controversy between phonics and look–say, and the question of the separation between units of processing and attention are all fundamental to the reading process. It is encouraging that the language and tools provided by mental chronometry provide a framework for discussing and investigating these effects. I have no answers that give a sure method of application, but this perspective does seem to provide a formulation that makes close connections with basic questions.

DEVELOPMENT OF INTELLIGENCE

Stages

Cognitive development has been dominated by theories that postulate a set of stages through which a person passes in reaching adulthood. These models are occasioned by the clear differences in performance capability on almost any task between children and adults. The stage theory that has been most dominant in the field of cognitive development is advocated by Piaget and Inhelder (1969). They argue that the underlying cognitive structures of one stage of development are replaced through the processes of accommodation and assimilation with new cognitive structures. These structures allow opportunities for new cognitive performances to emerge as a person develops. Although Piaget and Inhelder's theory allows adults to operate at any level of development, it stresses the discontinuities that occasion transfer from one cognitive structure to another.

A somewhat different stage view of cognitive development has been advocated by Bruner, Oliver, and Greenfield (1966). They postulate code-specific representations and an information-processing approach but attach them to the stage concepts of Piaget. Bruner et al. say:

> There are striking changes in emphasis that occur with the development of representation. At first the child's world is known to him principally by the habitual actions he uses for coping with it. In time there is added a technique of representation through imagery that is relatively free of action. Gradually there is added a new and powerful method of translating action and image into language, providing still a third system of representation. Each of the three modes of representation—enactive, ikonic, and symbolic—has its unique way of representing events. Each places a powerful impress on the mental life of human beings at different ages, and their interplay persists as one of the major features of adult intellectual life [p. 1].

Piaget and Bruner are alike in that they both stress the discontinuities that arise in development but differ in the changes that they think underlie such discontinuities. Piaget places his emphasis upon very abstract conceptual structures that allow different types of mental operations, whereas Bruner stresses the typical kind of concrete codes used by particular age groups.

How does the material presented in this book relate to the question of cognitive development? It is obvious that the approach used here with its emphasis upon multiple codes existing simultaneously in the nervous system (Chapter 2), the concrete nature of the thought processes (Chapter 3), and explicit recognition of individual differences in code selection (Chapter 3) would place less stress on the discontinuities that occur with development and more on continuous changes allowing the person to elaborate a larger number of codes and to select more accurately among them. If the child and the adult use fundamentally the same processing system, how then to account for the enormous differences in behavior shown by children and adults?

Immediate Memory

Information-processing theories of cognitive development place emphasis on things that vary quantitatively with age. The best documented such change is the increase in memory span from two to three items at the youngest age tested to seven items in adulthood. A number of studies have suggested that the ability to represent more items in immediate memory underlies much of the improved performance of adults in cognitive tasks (Pascual–Leone & Smith, 1969; Trabasso, 1975).

What seems to me even more impressive is evidence that even apparent changes in the size of the memory span may be due to increased familiarity of adults with the letters and digit items that usually comprise such tests (Chi, 1976; Huttenlocher & Burke, 1976). There is clear evidence that the reaction time for subjects to verify that a given item is a member of a prior list improves greatly as a function of age. However, neither the slope of the function relating size of the positive set to RT (Hoving et al., 1970) nor the time for phonetic retrieval changes at all (Hoving et al., 1974). Suppose that the increased efficiency of responding is due at least in part to faster and more automatic encoding of the probe item with age, as would be expected from most theories. It has been established that speed of encoding is closely related to the size of the memory span (Cavanaugh, 1972). These facts suggest that the improved memory span for adults could result mainly from the greater speed and automaticity of encoding rather than any more fundamental change in the capacity for memory.

Chi (1976) proposed exactly this view and found that when the rate of presentation of items was corrected for assumed differences in encoding rate between children and adults, differences in memory span were eliminated. Chi also suggests that an intuitive grasp of the importance of item familiarity in determining the size of the memory span can be obtained by comparing recall of a quick exposure to a string of digits and of Roman numerals. The span of immediate memory drops from about seven to eight items with digits and to about three items for the numerals. The latter figure is in line with more recent estimates of the adult memory span without use of chunking strategies (Broadbent, 1975).

Concrete Thought

Children often have trouble recognizing the difference between mirror-image letters (e.g., b vs. d). In the child's performance, this difficulty often shows up in reading errors. Such errors rarely if ever are found in adult performance, but chronometric studies indicate clearly that the time to decide that the letters of the pair "Bd" do not have the same name is much longer than it would be if "d" were not so easily confused with "b" (Posner, 1970). Thus a difficulty that is sufficient to cause substantial errors in the child does not disappear in the adult but is simply greatly reduced so that a more sensitive method must be used to observe it. Similarly, increasing the size of the smaller of two numbers that must be summed increases errors and dramatically influences RT in children, who can often be seen counting up from the larger of the two numbers on their fingers (Groen & Parkman, 1972). Much smaller increases in RT as a function of the minimum digit are found in the adult, but they are in the same direction and are measurable (Parkman & Groen, 1971).

These results suggest that the sensitivity of the tools of analysis will make a great deal of difference in whether one stresses continuities between children and adults or discontinuities.

Piaget and Bruner have considered in detail the inability of the child to conserve volume. Adults easily recognize that pouring a liquid from one vessel to another leads to conservation of liquid irrespective of the shape of the glass. Nonetheless, irrelevant dimensions such as size still affect the time it takes to decide that two shapes are identical (see Chapter 2). Piaget and Inhelder (1969) found that children tend to confuse a set with a supraset. When asked whether there are more beads or more black beads, they report that there are more black beads, because there are more black than white ones. Similar confusions between set and supraset have been reported by Meyer (1970), in which adults respond slowly as to whether all stones are rubies, because in fact all rubies are stones.

The concrete nature of adult thought is certainly not inconsistent with either Piaget's or Bruner's theory. Rather these theories simply place greater emphasis upon discontinuities than they do upon the continuities. This has tended to obscure the actual facts of adult thought by stressing its logical character in comparison with young children. The very concrete nature of adult thinking comes out very vividly in experimental analysis.

When adult subjects are asked to define an abstract category such as an animal, they frequently will begin to list the properties of a particular prototypical animal (e.g., dog). As Rosch (1973) has pointed out, categories seem to be organized in terms of concrete instances that serve as prototypical examples. The nature of statistical thinking has also been shown (Tversky & Kahneman, 1974) to depend upon the concrete representation of the situation. Statistical factors that cannot be easily included in such concrete representations tend not to affect decision making.

Piaget and Bruner fail to emphasize the importance of the concrete organization of categories in memory. The processes of abstract thought always remain difficult for the human, because they are superimposed upon categorization processes (Scribner & Cole, 1973) that are based upon concrete examples. The emphasis of experimental studies on categories that consist of concrete instances fits well with the common observation that the thinking of adults is heavily influenced by analogies or metaphors.

Halberstam (1969) suggested that the analogy between Munich and Vietnam had a strong influence upon the generation of leaders who controlled American policy in Vietnam. The use of this analogy was influential in the construction scenarios in which capitulation would lead to new demands and in the conclusion that a larger war might result from a failure to oppose demands at an early stage. Experimental studies of the organization of concepts suggest that once an analogy is used as a basis for thought, there is a strong tendency to confuse irrelevant features of the analogous situation with the real problem.

Intelligence

The view that the adult stage of thinking is typified by one particular code or a single brain system fits with a unitary view of intelligence. If development simply produces more advanced structures or codes, then the most intelligent people must reflect more completely these codes and structures. Despite evidence that intelligence consists of many only partially related skills and abilities (Guilford, 1967), the view of a single trait is still a strong one.

One basis for a unified view of intelligence emphasizes the central importance of language in communication and thought (Whorf, 1956). The ability of subjects to use language becomes the hallmark of their intelligence. The view that language is central to thought has been under continuous attack in modern information-processing research. There is much evidence that perceptual discriminations do not depend on linguistic recodings even when, as in the case of words, such recodings are readily available (e.g., Brown, 1976). Such findings lead away from the notion of a unified code underlying intelligence. Instead, intelligence can be seen as resulting from a federation of brain systems, each with its own unique capabilities.

There would be no a priori reason to suppose high correlations between these difficult systems. We know that deficits in verbal performance can occur as a result of brain lesions that spare spatial and other types of performance activity. This relative independence of deficit and of processing suggests that the efficiency of different processing systems is unrelated. Some have even proposed negative correlations, such that a highly developed verbal ability, for example, would be inconsistent with high spatial skill.

The relative importance of internal coding systems might be mainly a cultural phenomenon. In our heavily language-oriented Western culture, the importance of reading and smooth verbal communication is strongly emphasized and may thus be predictive of performance. A similar constellation of skills could be far less adaptive in a different environment.

This view is not to suggest that intelligence is entirely learned or easily modifiable. It could well be that the underlying ability to learn and perform different skilled acts is heavily influenced by the innate organization of the brain. Recent efforts to account for individual differences in memory span in terms of learned strategies have not been very successful. Even if the development of memory span with age is mainly due to improvements in encoding speed, the individual differences manifest in this skill seem to be unaffected by variation in speed of input. Whatever leads to differences in this memory skill seems to be sufficiently basic to transcend changes in input modality, rate of presentation, and mode of recall (Lyon, 1975).

A broader approach to the nature of human intellect might be based on views of separate brain processes (Jerison, 1973) and isolable processing codes (Hunt, Frost, & Lunneborg, 1973) and could serve to expand our appreciation of the diverse nature of intelligence. Emphasis in such theories would be more upon individual functioning than rank orders among people. The study of development of intelligence may then turn out to be much more closely aligned to the analysis of the unique set of capabilities of a given individual.

PERSONALITY

Fact and Affect

One aspect of personality to which chronometric methods have been applied with some success is the study of impression formation. The question of impression formation deals with how one forms and uses impressions of another person (Anderson, 1974; Asch, 1946). An aspect of the problem is the type of memorial representation that is produced when a series of trait-descriptive adjectives are given to an individual subject. In 1946 Asch investigated the impressions people formed of others based on a series of adjective traits describing a given individual. This led to a number of experimental investigations in which people have attempted to form deliberate, conscious impressions of others from listening to a set of trait-descriptive adjectives. It is certainly clear from these studies that people can form such impressions, and perhaps they could help tell us something about the way in which people represent to themselves their impressions of other people. However, since these studies have usually involved deliberate, conscious impressions that the subject is instructed to form, it is somewhat questionable that they have much to do with the type of implicit impressions that one individual might have of another.

Anderson and Hubert (1965) and Anderson and Farkas (1973) have argued that the storage of affect is separate from the specific set of adjectives by which the affect is conveyed. They argue that memories underlying emotion or evaluation are abstracted from the adjectives and stored separately from them. The basis of this view is that if asked to recall the adjectives in a list, subjects show a relatively strong recency effect; but if asked to rate their overall impressions of the person, the primacy effect is stronger.

Our studies (Posner & Snyder, 1975a) were undertaken to develop a firmer notion of the memory structures that underlie the emotional classification and to compare them with those that might mediate retention of the individual adjectives. In this way, it was felt one could understand some of the more fundamental processes involved in representing personalities of other people.

In order to observe the relationship between emotion and item information, we provided subjects with three kinds of sentences. The sentences always consisted of a single proper name followed by one to four adjectives. The adjectives might be all positive in emotional tone, all negative in emotional tone, or a mixture of positive and negative emotional tone. Words were selected from norms provided by Anderson (1974).

Following the sentences, subjects were given a single probe word. On half the trials the probe matched one of the words in the sentence, and on the other half it did not. Subjects were to respond as rapidly as possible to the question of whether the item in the probe matched an item in the sentence.

The basic results of the experiment are quite simple. For "yes" responses, reaction time did not differ for positive, negative, or neutral lists. The "no" responses can be broken down into two types—those in which the probe's emotional tone matched the list and those in which it did not. We compared the two types of "no" responses averaged across conditions where the list was positive and where it was negative. This is a particularly sensitive comparison, since the probes were the same words in both conditions but follow arrays of differing emotional tone. The results show a significantly faster reaction time when the emotional response is opposite to that of the list than when it is identical. This is accompanied by a reduction in error when the emotional response does not match the list. Although the difference in reaction time between matching and mismatching "no" responses did not change systematically as a function of size of the list, the error differences changed sharply as a function of the size of the list. When the list consisted of four items, there was a much higher probability that the subject would make an error when the emotional response matched the list than when it did not match. What do these results tell us about the relationship between item information and emotion?

Storage Models

There are clear effects of the impression upon the task. When the emotional tone of the probe does not match that of the list, subjects are facilitated in responding "no." There are several possible ways this result might occur. Suppose that the emotional information was present relatively more quickly than the factual information. This might be the case if the subject consciously prepared to match on the basis of emotional tone. One would expect subjects to be able to reject a mismatching emotional tone without any required search of the factual information, and this would produce a flat slope relating mismatching "no" responses to array size. However, there is no tendency for the slope to be reduced when the probe emotion mismatches. Another view supposes that each word consists of an item and an emotional attribute associated with it. Thus the adjective "loyal" is associated directly with the denotative and connotative meanings. In this view, a probe word may be rejected as matching an array word more quickly if the mismatch involves both item and emotion than if it involves only item information. Lively and Sanford (1972) have adopted exactly this model for the account of what happens when the subject receives a list consisting of digits and gets a probe that is a consonant. Such a model does not fit our data, since the slope of the "no" reaction times to mismatching emotions is at least as great as for matching emotions.

The overall results of the reaction time and error data obtained from our experiment seem most consistent with the following analysis of the relation of emotional information to item information. Suppose that there are two independent memory structures. These structures play much the same role as isolable subsystems have in the material presented in Chapter 2. One memory structure consists of a list of trait adjectives that the subject reads in a sentence. The other memory structure consists of an abstracted impression based on an integration of the values presented by the individual adjectives. The time to search the memory structure representing the traits would increase as a function of the number of items in the list. On the other hand, the impression would tend to get stronger as we increase the number of items on which it is based; thus one might expect a reduction in reaction time. Since judgments based on the emotional classification alone would be reliable for mismatching "no" responses, one would expect errors to pile up for matching "no" responses when the output of the emotional structure occurred prior to the output of the list array. This could account for the high error rate obtained with the four-item arrays.

To test this idea we performed an experiment in which the subjects receive the same list as described previously but were asked to determine if the probe item had the same emotional content as in the previous list. Two types of "yes" responses are possible—first, those to probe items that were actually in the list, and second, those that were not in the list but shared the same emotional tone. The results support a two-process view of the matching task. The role of the number of items is to increase reaction time for probes that are in the list but to reduce it for those that match only in affect. The two functions come together at about a four-item list.

In brief, what seems to happen in impression formation is that there are two memory structures or codes, one consisting of a list of item names and the other consisting of a generalized emotional response to those items. These separate memory structures appear to be oppositely affected by item length. The data seem most consistent with the view that each memory structure has an output that can be processed by the central processing system. In cases where the two decisions agree, there seems to be relatively little effect on overall reaction time or errors. In cases where they disagree, however, there appears to be a lengthened reaction time, as if there were some tendency to make the conflicting response. However, the tendency seems slight unless we let the times for the output get very close together. In that case, there seems to be a very difficult decision to be made and a high probability of error.

Judgment

One of the striking aspects of the experiments outlined above was provided by a discussion with the subjects following their experimental sessions. Since the adjectives we used were selected at random in accordance with their general emotional or connotative meaning, we often had personality descriptions that were difficult to integrate. Subjects invariably claimed that they had trouble coding them, because they did not make sense. In general they seemed to mean that people simply did not have that kind of personality.

That chronometric methods are appropriate for the analysis of this problem has been shown in a study by Diller (1971). He presented subjects with two trait-descriptive adjectives separated in time. When the second adjective was received, they were to combine and rate the overall impression created by the two adjectives. What was varied was the extent to which the two adjectives were consistent with each other. It was found that the reaction time for making the judgment and the degree of interference with a probe tone were both affected by the consistency of the two traits. If the traits were consistent, the task was much easier for the subject, probe reaction time suffered less, and the overall reaction time to make the judgment was reduced. These data indicate that the kinds of judgments involved in impression formation can be studied through the same processes that have been examined in Chapter 6.

Laboratory experiments of impression formation seem to lend themselves well to chronometric analysis. It appears that laying down a number of trait-descriptive adjectives leads to discriminably different memory structures representing the content of the adjectives used and the overall emotional connotation that they convey. A portion of this process seems to be automatic in the sense that we have been discussing previously. The emotional information seems to influence a judgment for which no emotional analysis is necessary, such as whether the adjective had occurred in the previous list. Moreover, increasing amounts of conscious effort seem to be involved as the discrepancy between adjectives that must be combined by the subject in producing the impression increased.

Emotion

These investigations lead to a principle that can be important in the study of personality. They suggest that emotional information can be stored and accessed separately from content information. This principle is of importance, because it is one of the main points of contact between Freudian theory of personality and information-processing approaches. Freud held that ego mechanisms that were largely unconscious protected the consciousness from unacceptable thoughts. It has always seemed paradoxical to experimental psychologists that an input item could be analyzed for its emotion prior to its reaching consciousness. The reason for this paradox is the implicit notion that semantic processing of input items was, of necessity, conscious. Chronometric studies have shown that the question of semantic analysis is quite separate from that of our conscious awareness. Thus, like other semantic analyses, emotional information can be contacted by input without the necessity of subjects being aware of the item. An example of this is that a previously shocked item might produce a GSR response, even when it was on an unattended ear (Von Wright, Anderson, & Stenman, 1975). Although one can argue that emotional information is available to input without conscious processing, it should not be held that in every case emotional responding to input items will be independent of conscious processing. As we have seen, it is also quite possible for semantic analysis in general to be accompanied by conscious awareness, and the same should be true of emotional processing. If emotions can be released by input independently of the subject's awareness, feedback from the emotion could affect the direction of the central processing system.

Some evidence for this view (Broadbent, 1975) is that words that lead to emotional arousal can affect the quality of processing on the next word in a list. Thus the direction of the subject's conscious processing of the next word is influenced by the extent of the arousal on a previous word. Carrying the argument a bit further, it may be possible that feedback from the emotional arousal of a given word can influence the conscious processing of that word itself. This provides a mechanism whereby an emotional word can influence the direction of our attention to itself. Since many tasks are extended in time, this principle becomes more important as the length of time the emotion has to affect the direction of conscious attention is increased (Erdelyi, 1974).

Though the information-processing results suggest a mechanism by which perceptual defense might occur, they do not really provide any strong evidence on the direction of the attentional effects of emotional information. This could be in the direction of more intense attention given to processing in the presence of emotion, or it may be that feedback from the emotional information reduces attention. Studies of the relationship between arousal and attention have suggested that the major mechanism involved here is that the attentional processes are more focused in conditions of high arousal (Kahneman, 1973).

Cognitive Training

The processes reviewed above suggest that mental structures have important influences upon the direction of current attention. This is one of many places where bias from stored information can influence the direction of current attention. The importance of this factor in human information processing should not be underestimated. For example, in the case of the formation of stereotypes, it may well be that people who believe that blondes have more fun in fact code the world in such a way that they are more likely to see and retain instances that confirm their hypothesis (Rothbart, Evans, & Fulero, Note 20). Although economic, political, and emotional factors are also likely to be important in the way in which people react to their natural and human environment, one should not discount the role of perfectly normal biases in distorting one's experience and memory. This view is in some ways consistent with the psychoanalytic approach to personality but in other ways quite different. Freudian views stress very early experience as providing the structures that subsequently control the direction of ego defense mechanisms. On the other hand, much of current cognitive psychology argues that the relatively less dramatic principles of conscious and unconscious processing emerging from studies of human performance may account for many of the things that we have in the past attributed to cognitive processes lying deep within the unconscious.

One type of evidence that to me seems to favor the importance of such a shallow, rather than a deep,[1] psychology is the work of McClelland and his associates (1961). McClelland has linked a number of human motives, including the need for achievement[2] and the need for power, with important cultural changes that take place in the growth of societies such as the ability to develop high levels of entrepreneurial achievement and cycles of war and peace. McClelland's original work was based upon derivatives of Freudian depth psychology and stressed the importance of early training of the child in these later cultural events. However, as a part of the efforts to test the models of achievement motivation presented in McClelland's book, *The Achieving Society,* he attempted to develop adult courses that might influence the direction or extent of achievement of those who were to take the courses. These courses in achievement

---

[1]The term *shallow psychology* is taken from a recent paper by Dawes (1977), who makes a similar argument for the relevance of cognitive structures and limitation in the occurrence of many things that are often attributed to deeper motivational causes.

[2]Much of the criticism of *The Achieving Society* has centered upon the rather weak evidence that achievement motivation as a trait of individuals holds up across different situations. Recently, Bem and Allen (1974) have argued that many so-called human traits are really only characteristic of a subsection of the population, and not all people can reasonably be said to be characterized either by the presence or the absence of that trait. For this reason, Bem and Allen argue that such traits do not show high correlations when measured psychometrically. Note that even if achievement motives are only characteristic of small numbers of people, it still may well be that they are predictive of changes in the society at large, which after all are often shaped by only a small minority of the population.

motivation were given and evaluated in India in the mid-1960s (McClelland & Winter, 1969). The results produced some evidence that those people receiving achievement training in a 2-week course were more likely to start new businesses, to work longer hours, and to show other evidence of achievement-oriented behavior over the next 2-year period.

There has been much controversy about the McClelland work, but one of the most dramatic aspects of this work is that a 2-week course on achievement motivation appears to have the power of changing what was in the original theory a trait that was laid down by a person's early experience. How can this be? One wonders whether the semantic structures developed during the 2-week course that tend to allow people to consciously encode opportunities in their environments in terms of the language of achievement motivation might not have powerful behavioral effects. If everything one sees is interpreted in terms of the opportunity that one might have to achieve economic wealth, is it not likely that a fundamental change in the behavioral patterns of at least some persons might emerge?[3]

I am aware of the speculative nature of these relationships between the findings of experimental studies and their application to the large problems of personality development in different cultures. I dwell on them mainly to show the extent of our ignorance of the complex cognitive mechanisms that might underlie the development of individual personality. Whether or not the principles emerging from experimental laboratories and the methods of mental chronometry will be helpful in laying bare some of these mechanisms will remain for the future to determine. However, I do believe that the complex interplay between emotion, cognition, arousal, and motivation can be studied in simpler situations and the principles at least to some degree brought to bear upon our understanding of the nature of human information processing, even in these complicated situations.[4]

SUMMARY

Although it is not likely that the experiments discussed in previous chapters can be applied directly to real life, it is reasonable to expect the tools of mental chronometry and the general principles developed from their use to have broad

---

[3]Of course it is difficult to explain exactly what it was about this particular course that produced change. McClelland and Winter (1969) argue that the course produced important changes in intrapersonal goals and methods and the needed social support to maintain these changes over a period of time. Obviously, training is not always successful in producing such important alterations in behavior, and it remains for research to determine the crucial intrapersonal and social factors. The only point to be made here is that there is evidence that cognitive training at a relative late stage in life can produce changes in behavior that have usually been interpreted in terms of a personality change.

[4]The reader should keep in mind that the kinds of implications I have in mind here are the relatively gentle ones discussed on page 221, not detailed predictions of exactly how they might interact in a given situation.

implications for many aspects of everyday life performance. The multicode viewpoint, separation of conscious and unconscious processes, limited capacity for conscious attention to items and codes, categories defined by prototypes, and the importance of prior set in directing orientation are all ideas that may be applied broadly to human activities. In this chapter, I have tried to apply these principles together with the tools of mental chronometry to broader issues such as learning to read, the development of intelligence, and the relation between content and emotion in the formation of the individual personality. In each of these cases, viewpoints arising from our research are contrasted with views based upon behaviorism, Piagetian psychology, Freudian psychology, and other general approaches toward the analysis of human problems. Experimental studies of the time course of information flow add some new insights to those available through the use of other approaches.

Bibliography

REFERENCE NOTES

1. Goff, W. R., Williamson, P. D., Van Gilder, J. C., Allison, T., & Fisher, T. C. *Neural origins of long latency evoked responses recorded from the depth and cortical surface of the brain in man and animals.* Paper presented at the Brussels International Symposium on Cerebral Evoked Potentials in Man, Brussels, April 1974.
2. Posner, M. I., & Wilkinson, R. T. *On the process of preparation.* Paper presented at the meeting of the Psychonomic Society, St. Louis, November 1969.
3. Miller, G. A. *The subjective lexicon.* Paper presented at the American Psychological Association, Miami Beach, September 1970.
4. Cole, R. Personal communication, May 1974.
5. Beller, K. H., & Schaeffer, B. *Studies of word matching.* Unpublished manuscript, University of Oregon, 1970.
6. Posner, M. I., & Hanson, V. L. *Cross-modality matching study.* Unpublished studies, University of Oregon, 1976.
7. Day, R. *Temporal order judgments in speech: Are individuals language-bound or stimulus-bound?* (Status Report, SR 21/22). New Haven, Conn.: Haskins Laboratory, 1970.
8. Posner, M. I., & Summers, J. Unpublished studies, University of Oregon, 1972.
9. Meyer, D. E., Schvaneveldt, R. W., & Ruddy, M. G. *Activation of lexical memory.* Paper presented at the meeting of the Psychonomic Society, St. Louis, Missouri, November 1973.
10. Snyder, C. R. R., & Posner, M. I. *The economics of attention: A cost–benefit analysis of priming.* Unpublished manuscript, University of Oregon, 1974.
11. Farrar, P. Unpublished experiments, University of Oregon, 1973.
12. Posner, M. I., & Ogden, W. C. Unpublished experiments, University of Oregon, 1975.
13. Hines, T. M. *Differential use of feedback by old and young subjects.* Paper presented at the Western Psychological Association, Seattle, Washington, April 1977.
14. Hines, T. M., & Posner, M. I. *Slow but sure: A chronometric analysis of the process of aging.* Paper presented at the American Psychological Association, Washington, D.C., September 1976.

15. Sternberg, S., Knoll, R. L., & Leuin, T. C. *Existence and transformation of iconic memory revealed by search rates*. Paper presented at the Meeting of the Psychonomic Society, Boston, November 1974.
16. Posner, M. I., Snyder, C. R. R., & Nissen, M. J. *Stimulus and response set: A cost-benefit analysis*. Paper presented at the meeting of the Psychonomic Society, St. Louis, November 1973.
17. Smith, S. W., & Blaha, J. *Preliminary report summarizing the results of location uncertainty experiments I-VII*. Unpublished experiments, Ohio State University, 1969.
18. Posner, M. I., Nissen, M. J., & Ogden, W. *Attending to a position in space*. Paper presented at the meeting of the Psychonomic Society, Denver, November 1976.
19. Posner, M. I., Davidson, B. J., & Nissen, M. J. *The process of stimulus detection*. Paper presented at the meeting of the Psychonomic Society, St. Louis, November 1976.
20. Rothbart, M., Evans, M., & Fulero, S. *Mnemonic factors in the maintenance of social stereotypes*. Unpublished manuscript, University of Oregon, 1977.

REFERENCES

Aderman, D., & Smith, E. E. Expectancy as a determinant of function units in perceptual recognition. *Cognitive Psychology*, 1971, *2*, 117–129.

Alegria, J., & Bertelson, P. Time uncertainty, number of alternatives and particular signal response pair as determinants of choice reaction time. In A. F. Sanders (Ed.), *Attention and performance III*. Amsterdam: North-Holland, 1970. (*Acta Psychologica*, 1970, *33*, 36–44.)

Ambler, B. A., & Proctor, J. D. The familiarity effect for single letter pairs. *Journal of Experimental Psychology: Human Perception and Performance*, 1976, *2*, 222–234.

Anders, T., & Fozard, J. Effects of age upon retrieval from primary and secondary memory. *Developmental Psychology*, 1973, *9*, 411–415.

Anderson, J. R., & Bower, G. H. *Human associative memory*. Washington, D.C.: Winston, 1973.

Anderson, C. M. B. *An analysis of the memorial and processing components of a simple letter matching task*. Unpublished doctoral dissertation, University of Toronto, 1975.

Anderson, N. H. Information integration: A brief survey. In D. H. Krantz, R. C. Atkinson, R. D. Luce, & P. Suppes (Eds.), *Contemporary developments in mathematical psychology*. San Francisco: Freeman, 1974.

Anderson, N. H., & Farkas, A. J. New light on order effects in attitude change. *Journal of Social Psychology*, 1973, *28*, 88–93.

Anderson, N. H., & Hubert, S. Effects of concomitant verbal recall on order effects in personality impression formation. *Journal of Verbal Learning and Verbal Behavior*, 1965, *2*, 531–539.

Angel, A. The central control of sensory transmission and its possible relation to reaction time. *Acta Psychologica*, 1969, *30*, 339–357.

Arbib, M. *The metaphorical brain*. New York: Wiley, 1972.

Asch, S. Forming impressions of personality. *Journal of Abnormal and Social Psychology*, 1946, *41*, 258–290.

Atkinson, R. C., & Juola, J. F. Factors influencing speed and accuracy of word recognition. In S. Kornblum (Ed.), *Attention and performance IV*. New York: Academic Press, 1973.

Attneave, F. In defense of homonculi. In W. Rosenblith (Ed.), *Sensory communication*. Cambridge, Mass.: MIT Press, 1960.

Ball, F., Wood, D., & Smith, E. E. When are semantic targets detected faster than visual or acoustic ones? *Perception & Psychophysics*, 1975, *17*, 1–8.

Baron, J. Phonemic stage not necessary for reading. *Quarterly Journal of Experimental Psychology*, 1973, *25*, 241–246.

Baron, J., & Strawson, C. Use of orthographic and word-specific knowledge in reading words aloud. *Journal of Experimental Psychology: Human Perception and Performance*, 1976, *2*, 386–393.

Bartlett, J. R., & Doty, R. W., Sr. Response of units in the striate cortex of squirrel monkeys to visual and electrical stimuli. *Journal of Neurophysiology*, 1974, *37*, 621–641.

Beck, J., & Ambler, B. The effects of concentrated and distributed attention on peripheral acuity. *Perception & Psychophysics*, 1973, *14*, 225–230.

Becker, C. A. Allocation of attention during visual word recognition. *Journal of Experimental Psychology: Human Perception and Performance*, 1976, *2*, 556–566.

Becker, C. A., & Killion, T. H. Interaction of visual and cognitive effects in word recognition. *Journal of Experimental Psychology: Human Perception and Performance*, 1977, *3*, 389–401.

Beller, H. K. Parallel and serial stages in matching. *Journal of Experimental Psychology*, 1970, *84*, 213–219.

Bem, D. J., & Allen, A. On predicting some of the people some of the time: The search for cross-situational consistencies in behavior. *Psychological Review*, 1974, *81*, 506–520.

Berlyne, D. *Studies in the new experimental aesthetics*. New York: Halsted, 1974.

Bernstein, I. Can we see and hear at the same time? *Acta Psychologica*, 1970, *33*, 21–35.

Bernstein, I., Chu, P., Briggs, P., & Schurman, D. Stimulus intensity and foreperiod effects in intersensory facilitation. *Quarterly Journal of Experimental Psychology*, 1973, *25*, 171–181.

Bertelson, P. The time course of preparation. *Quarterly Journal of Experimental Psychology*, 1967, *19*, 272–279.

Bertelson, P., & Barzeele, J. Interaction of time uncertainty and relative signal frequency in determining choice reaction time. *Journal of Experimental Psychology*, 1965, *70*, 448–451.

Blake, M. J. F. Temperature and time of day. In W. P. Colquhoun (Ed.), *Biological rhythms and human performance*. New York: Academic Press, 1971.

Blake, R. R., Fox, R., & Lappin, J. S. Invariance in reaction time classification of same and different letter pairs. *Journal of Experimental Psychology*, 1970, *85*, 133–137.

Boies, K. *An experimental study of aphasia: An investigation of the naming process in brain-damaged populations*. Unpublished doctoral dissertation, University of Oregon, 1971.

Boies, S. J. *Rehearsal of visual codes of single letters*. Unpublished master's thesis, University of Oregon, 1969.

Boies, S. J. *Memory codes in a speeded classification task*. Unpublished doctoral dissertation, University of Oregon, 1971.

Botwinick, J. *Aging and behavior*. New York: Springer, 1973.

Botwinick, J., & Thompson, L. Components of reaction time in relation to age and sex. *Journal of Genetic Psychology*, 1966, *108*, 175–183.

Bransford, J., & Franks, J. The abstraction of linguistic ideas. *Cognitive Psychology*, 1971, *2*, 331–350.

Broadbent, D. E. *Perception and communication*. London: Pergamon, 1958.

Broadbent, D. E. *Decision and stress*. London: Academic Press, 1971.

Broadbent, D. E. *In defence of empirical psychology*. London: Methuen, 1973.

Broadbent, D. E. The magic number seven after fifteen years. In A. Kennedy & A. Wilkes (Eds.), *Studies in long-term memory*. New York: Wiley, 1975.

Brooks, L. R. Spatial and verbal components of the act of recall. *Canadian Journal of Psychology*, 1968, *22*, 349–368.

Brooks, L. Visual patterns in fluency word identification. In A. Reber & D. Scarborough (Eds.), *Reading: The CUNY Conference*. Hillsdale, N.J.: Lawrence Erlbaum Associates, 1977.

Broota, K. D., & Epstein, W. The time it takes to make veridical size and distance judgments. *Perception & Psychophysics*, 1973, *14*, 358–364.

Brown, I. D. Measuring the spare mental capacity of drivers by a subsidiary task. *Ergonomics*, 1962, *5*, 247–250.

Brown, R. Reference: In memorial tribute to Eric Lenneborg. *Cognition*, 1976, *4*, 125–153.

Bruner, J. S., Oliver, R. R., & Greenfield, P. M. *Studies in cognitive growth*. New York: Wiley, 1966.

Bruner, J. S., & Potter, M. C. Interference in visual recognition. *Science*, 1964, *144*, 424–425.

Brunning, E. *The physiological clock* (3rd ed.). New York: Springer-Verlag, 1973.

Buggie, S. *Stimulus preprocessing and abstraction in the recognition of disoriented forms*. Unpublished master's thesis, University of Oregon, 1970.

Bundesen, C., & Larsen, A. Visual transformation of size. *Journal of Experimental Psychology: Human Perception and Performance*, 1975, *1*, 214–220.

Carpenter, P., & Just, M. Sentence comprehension: A psycholinguistic processing model of verification. *Psychological Review*, 1975, *82*, 45–73.

Caspers, H. Relations of steady potential shifts in the cortex to wakefulness–sleep spectrum. In M. A. B. Brazier (Ed.), *Brain function* (Vol. 1). Berkeley, Calif.: University of California Press, 1963.

Cavanaugh, J. P. Relation between the immediate memory span and the memory search rate. *Psychological Review*, 1972, *79*, 525–530.

Chapman, R. M. Evoked potentials of the brain related to thinking. In F. J. McGuigan & R. Schoonover (Eds.), *Psychophysiology of thinking*. New York: Academic Press, 1973.

Chi, M. T. H. Short-term memory limitations in children: Capacity or processing deficits? *Memory & Cognition*, 1976, *4*, 559–572.

Clark, H. H., & Chase, W. G. On the process of comparing sentences against pictures. *Cognitive Psychology*, 1972, *3*, 472–517.

Cohen, G. Some evidence for parallel comparisons in letter recognition tasks. *Quarterly Journal of Experimental Psychology*, 1969, *21*, 272–279.

Cohen, G. Hemispheric differences in letter classification tasks. *Perception & Psychophysics*, 1972, *11*, 139–142.

Colavita, F. B. Human sensory dominance. *Perception & Psychophysics*, 1974, *16*, 409–412.

Cole, R. A., Coltheart, M., & Allard, F. Memory of a speaker's voice: Reaction time to same or different voiced letter. *Quarterly Journal of Experimental Psychology*, 1974, *26*, 1–7.

Cole, R. A., Cooper, W. E., Singer, J., & Allard, F. Selective adaptation of English consonants using real speech. *Perception & Psychophysics*, 1975, *18*, 227–244.

Collins, A. M., & Loftus, E. F. A spreading-activation theory of semantic processing. *Psychological Review*, 1975, *82*, 407–428.

Colquhoun, W. P. (Ed.). *Biological rhythms and human performance*. New York: Academic Press, 1971.

Coltheart, M. Visual information processing. In P. C. Dodwell (Ed.), *New horizons in psychology 2*. Baltimore, Md.: Penguin Books, 1972.

Coltheart, M., & Freeman, R. Case alternation impairs word identification. *Bulletin of the Psychonomic Society*, 1974, *3*, 102–104.

Comstock, E. M. Processing capacity in a letter matching task. *Journal of Experimental Psychology*, 1973, *100*, 63–72.

Conrad, C. Context effects in sentence comprehension: A study of the subjective lexicon. *Memory & Cognition*, 1974, *2*, 130–138.

Conrad, R. Acoustic confusions in immediate memory. *British Journal of Psychology*, 1965, *55*, 75–84.

Cooper, L. A. Mental rotation of random two-dimensional forms. *Cognitive Psychology*, 1975, *7*, 20–43.

Cooper, L. A. Demonstration of a mental analog of an external rotation. *Perception & Psychophysics*, 1976, *19*, 296–302.

Cooper, L. A., & Shepard, R. N. Mental rotation of letters. In W. G. Chase (Ed.), *Visual information processing*. New York: Academic Press, 1973.

Corcoran, D. W. J., & Besner, D. Application of the Posner technique to the study of size and brightness irrelevancies in letter pairs. In P. M. A. Rabbitt (Ed.), *Attention and performance V*. London: Academic Press, 1975.

Corteen, R. S., & Wood, B. Autonomic responses to shock-associated words in an unattended channel. *Journal of Experimental Psychology*, 1972, *94*, 308–313.

Craik, F. I. M., & Lockhart, R. S. Levels of processing: A framework for memory research. *Journal of Verbal Learning and Verbal Behavior*, 1972, *11*, 671–684.

Critchley, M. *Developmental dyslexia*. London: Heinemann, 1967.

Cruse, D., & Clifton, C. Recoding strategies and the retrieval of information from memory. *Cognitive Psychology*, 1973, *4*, 157–193.

Cutting, J. E. Auditory and linguistic processes in speech perception: Inferences from six fusions in dichotic listening. *Psychological Review*, 1976, *83*, 114–140.

Dainoff, M. J., & Haber, R. N. Effects of acoustic confusability on levels of information processing. *Canadian Journal of Psychology*, 1970, *24*, 98–108.

Davidson, B. J. *Coding strategies in word recognition*. Unpublished master's thesis, University of Oregon, 1977.

Davis, H., Osterhammel, P. A., Wier, C. C., & Gjerdingen, D. Slow vertex potentials: Interactions between auditory, tactile, electric and visual stimuli. *EEG and Clinical Neurophysiology*, 1967, *22*, 537–546.

Dawes, R. M. Shallow psychology. In J. S. Carroll & R. Payne (Eds.), *Cognitive and social decisions*. Hillsdale, N.J.: Lawrence Erlbaum Associates, 1977.

Deutsch, D., & Roll, P. L. Separate "what" and "where" decision mechanisms in processing a dichotic tonal sequence. *Journal of Experimental Psychology: Human Perception and Performance*, 1976, *2*, 23–29.

Diller, R. *Reaction time characteristics of an impression-formation task*. Unpublished doctoral dissertation, University of Oregon, 1971.

Donchin, E., Kubovy, M., Kutas, M., Johnson, R., & Herning, R. Graded changes in evoked response amplitude as a function of cognitive activity. *Perception & Psychophysics*, 1973, *14*, 319–324.

Donchin, E., & Lindsley, D. B. *Averaged evoked potentials: Methods, results and evaluations*. NASA SP-191, Washington, D.C., 1969.

Dyer, F. H. The Stroop phenomenon and its use in the study of perceptual, cognitive and response processes. *Memory & Cognition*, 1973, *1*, 106–120.

Eason, R. G., Harter, R., & White, C. T. Effects of attention and arousal on visually evoked cortical potentials and reaction time in man. *Physiology and Behavior*, 1969, *4*, 283–289.

Egeth, H., & Blecker, D. Differential effects of familiarity on judgments of sameness and difference. *Perception & Psychophysics*, 1971, *9*, 321–326.

Egeth, H. E., Brownell, H. H., & Geoffrion, L. D. Testing the role of vertical symmetry in letter matching. *Journal of Experimental Psychology: Human Perception and Performance*, 1976, *2*, 429–434.

Egger, M. D., & Miller, N. E. Secondary reinforcement in rats as a function of information value and reliability of the stimulus. *Journal of Experimental Psychology*, 1962, *64*, 97–104.

Eggers, S. J. *A comparison of physical and name matches in a letter matching task*. Unpublished doctoral dissertation, University of Western Australia, 1975.

Eichelman, W. H. Familiarity effects in the simultaneous matching task. *Journal of Experimental Psychology*, 1970, *86*, 275–282. (a)

Eichelman, W. H. Stimulus and response repetition effects for naming letters. *Perception & Psychophysics*, 1970, *7*, 94–96. (b)

Eimas, P. D., & Corbit, J. D. Selective adaptation of linguistic feature detectors. *Cognitive Psychology*, 1973, *6*, 99–109.

Elias, M. F., & Kinsbourne, M. Time course of identity and category matching by spatial orientation. *Journal of Experimental Psychology*, 1972, *95*, 177-183.

Ells, J. G. Analysis of temporal and attentional aspects of movement control. *Journal of Experimental Psychology*, 1973, *99*, 10-21.

Engle, F. L. Visual conspicuity, directed attention and retinal locus. *Vision Research*, 1971, *11*, 563-576.

Erdelyi, M. A new look at the new look: Perceptual defense and vigilance. *Psychological Review*, 1974, *81*, 1-25.

Eriksen, D. W., & Hoffman, J. E. The extent of processing of noise elements during selective encoding from visual displays. *Perception & Psychophysics*, 1973, *14*, 155-160.

Esposito, N. J., & Pelton, L. H. Review of the measurement of semantic satiation. *Psychological Bulletin*, 1971, *75*, 330-346.

Estes, W. K. Memory, perception and decision in letter identification. In R. Solso (Ed.), *Information processing and cognition*. Hillsdale, N.J.: Lawrence Erlbaum Associates, 1975.

Evarts, E. V. Motor cortex reflexes associated with learned movement. *Science*, 1973, *179*, 501-503.

Feynman, R. *The character of physical law*. Cambridge, Mass.: MIT Press, 1965.

Fischler, I. Associative facilitation in a lexical decision task. *Journal of Experimental Psychology: Human Perception and Performance*, 1977, *3*, 18-26.

Fitts, P. M. Perceptual-motor skill learning. In A. W. Melton (Ed.), *Categories of human learning*. New York: Academic Press, 1964.

Fitts, P. M., & Seeger, C. M. S-R compatibility: Spatial characteristics of stimulus and response codes. *Journal of Experimental Psychology*, 1953, *46*, 199-210.

Fox, J. The use of structural diagnostics in recognition. *Journal of Experimental Psychology: Human Perception and Performance*, 1975, *104*, 57-67.

Fuster, J. M. Effects of stimulation of brain stem on tachistoscopic perception. *Science*, 1958, *127*, 150.

Gaillard, A. W., & Näätänen, R. Slow potential changes and choice reaction time as a function of interstimulus interval. *Acta Psychologica*, 1973, *37*, 173-186.

Galton, Sir F. *Inquiries into human faculty and its development*. London: J. M. Dent & Sons, 1907.

Garner, W. R. *The processing of information and structure*. Hillsdale, N.J.: Lawrence Erlbaum Associates, 1974.

Garner, W. R., & Felfoldy, G. L. Integrality of stimulus dimensions in various types of information processing. *Cognitive Psychology*, 1970, *1*, 225-241.

Gazzaniga, M. S. *The bisected brain*. New York: Appleton-Century-Crofts, 1970.

Gazzaniga, M. S., Glass, A. V., Sarno, M. T., & Posner, J. B. Pure word deafness and hemispheric dynamics: A case history. *Cortex*, 1973, *9*, 136-143.

Gazzaniga, M. S., & Hillyard, S. A. Attention mechanisms following brain bisection. In S. Kornblum (Ed.), *Attention and performance IV*. New York: Academic Press, 1973.

Geffen, G., Bradshaw, J. L., & Nettleton, N. C. Hemispheric asymmetry: Verbal and spatial encoding of visual stimuli. *Journal of Experimental Psychology*, 1972, *95*, 25-31.

Geschwind, N. Disconnection syndromes in animals and man. *Brain*, 1968, *88*, 237-294; 585-644.

Gibson, E., & Levin, H. *The psychology of reading*. Cambridge, Mass.: MIT Press, 1975.

Gibson, J. J. Adaptation, after-effect and contrast in the perception of curved lines. *Journal of Experimental Psychology*, 1933, *16*, 1-31.

Gibson, J. J. A critical review of the concept of set in contemporary experimental psychology. *Psychological Bulletin*, 1941, *38*, 781-815.

Gibson, J. J. *The senses considered as perceptual systems*. Boston: Houghton Mifflin, 1966.

Gleitman, L., & Rozin, P. The structure and acquisition of reading I: Relations between orthographies and the structure of language. In A. S. Reber & D. L. Scarborough (Eds.), *Toward a psychology of reading: The proceedings of the CUNY conferences*. Hillsdale, N.J.: Lawrence

Erlbaum Associates, 1977.

Globus, G. Rapid eye movement cycle in real time. *Archives of General Psychiatry*, 1966, *15*, 654–659.

Glucksberg, S., & Danks, J. Grammatical structure and recall: A function of space in immediate memory or of recall delay? *Perception & Psychophysics*, 1969, *6*, 113–117.

Glucksberg, S., & Weisberg, R. W. Verbal behavior and problem solving: Some effects of labeling in a functional fixity problem. *Journal of Experimental Psychology*, 1966, *71*, 659–664.

Goff, W. R. Evoked potential correlates of perceptual organization in man. In C. R. Evans & T. B. Mulholland (Eds.), *Attention in neurophysiology*. New York: Appleton, 1969.

Goldberg, M. E., & Wurtz, R. H. Activity of superior colliculus in behaving monkeys. II. Effect of attention on neuronal responses. *Journal of Neurophysiology*, 1972, *35*, 560–574.

Gormezano, I. Yoked comparisons of classical and instrumental conditioning of the eyelid response: And an addendum on "voluntary responders." In W. F. Prokasy (Ed.), *Classical conditioning*. New York: Appleton-Century-Crofts, 1968.

Gostnell, D. R. *The functions of tonic and phasic arousal in reaction times and memory span of normal and retarded subjects*. Unpublished doctoral dissertation, University of Oregon, 1976.

Grant, D. A. A preliminary model for processing information conveyed by verbal conditioned stimuli in classical conditioning. In A. H. Black & W. F. Prokasy (Eds.), *Classical conditioning II: Current theory and research*. New York: Meredith, 1972.

Greenwald, A. G. A double stimulation test of ideo-motor theory with implications for selective attention. *Journal of Experimental Psychology*, 1970, *84*, 392–398.

Grice, G. R. Stimulus intensity and response evocation. *Psychological Review*, 1968, *75*, 359–373.

Grice, G. R., & Hunter, J. Stimulus intensity effects depend upon the type of experimental design. *Psychological Review*, 1964, *71*, 247–256.

Griffith, D., & Johnston, W. A. An information processing analysis of visual imagery. *Journal of Experimental Psychology*, 1973, *100*, 141–146.

Grindley, C. G., & Townsend, V. Voluntary attention in peripheral vision and its effects on acuity and differential thresholds. *Quarterly Journal of Experimental Psychology*, 1968, *20*, 11–19.

Groen, G. J., & Parkman, J. M. A chronometric analysis of simple addition. *Psychological Review*, 1972, *79*, 329–343.

Groves, P. M., & Thompson, R. F. Habituation: A dual process theory. *Psychological Review*, 1970, *77*, 419–450.

Guilford, J. P. *The nature of human intelligence*. New York: McGraw-Hill, 1967.

Halberstam, D. *The best and the brightest*. New York: Random House, 1969.

Hanson, V. L. Within category discriminations in speech perception. *Perception & Psychophysics*, 1977, *21*, 423–430.

Hawkins, H. L. Parallel processes in complex visual discrimination. *Perception & Psychophysics*, 1969, *5*, 56–64.

Hawkins, H. L., Reicher, G. M., Rogers, M., & Peterson, L. Flexible coding in word recognition. *Journal of Experimental Psychology: Human Perception and Performance*, 1976, *2*, 380–385.

Hebb, D. O. *Organization of behavior*. New York: Wiley, 1949.

Henderson, L. A word superiority effect without orthographic assistance. *Quarterly Journal of Experimental Psychology*, 1974, *26*, 301–311.

Heninger, G. R., McDonald, R. K., Goff, W. R., & Sollberger, A. Diurnal variations in the cerebral evoked response and EEG. *Archives of Neurology*, 1969, *21*, 330–337.

Henkin, R. I. The neuroendocrine control of perception. In *Perception and its disorders* (Research Publication ARNMD), *48*, 1970, 54–107.

Hick, W. G. On the rate of gain of information. *Quarterly Journal of Experimental Psychology*, 1952, *4*, 11–26.

Hillyard, S. A., Hink, R. F., Schwent, V. L., & Picton, T. W. Electrical signs of selective attention in the human brain. *Science*, 1973, *182*, 177–180.

Hillyard, S. A., & Picton, T. W. Cognitive components in cerebral event-related potentials and selective attention. In J. E. Desmedt (Ed.), *Progress in clinical neurophysiology* (Vol. VI). Basel, Germany: Karger, in press.

Hinrich, J. V., & Craft, J. L. Verbal expectancy and probability in two-choice reaction time. *Journal of Experimental Psychology,* 1971, *88,* 367–371.

Hintzman, D. L. Repetition and memory. In G. H. Bower (Ed.), *The psychology of learning and motivation* (Vol. 10). New York: Academic Press, 1976.

Hintzman, D. L., Block, R. A., & Inskeep, N. Memory for mode of input. *Journal of Verbal Learning and Verbal Behavior,* 1972, *11,* 741–749.

Hintzman, D. L., Carre, F. A., Eskridge, V. L., Owens, A. M., Shaff, S. S., & Sparks, E. M. "Stroop" effect: input or output phenomenon? *Journal of Experimental Psychology,* 1972, *95,* 458–459.

Hintzman, D. L., & Summers, J. J. Long-term visual traces of visually presented words. *Psychonomic Bulletin,* 1973, *1,* 325–327.

Holender, D., & Bertelson, P. Selective preparation and time uncertainty. *Acta Psychologica,* 1975, *39,* 193–203.

Holyoak, K. The form of analog size information in memory. *Cognitive Psychology,* 1977, *9,* 31–51.

Hoving, K. L., Morin, R. E., & Konick, D. S. Recognition reaction time and size of the memory set: A developmental study. *Psychonomic Science,* 1970, *21,* 248–249.

Hoving, K. L., Morin, R. E., & Konick, D. S. Age-related changes in the effectiveness of name and visual codes in recognition memory. *Journal of Experimental Child Psychology,* 1974, *18,* 349–361.

Hoyle, G. Neural mechanisms underlying behavior of invertebrates. In M. S. Gazzaniga & C. Blakemore (Eds.), *Handbook of psychobiology.* New York: Academic Press, 1975.

Hubel, D. H., & Wiesel, T. N. Receptive fields, binocular interaction and functional architecture in the cat's visual cortex. *Journal of Physiology,* 1962, *160,* 106–154.

Hunt, E., Frost, N., & Lunneborg, C. Individual differences in cognition: A new approach to intelligence. In G. Bower (Ed.), *Advances in learning and motivation* (Vol. 7). New York: Academic Press, 1973.

Hunt, E., Lunneborg, C., & Lewis, J. What does it mean to be high verbal? *Cognitive Psychology,* 1975, *7,* 194–227.

Huttenlocher, J., & Burke, D. Why does memory span increase with age? *Cognitive Psychology,* 1976, *8,* 1–32.

Hyman, R. Stimulus information as a determinant of reaction time. *Journal of Experimental Psychology,* 1953, *45,* 188–196.

James, C. T. The role of semantic information in lexical decisions. *Journal of Experimental Psychology: Human Perception and Performance,* 1975, *1,* 130–136.

James, W. *Principles of psychology* (Vol. 1). New York: Holt, 1890.

Jerison, B. J. *Evolution of the brain and intelligence.* New York: Academic Press, 1973.

Johnston, W. A., Wagstaff, R. R., & Griffith, D. Information processing analysis of verbal learning. *Journal of Experimental Psychology,* 1972, *96,* 307–314.

Jones, B., & Kabanoff, B. Eye movements in auditory space perception. *Perception & Psychophysics,* 1975, *17,* 241–245.

Kahneman, D. Method, findings and theory in studies of visual masking. *Psychological Bulletin,* 1969, *70,* 404–425.

Kahneman, D. *Attention and effort.* Englewood Cliffs, N.J.: Prentice-Hall, 1973.

Karlin, L., & Kestenbaum, R. Effects of number of alternatives on the psychological refractory period. *Quarterly Journal of Experimental Psychology,* 1968, *20,* 167–178.

Keele, S. W. *Attention and human performance.* Pacific Palisades, Calif.: Goodyear, 1973.

Kerr, B. Processing demands during mental operations. *Memory & Cognition,* 1973, *1,* 401–412.

Kimura, P. Functional asymmetries of the brain in dichotic listening. *Cortex,* 1967, *3,* 165–178.

Kirsner, K. Naming latency facilitation: An analysis of the encoding component in reaction time. *Journal of Experimental Psychology,* 1972, *95,* 171-176.

Kirsner, K., & Smith, M. C. Modality effects in word recognition. *Memory & Cognition,* 1974, *2,* 637-640.

Klein, R. M. *The role of attention in the processing of visual and kinesthetic information.* Unpublished doctoral dissertation, University of Oregon, 1974.

Klein, R. M. Attention and visual dominance: A chronometric analysis. *Journal of Experimental Psychology: Human Perception and Performance,* 1977, *3,* 365-378.

Klein, R. M., & Kerr, B. Visual signal detection and the locus of foreperiod effects. *Memory & Cognition,* 1974, *2,* 431-435.

Klein, R. M., & Posner, M. I. Attention to visual and kinesthetic components of skills. *Brain Research,* 1974, *71,* 401-411.

Kleitman, N. *Sleep and wakefulness.* Chicago: University of Chicago Press, 1963.

Kolers, P. A. Some problems of classification. In J. F. Kavanaugh & I. G. Mattingly (Eds.), *Language by ear and by eye.* Cambridge, Mass.: MIT Press, 1972.

Komoda, M., Festinger, L., Phillips, L., Duckman, R., & Young, R. Some observations concerning saccadic eye movements. *Vision Research,* 1973, *13,* 1009-1020.

Konorski, J. *Integrative activity of the brain.* Chicago: University of Chicago Press, 1967.

Kornhuber, H. H., & Deecke, L. Hirnpotentialänderungen bei wilkürbewegungen und passiven bewegungen des menschen: Bereitschaftspotential und reafferente potentiale. *Pflügers Archiv für die gesamte Physiologie des Menschen und der Tiere,* 1965, *284,* 1-17.

Kosslyn, S. M., & Pomerantz, J. R. Imagery, propositions, and the form of internal representation. *Cognitive Psychology,* 1977, *9,* 52-76.

Kraut, A. G. Effects of familiarization on alertness and encoding in children. *Developmental Psychology,* 1976, *12,* 491-496.

Kroll, N. E. A. Visual short-term memory. In D. Deutsch & J. A. Deutsch (Eds.), *Short-term memory.* New York: Academic Press, 1975.

Kroll, N. E. A., Kellicutt, M. H., Berrian, R. W., & Kreisler, A. F. The effects of irrelevant color changes on speed of visual recognition following short retention intervals. *Journal of Experimental Psychology,* 1974, *103,* 97-106.

Krueger, L. E. Effect of bracketing lines on the speed of "same"-"different" judgment of two adjacent letters. *Journal of Experimental Psychology,* 1970, *84,* 324-330.

Kumnick, L. S. Aging and pupillary response to light and sound stimuli. *Journal of Gerontology,* 1956, *11,* 38-45.

LaBerge, D. H. Identification of two components of the time to switch attention: A test of a serial and a parallel model of attention. In S. Kornblum (Ed.), *Attention and performance IV.* New York: Academic Press, 1973.

LaBerge, D., & Samuels, J. Toward a theory of automatic information processing in reading. *Cognitive Psychology,* 1974, *6,* 293-323.

Lackner, J. R., & Garrett, M. F. Resolving ambiguity effects of biasing context in the unattended ear. *Cognition,* 1973, *1,* 359-374.

Lansing, R. W., Schwartz, E., & Lindsley, D. Reaction time and EEG activation under alerted and non-alerted conditions. *Journal of Experimental Psychology,* 1959, *58,* 1-7.

Lappin, J. E., & Disch, K. The latency operating characteristic: II. Effects of visual stimulus intensity on choice reaction time. *Journal of Experimental Psychology,* 1972, *79,* 14-57.

Leavitt, F. Accuracy of report and central readiness. *Journal of Experimental Psychology,* 1969, *81,* 542-546.

Levy, J. Psychobiological implications of bilateral asymmetry. In S. J. Dimond & J. G. Beaumont (Eds.), *Hemisphere function in the human brain.* London: Paul Elek Ltd., 1974.

Lewis, J. Semantic processing of unattended messages using dichotic listening. *Journal of Experimental Psychology,* 1970, *85,* 225-228.

Liberman, A. M., Cooper, F. S., Shankweiler, D. P., & Studdert-Kennedy, P. Perception of the speech code. *Psychological Review,* 1967, *74,* 431–461.

Lively, B. L., & Sanford, B. J. The use of category information in a memory search task. *Journal of Experimental Psychology,* 1972, *93,* 379–385.

Loveless, N. E., & Sanford, A. J. Slow potential correlates of preparatory set. *Biological Psychology,* 1974, *1,* 303–314.

Luce, R. D., & Green, D. M. A neural timing theory for response times and the psychophysics of intensity. *Psychological Review,* 1972, *79,* 14–57.

Lyon, D. *Individual differences in memory span.* Unpublished doctoral dissertation. University of Oregon, 1975.

Lyon, J. J. The encoding of ignored information. *Memory & Cognition,* 1974, *2,* 161–168.

MacKay, D. G. Aspects of the theory of comprehension, memory and attention. *Quarterly Journal of Experimental Psychology,* 1973, *25,* 22–40.

Mackworth, J. F. *Vigilance and habituation.* Harmondsworth, England: Penguin Books, 1969.

Marcel, T., & Forrin, B. Naming latency and repetition of stimulus categories. *Journal of Experimental Psychology,* 1974, *103,* 450–460.

March, J. G., & Simon, H. A. *Organizations.* New York: Wiley, 1958.

Marler, P. R., & Hamilton, W. J., III. *Mechanisms of animal behavior.* New York: Wiley, 1967.

Marshall, J. C., & Newcombe, F. Patterns of paralexia: A psycholinguistic approach. *Journal of Psycholinguistic Research,* 1973, *2,* 175–198.

Mattingly, I. G. Reading, the linguistic process, and linguistic awareness. In J. F. Kavanaugh & I. G. Mattingly (Eds.), *Language by ear and by eye.* Cambridge, Mass.: MIT Press, 1972.

McAdams, D. W., Irwin, D. A., Rebert, C. S., & Knott, J. P. Conative control of the contingent negative variation. *EEG and Clinical Neurophysiology,* 1969, *21,* 194–195.

McClelland, D. C. *The achieving society.* New York: Van Nostrand Co., 1961.

McClelland, D. C., & Winter, D. G. *Motivating economic achievement.* New York: Free Press, 1969.

McClelland, J. Preliminary letter identification in the perception of words and nonwords. *Journal of Experimental Psychology: Human Perception and Performance,* 1976, *2,* 80–91.

McLean, J. P. *Strategic and ballistic aspects of attention.* Unpublished master's thesis, University of Oregon, 1977.

McLeod, P. D. Does probe RT measure central processing demand? *Quarterly Journal of Experimental Psychology,* in press.

Megaw, E. D., & Armstrong, W. Individual and simultaneous tracking of a step input by the horizontal saccadic eye movement and manual control systems. *Journal of Experimental Psychology,* 1973, *100,* 18–28.

Melzack, R. *The puzzle of pain.* New York: Basic Books, 1973.

Mertens, J. J. Influence of knowledge of target location upon the probability of obsecuation of peripherally observable test flashes. *Journal of the Optical Society of America,* 1956, *46,* 1069–1070.

Meyer, D. E. On the representation and retrieval of stored semantic information. *Cognitive Psychology,* 1970, *1,* 242–299.

Meyer, D. E., & Schvaneveldt, R. W. Meaning, memory structure and mental processes. *Science,* 1976, *192,* 27–33.

Meyer, D. E., Schvaneveldt, R. W., & Ruddy, M. G. Loci of contextual effects on visual word-recognition. In P. M. A. Rabbitt & S. Dornic (Eds.), *Attention and performance V.* London: Academic Press, 1975.

Mezrich, J. J. The word familiarity effect in brief visual displays: Elimination by vocalization. *Perception & Psychophysics,* 1973, *13,* 45–48.

Miller, N. E. Learning of visceral and glandular responses. *Science,* 1969, *163,* 434–445.

Milner, B. Memory disturbances after bilateral hippocampal lesions. In P. N. Milner & S. E. Glickman (Eds.), *Cognitive processes and the brain.* New York: Van Nostrand, 1967.

Mischel, W. Toward a cognitive social learning reconceptualization of personality. *Psychological Review*, 1973, *80*, 252–283.

Morton, J., & Chambers, S. M. Selective attention to words and colors. *Quarterly Journal of Experimental Psychology*, 1973, *25*, 387–397.

Mountcastle, V. The world around us: Neural command functions for selective attention. *Neural Sciences Research Bulletin*, 1976, *16*, #2 Supp.

Mowrer, O. H. Preparatory set (expectancy)—Further evidence of its "central" locus. *Journal of Experimental Psychology*, 1941, *28*, 116–133.

Murray, D. J., Mastronadi, J., & Duncan, S. Selective attention to "physical" versus "verbal" aspects of colored words. *Psychonomic Science*, 1972, *26*, 305–307.

Murray, H. Stimulus intensity and reaction time: Evaluation of a decision-theory model. *Journal of Experimental Psychology*, 1970, *84*, 383–391.

Neely, J. H. Semantic priming and retrieval from lexical memory: Roles of inhibitionless spreading activation and limited-capacity attention. *Journal of Experimental Psychology: General*, 1977, *106*, 226–254.

Neisser, U. *Cognitive psychology*. Englewood Cliffs, N.J.: Prentice-Hall, 1967.

Neisser, U. *Cognition and reality*. San Francisco: Freeman, 1976.

Newell, A., Shaw, J. C., & Simon, H. A. Elements of a theory of human problem solving. *Psychological Review*, 1958, *65*, 151–165.

Newell, A., & Simon, H. A. *Human problem solving*. Englewood Cliffs, N.J.: Prentice-Hall, 1972.

Nickerson, R. Intersensory facilitation of reaction time: Energy summation or preparation enhancement? *Psychological Review*, 1973, *80*, 489–509.

Niemi, P. The locus of stimulus intensity effects in auditory and visual reaction processes. *Acta Psychologica*, in press.

Ninio, A. *The rate of expenditure of effort in RT tasks of varying difficulty*. Unpublished doctoral dissertation, The Hebrew University, Jerusalem, 1974.

Nissen, M. J. M. *Facilitation and selection: Two modes of sensory interaction*. Unpublished master's thesis, University of Oregon, 1974.

Nissen, M. J. M. *Semantic activation and levels of processing*. Unpublished doctoral dissertation, University of Oregon, 1976.

Norman, D. A., & Bobrow, D. G. On data-limited and resource-limited processes. *Cognitive Psychology*, 1975, *7*, 44–64.

Olds, J., Disterhoft, J. F., Segal, M., Kornblith, C. L., & Hirsh, R. Learning centers of rat brain mapped by measuring latencies of conditioned unit responses. *Journal of Neurophysiology*, 1972, *35*, 202–219.

Orton, S. T. Word-blindness in school-children. *Archives of Neurology and Psychiatry*, 1925, *14*, 581–615.

Ostry, D., Moray, N., & Marks, G. Attention, practice and semantic targets. *Journal of Experimental Psychology: Human Perception and Performance*, 1976, *2*, 326–336.

Pachella, R. G. The interpretation of reaction time in information-processing research. In B. Kantowitz (Ed.), *Human information processing: Tutorials in performance and cognition*. Hillsdale, N.J.: Lawrence Erlbaum Associates, 1974.

Pachella, R. G., & Fisher, D. F. Effects of stimulus degradation and similarity on the trade-off between speed and accuracy in absolute judgment. *Journal of Experimental Psychology*, 1969, *81*, 7–9.

Pachella, R. G., & Miller, J. O. Stimulus probability and same–different classification. *Perception & Psychophysics*, 1976, *19*, 29–34.

Paivio, A. Mental imagery in associative learning and memory. *Psychological Review*, 1969, *76*, 241–263.

Paivio, A., & Ernest, C. H. Imagery ability and visual perception of verbal and nonverbal stimuli. *Perception & Psychophysics*, 1971, *10*, 429–432.

Parasuraman, R., & Davies, D. R. Decision theory analysis of response latencies in vigilance.

Journal of Experimental Psychology: Human Perception and Performance, 1976, *2,* 578–590.

Parkman, J. M., & Groen, G. Temporal aspects of simple additions and comparison. *Journal of Experimental Psychology,* 1971, *89,* 335–342.

Parks, T. E., Kroll, N. E. A., Salzberg, P. M., & Parkinson, S. R. Persistence of visual memory as indicated by decision time in a matching task. *Journal of Experimental Psychology,* 1972, *92,* 437–438.

Pascual-Leone, J., & Smith, J. The encoding and decoding of symbols by children: A new experimental paradigm and a neo-Piagetian model. *Journal of Experimental Child Psychology,* 1969, *8,* 328–355.

Pavlov, I. P. *Conditioned reflex.* New York: Dover, 1960.

Peterson, M. J., & Graham, S. E. Visual detection and visual imagery. *Journal of Experimental Psychology,* 1974, *103,* 509–514.

Pfautz, P. L., & Wagner, A. R. Transient variations in responding to Pavlovian conditioned stimuli have implications for mechanisms of "priming." *Animal Learning and Behavior,* 1976, *4,* 107–112.

Piaget, J., & Inhelder, B. [*The psychology of the child*] (H. Weaver, trans.). New York: Basic Books, 1969.

Pick, H. L., Warren, D. H., & Hay, J. C. Sensory conflict in judgments of spatial direction. *Perception & Psychophysics,* 1969, *6,* 203–205.

Picton, T. W., Hillyard, S. A., Krausz, H. I., & Galambos, R. Human auditory evoked potentials. I: Evaluation of components. *Electroencephalography and Clinical Neurophysiology,* 1974, *36,* 179–190.

Pisoni, D. B., & Tash, J. Reaction times to comparisons within and across phonetic categories. *Perception & Psychophysics,* 1974, *15,* 201–209.

Polf, J. *The word superiority effect: A speed–accuracy analysis and test of a decoding hypothesis.* Unpublished doctoral dissertation, University of Oregon, Eugene, 1976.

Pollatsek, A., Well, A., & Schindler, R. Familiarity affects visual processing of words. *Journal of Experimental Psychology: Human Perception and Performance,* 1975, *1,* 328–338.

Pomerantz, J. R., Kaplan, S., & Kaplan, R. Satiation effects in the perception of single letters. *Perception & Psychophysics,* 1969, *6,* 129–132.

Posner, M. I. Information reduction in the analysis of sequential tasks. *Psychological Review,* 1964, *71,* 491–504.

Posner, M. I. Characteristics of visual and kinesthetic memory codes. *Journal of Experimental Psychology,* 1967, *75,* 103–107.

Posner, M. I. Abstraction and the process of recognition. In G. Bower & J. T. Spence (Eds.), *Psychology of learning and motivation* (Vol. 3). New York: Academic Press, 1969.

Posner, M. I. On the relationship between letter names and superordinate categories. *Quarterly Journal of Experimental Psychology,* 1970, *22,* 279–287.

Posner, M. I. Coordination of internal codes. In W. G. Chase (Ed.), *Visual information processing.* New York: Academic Press, 1972.

Posner, M. I. Psychobiology of attention. In M. Gazzaniga & C. Blakemore (Eds.), *Handbook of psychobiology.* New York: Academic Press, 1975. (a)

Posner, M. I. The temporal course of pattern recognition in the human brain. In G. F. Inbar (Ed.), *Signal analysis and pattern recognition in biomedical engineering.* New York: Wiley, 1975. (b)

Posner, M. I. Applying theories and theorizing about applications. In L. Resnick & P. Weaver (Eds.), *Theory and practice in early reading.* Hillsdale, N.J.: Lawrence Erlbaum Associates, in press.

Posner, M. I., & Boies, S. J. Components of attention. *Psychological Review,* 1971, *78,* 391–408.

Posner, M. I., Boies, S. J., Eichelman, W. H., & Taylor, R. L. Retention of visual and name codes of single letters. *Journal of Experimental Psychology,* 1969, *79,* 1–16.

Posner, M. I., & Davidson, B. J. Automatic and attended components of orienting. *Proceedings of the International Congress of Official Physical Activity Sciences,* Quebec City, July 1976 (Monograph No. 5).

Posner, M. I., & Keele, S. W. Decay of visual information from a single letter. *Science,* 1967, *158,* 137-139.

Posner, M. I., & Keele, S. W. On the genesis of abstract ideas. *Journal of Experimental Psychology,* 1968, *77,* 353-363.

Posner, M. I., & Klein, R. M. On the functions of consciousness. In S. Kornblum (Ed.), *Attention and performance IV.* New York: Academic Press, 1973.

Posner, M. I., Klein, R., Summers, J., & Buggie, S. On the selection of signals. *Memory & Cognition,* 1973, *1,* 2-12.

Posner, M. I., Lewis, J., & Conrad, C. Component processes in reading: A performance analysis. In J. Kavanaugh & I. Mattingly (Eds.), *Language by ear and by eye.* Boston: MIT Press, 1972.

Posner, M. I., & Mitchell, R. F. Chronometric analysis of classification. *Psychological Review,* 1967, *74,* 392-409.

Posner, M. I., Nissen, M. J., & Klein, R. Visual dominance: An information-processing account of its origins and significance. *Psychological Review,* 1976, *83,* 157-171.

Posner, M. I., Nissen, M. J., & Ogden, W. C. Attended and unattended processing modes: The role of set for spatial location. In H. L. Pick & I. J. Saltzman (Eds.), *Modes of perceiving and processing information.* Hillsdale, N.J.: Lawrence Erlbaum Associates, 1978.

Posner, M. I., & Rossman, E. The effect of size and location of interpolated information reducing transforms upon short term retention. *Journal of Experimental Psychology,* 1965, *70,* 496-505.

Posner, M. I., & Snyder, C. R. R. Attention and cognitive control. In R. L. Solso (Ed.), *Information processing and cognition: The Loyola Symposium.* Hillsdale, N.J.: Lawrence Erlbaum Associates, 1975. (a)

Posner, M. I., & Snyder, C. R. R. Facilitation and inhibition in the processing of signals. In P. M. A. Rabbitt & S. Dornic (Eds.), *Attention and performance V.* New York: Academic Press, 1975. (b)

Posner, M. I., & Taylor, R. L. Subtractive method applied to separation of visual and name components of multiletter arrays. *Acta Psychologica,* 1969, *30,* 104-114.

Posner, M. I., & Warren, R. Traces, concepts and conscious constructions. In A. W. Melton & E. Martin (Eds.), *Coding theory in learning and memory.* New York: Winston, 1972.

Powers, W. T. *Behavior: The control of perception.* Chicago: Aldine, 1973.

Pushkin, V. N. Vigilance as a function of strength of the nervous system. In V. Nebylitsyn & J. Gray (Eds.), *Biological bases of individual behavior.* New York: Academic Press, 1972.

Pylyshyn, A. What the mind's eye tells the mind's brain: A critique of mental imagery. *Psychological Bulletin,* 1973, *80,* 1-24.

Rabbitt, P. M. A. Set and age in a choice-response task. *Journal of Gerontology,* 1964, *19,* 301-306.

Radeau, M., & Bertelson, P. The aftereffects of ventriloquism. *Quarterly Journal of Experimental Psychology,* 1974, *26,* 63-71.

Razran, G. *Mind in evolution.* New York: Houghton Mifflin, 1971.

Regan, D. *Evoked potentials.* New York: Wiley, 1972.

Reicher, G. M. Perceptual recognition as a function of meaningfulness of stimulus material. *Journal of Experimental Psychology,* 1969, *81,* 275-280.

Reiter, L. A., & Ison, J. R. Inhibition of the human eyeblink reflex. *Journal of Experimental Psychology: Human Perception and Performance,* 1977, *3,* 325-336.

Rescorla, R. A., & Wagner, A. R. A theory of Pavlovian conditioning: Variations in the effectiveness of reinforcement and nonreinforcement. In A. H. Black & W. F. Prokasy (Eds.), *Classical conditioning II: Current theory and research.* New York: Meredith, 1972.

Requin, J. Some data on neurophysiological processes involved in the preparatory motor activity to reaction performance. *Acta Psychologica,* 1969, *30,* 358-367.

Richards, J. T. Interitem structure and the facilitation of simultaneous comparison. *Journal of*

Experimental Psychology: Human Perception and Performance, 1978, *4,* 72–87.

Rips, L. J., Shoben, E. J., & Smith, E. E. Semantic distance and the verification of semantic relations. *Journal of Verbal Learning and Verbal Behavior,* 1973, *12,* 1–20.

Ritter, W., Simpson, R., & Vaughan, H. G. Association cortex potentials and reaction time in auditory discrimination. *EEG and Clinical Neurophysiology,* 1972, *33,* 547–555.

Rock, I., & Victor, J. Vision and touch: An experimentally created conflict between the two senses. *Science,* 1964, *143,* 594–596.

Rogers, M. G. K. *Visual generation in the recognition of faces.* Unpublished master's thesis, University of Oregon, 1972.

Rogers, M. G. K. *Visual and verbal processes in the recognition of names and faces.* Unpublished doctoral dissertation, University of Oregon, 1974.

Rohrbaugh, J. W., Syndulko, K., & Lindsley, D. B. Brain wave components of the contingent negative variation in humans. *Science,* 1976, *191,* 1055–1057.

Rosch, E. On the internal structure of perceptual and cognitive categories. In T. E. Moore (Ed.), *Cognitive development and the acquisition of language.* New York: Academic Press, 1973.

Rosch, E. The nature of mental codes for color categories. *Journal of Experimental Psychology: Human Perception and Performance,* 1975, *4,* 302–322. (a)

Rosch, E. Cognitive representations of semantic categories. *Journal of Experimental Psychology: General,* 1975, *104,* 192–233. (b)

Rosch, E., Mervis, C. B., Grey, W. D., Johnson, D. M., & Boyes-Braem, P. Basic objects in natural categories. *Cognitive Psychology,* 1976, *8,* 382–439.

Ross, L. R., & Ross, S. M. Cognitive factors in classical conditioning. In W. K. Estes (Ed.), *Handbook of learning and cognitive processes* (Vol. 3). Hillsdale, N.J.: Lawrence Erlbaum Associates, 1976.

Rozin, P. The evolution of intelligence and access to the cognitive unconscious. In J. M. Sprague & A. N. Epstein (Eds.), *Progress in psychobiology and physiological psychology.* New York: Academic Press, 1976.

Rozin, P., & Gleitman, L. The reading process and the acquisition of the alphabetic principle. In A. Reber & D. Scarborough (Eds.), *Toward a psychology of reading: The proceedings of the CUNY conferences.* Hillsdale, N.J.: Lawrence Erlbaum Associates, 1977.

Rubenstein, H., Lewis, S. S., & Rubenstein, M. A. Evidence for phonemic recoding in visual word recognition. *Journal of Verbal Learning and Verbal Behavior,* 1971, *10,* 645–657.

Rudell, A. P., & Fox, S. S. Operant controlled neural event: Functional bioelectric coding in primary components of cortical evoked potential in cat brain. *Journal of Neurophysiology,* 1972, *35,* 892–902.

Sabol, M. A., & DeRosa, D. V. Semantic encoding of isolated words. *Journal of Experimental Psychology: Human Learning and Memory,* 1976, *2,* 58–68.

Sanders, A. F. Foreperiod duration and the time course of preparation. *Acta Psychologica,* 1972, *36,* 60–71.

Sanders, A. F. The foreperiod effect revisited. *Quarterly Journal of Experimental Psychology,* 1975, *27,* 591–598.

Saslow, M. G. Latency for saccadic eye movement. *Journal of the Optical Society of America,* 1967, *57,* 1030–1033.

Scarborough, D. L., Cortese, C., & Scarborough, H. S. Frequency and repetition effects in lexical memory. *Journal of Experimental Psychology: Human Perception and Performance,* 1977, *3,* 1–17.

Schindler, R., Well, A., & Pollatsek, A. Inducing the familiarity effect. *Perception & Psychophysics,* 1976, *19,* 425–432.

Schroeder, R. *Information processing of color and form.* Unpublished honors thesis, University of Oregon, 1976.

Schvaneveldt, R., & Meyer, D. E. Retrieval and comparison processes in semantic memory. In S. Kornblum (Ed.), *Attention and performance IV.* New York: Academic Press, 1973.

Schvaneveldt, R. W., Meyer, D. E., & Becker, C. A. Lexical ambiguity, semantic context and visual word recognition. *Journal of Experimental Psychology: Human Perception and Performance,* 1976, *2,* 243–256.

Scribner, S., & Cole, M. Cognitive consequences of formal and informal education. *Science,* 1973, *182,* 553–559.

Sechenov, I. M. *Reflexes of the brain.* Cambridge, Mass.: MIT Press, 1965.

Sekuler, R. Spatial vision. *Annual Review of Psychology,* 1974, *25,* 195–232.

Selfridge, O. Pandemonium: A paradigm for learning. In *Symposium on the mechanization of the thought processes.* London: Houghton Mifflin Stationery Office, 1959.

Senders, J. W. The human operator as a monitor and controller of multidegree of freedom systems. *IEEE Transactions of Human Factors in Electronics,* 1964, *5,* 1.

Shallice, T. Dual functions of consciousness. *Psychological Review,* 1972, *79,* 383–393.

Shallice, T., & Warrington, E. Word recognition in a phonemic dyslexic patient. *Quarterly Journal of Experimental Psychology,* 1975, *27,* 187–199.

Shannon, C. E., & Weaver, W. *The mathematical theory of communication.* Urbana: University of Illinois Press, 1949.

Shepard, R. Form, formation, and transformation of internal representations. In R. L. Solso (Ed.), *Information processing and cognition: The Loyola Symposium.* Hillsdale, N.J.: Lawrence Erlbaum Associates, 1975.

Shepard, R. N., & Metzler, J. Mental rotation of three-dimensional objects. *Science,* 1971, *171,* 701–703.

Sherrington, C. *The integrative action of the nervous system.* New Haven, Conn.: Yale University Press, 1906.

Shiffrin, R. M., & Gardner, G. T. Visual processing capacity and attentional control. *Journal of Experimental Psychology,* 1972, *93,* 72–82.

Shwartz, S. P. Capacity limitations in human information processing. *Memory & Cognition,* 1976, *4,* 763–768.

Shwartz, S. P., Pomerantz, J. R., & Egeth, H. E. State and process limitations in information processing: An additive factors analysis. *Journal of Experimental Psychology: Human Perception and Performance,* 1977, *3,* 402–410.

Simon, H. A. *The sciences of the artificial.* Cambridge, Mass.: MIT Press, 1969.

Simon, J. R. Reaction toward the source of stimulation. *Journal of Experimental Psychology,* 1969, *81,* 174–176.

Skinner, B. F. *Behavior of organisms.* New York: Appleton-Century-Crofts, 1938.

Smith, E. E., Haviland, S. E., Reder, L. M., Brownell, H. M., & Adams, N. When preparation fails: Disruptive effects of prior information on perceptual recognition. *Journal of Experimental Psychology: Human Perception and Performance,* 1976, *2,* 151–161.

Smith, E. E., & Spoehr, K. T. The perception of printed English: A theoretical perspective. In B. H. Kantowitz (Ed.), *Human information processing: Tutorials in performance and cognition.* Hillsdale, N.J.: Lawrence Erlbaum Associates, 1974.

Snyder, C. R. R. *Individual differences in imagery and thought.* Unpublished doctoral dissertation, University of Oregon, 1972.

Sokolov, E. N. *Perception and the conditioned reflex.* New York: Macmillan, 1963.

Spelke, E. Infants' intermodal perception of events. *Cognitive Psychology,* 1976, *8,* 553–560.

Sperling, G. The information available in brief visual presentations. *Psychological Monographs,* 1960, *74* (11, Whole No. 498).

Stanovich, K. E., & Pachella, R. G. Encoding, stimulus–response compatibility, and stages of processing. *Journal of Experimental Psychology: Human Perception and Performance,* 1977, *3,* 411–421.

Stein, B. E., Magalhães-Castro, B., & Kruger, L. Superior colliculus: Visuotopic-somatotopic overlap. *Science,* 1975, *189,* 224–225.

Sternberg, S. High speed scanning in human memory. *Science,* 1966, *153,* 652–654.

Sternberg, S. The discovery of processing stages: Extensions of Donders' method. In W. G. Koster (Ed.), *Attention and performance II*. Amsterdam: North-Holland, 1969. (*Acta Psychologica, 1969, 30,* 276–315).

Stone, J. Morphology and physiology of the geniculo-cortical synapse in the cat: The question of parallel input to the striate cortex. *Investigative Ophthalmology,* 1972, *11,* 338–346.

Sutton, S., Braren, M., & Zubin, J. Evoked potential correlates of stimulus uncertainty. *Science,* 1965, *150,* 1187–1188.

Swanson, J. M., Johnsen, A. M., & Briggs, G. E. Recoding in a memory search task. *Journal of Experimental Psychology,* 1972, *93,* 1–9.

Tanner, W. P., Jr., & Swets, J. A. A decision-making theory of visual detection. *Psychological Review,* 1954, *61,* 401–409.

Taylor, F. W. *The principles of scientific management.* New York: Norton Library, 1967.

Taylor, R. L., & Reilly, S. Naming and other methods of decoding visual information. *Journal of Experimental Psychology,* 1970, *83,* 80–83.

Teichner, W. H., & Krebs, M. J. Laws of the simple reaction time. *Psychological Review,* 1972, *79,* 344–358.

Thomas, E. The selectivity of preparation. *Psychological Review,* 1974, *81,* 442–464.

Thompson, R. F. *Foundations of physiological psychology.* New York: Harper, 1967.

Thorson, G., Hockhaus, L., & Stanners, R. F. Temporal changes in visual and acoustic codes in a letter-matching task. *Perception & Psychophysics,* 1976, *19,* 346–348.

Titchener, E. B. *Lectures on the elementary psychology of feeling and attention.* New York: Macmillan, 1908.

Trabasso, T. Representation, memory and reasoning: How do we make transitive inferences? In A. D. Pick (Ed.), *Minnesota symposium on child psychology* (Vol. 9). Minneapolis, Minn.: University of Minnesota Press, 1975.

Treisman, A. Strategies and models of selective attention. *Psychological Review,* 1969, *76,* 282–299.

Treisman, A., & Geffen, G. Selective attention: Perception or response? *Quarterly Journal of Experimental Psychology,* 1967, *19,* 1–17.

Treisman, A. M., Squire, R., & Green, J. Semantic processing in dichotic listening: A replication. *Memory & Cognition,* 1974, *2,* 641–649.

Tversky, A., & Kahneman, D. Judgment under uncertainty: Heuristics and biases. *Science,* 1974, *185,* 1124–1130.

Tversky, B. Pictorial and verbal encoding in a short-term memory task. *Perception & Psychophysics,* 1969, *6,* 225–233.

Tweedy, J. R., Lapinski, R. H., & Schaneveldt, R. W. Semantic context effects on word recognition: Influence of varying the proportion of items presented in an appropriate context. *Memory & Cognition,* 1977, *5,* 84–89.

Umilta, C., Frost, N., & Hyman, R. Interhemispheric effects on choice reaction times to one-, two- and three-letter displays. *Journal of Experimental Psychology,* 1972, *93,* 198–204.

Underwood, B. J. False recognition produced by implicit verbal responses. *Journal of Experimental Psychology,* 1965, *70,* 122–129.

Underwood, B. J. Attributes of memory. *Psychological Review,* 1969, *76,* 559–573.

Underwood, B. J. Individual differences as a crucible in theory construction. *American Psychologist,* 1975, *12,* 128–135.

Uttal, W. R. The psychobiological silly season, or what happens when neurophysiological data becomes psychological theory. *Journal of General Psychology,* 1971, *84,* 151–166.

Vaughan, H. G., & Ritter, W. The sources of auditory evoked responses recorded from the human scalp. *EEG and Clinical Neurophysiology,* 1970, *28,* 360–367.

Von Wright, J. M., Anderson, K., & Stenman, U. Generalization of conditioned GSRs in dichotic listening. In P. M. A. Rabbitt & S. Dornic (Eds.), *Attention and performance V.* London: Academic Press, 1975.

Walter, W. G. The convergence and interaction of visual, auditory and tactile responses in human non-specific cortex. *Annals of the New York Academy of Sciences*, 1964, *112*, 320-361.

Wardlaw, K. A., & Kroll, N. E. A. Autonomic responses to shock-associated words in a nonattended message: A failure to replicate. *Journal of Experimental Psychology: Human Perception and Performance*, 1975, *1*, 257-259.

Warren, R. E. Stimulus encoding and memory. *Journal of Experimental Psychology*, 1972, *94*, 90-100.

Warren, R. E. Association, directionality, and stimulus encoding. *Journal of Experimental Psychology*, 1974, *102*, 151-158.

Warren, R. E., & Warren, N. T. Dual semantic encoding of homographs and homophones embedded in context. *Memory & Cognition*, 1976, *4*, 586-592.

Warren, R. M., & Warren, R. P. Auditory illusions and confusions. *Scientific American*, 1970, *233*, 30-36.

Warrington, E. K., & Weiskrantz, L. New method of testing long-term recognition with special reference to amnesic patients. *Nature*, 1968, *217*, 972-974.

Webb, R. A., & Obrist, P. S. The physiological concomitants of reaction time performance as a function of preparatory interval and preparatory interval series. *Psychophysiology*, 1970, *6*, 389-403.

Weber, R. J., & Harish, R. Visual imagery for words: The Hebb test. *Journal of Experimental Psychology*, 1974, *102*, 409-414.

Webster, W. R., & Aitkin, L. M. Central auditory processing. In M. S. Gazzaniga & C. Blakemore (Eds.), *Handbook of psychobiology*. New York: Academic Press, 1975.

Weitzman, E. D., Fukushima, D., Nogeire, C., Roffwarg, H., Gallagher, T. F., & Hellman, L. Twenty-four hour pattern of the episodic secretion of cortisol in normal subjects. *Journal of Clinical Endocrinology and Metabolism*, 1971, *33*, 14-22.

Welch, J. On the measurement of mental activity through muscular activity and the determination of a constant of attention. *American Journal of Physiology*, 1898, *1*, 288-306.

Welford, A. Changes of performance time with age: A correction and methodological note. *Ergonomics*, 1962, *5*, 581-582.

Well, A. D., & Green, J. Effects of color differences in a letter-matching task. *Bulletin of the Psychonomic Society*, 1972, *29*, 109-110.

Westheimer, G. Eye movement responses to a horizontally moving visual stimulus. *Archives of Ophthalmology*, 1954, *52*, 939-941.

Whorf, B. L. *Language, thought and reality*. Cambridge, Mass.: MIT Press, 1956.

Wilkinson, R. T. Evoked response and reaction time. *Acta Psychologica*, 1967, *27*, 235-245.

Wilson, E. O. *Sociobiology: The new synthesis*. Cambridge, Mass.: Belknap Press of Harvard University Press, 1975.

Winkelman, J. H., & Schmidt, J. Associative confusions in mental arithmetic. *Journal of Experimental Psychology*, 1974, *102*, 734-737.

Wood, C. C. Auditory and phonetic levels of processing in speech perception: Neurophysiological and information processing analysis. *Journal of Experimental Psychology: Human Perception and Performance*, 1975, *1*, 3-20.

Wood, L. E. Visual and auditory coding in a memory matching task. *Journal of Experimental Psychology*, 1974, *102*, 106-113.

Wündt, W. [*Introduction to psychology*] (R. Pinter, trans.). London: George Allen, 1912.

Author Index

Italicized page numbers indicate pages that contain complete reference information.

Subject Index